Japanese Workers in Protest

Japanese Workers in Protest

An Ethnography of Consciousness
and Experience

Christena L. Turner

UNIVERSITY OF CALIFORNIA PRESS

Berkeley / Los Angeles / London

University of California Press
Berkeley and Los Angeles, California

University of California Press, Ltd.
London, England

© 1995 by
The Regents of the University of California

Library of Congress Cataloging-in-Publication Data

Turner, Christena L., 1949–
    Japanese workers in protest : an ethnography of consciousness and
experience / Christena L. Turner.
      p.   cm.
    Includes bibliographical references and index.
    ISBN 0-520-08570-1 (alk. paper)
    1. Trade-unions—Japan. 2. Working class—Japan. 3. Labor
movement—Japan. 4. Class consciousness—Japan. 5. Industrial
relations—Japan. 6. Japan—Social conditions—1945– I. Title.
HD6832.T87   1995
331.88'0952—dc20   94-20207

Printed in the United States of America

9   8   7   6   5   4   3   2   1

The paper used in this publication meets the minimum requirements of
American National Standard for Information Sciences—Permanence of
Paper for Printed Library Materials, ANSI Z39.48-1984.∞

To the memory of my parents,
Nellie B. and Charles E. Turner

Contents

viii   CONTENTS

Acknowledgments

The people of Unikon Camera and Universal Shoes accepted me into their daily work routine and regular political and social activities at a time when their organizational and personal resources were already strained by the labor disputes they were fighting and by the demands of worker-controlled production. I am deeply indebted to the people in these unions for an unusual research opportunity, for their patience and good humor, and for their insightful and enthusiastic participation in my work.

There were a number of people involved in setting up this project. Harumi Befu has guided it from the very beginning with wisdom and enthusiasm, and he began the chain of introductions and efforts on my behalf which led me into these two workplaces. That chain includes Kawanishi Hirosuke, Totsuka Hideo, and Hara Hiroko. In addition to the original introduction, Totsuka Hideo has offered important insights into the Japanese labor movement as well into these two companies, and he has become a valued friend and *sensei* as well.

There are a number of people who have made invaluable contributions to this project. Thomas Rohlen inspired this work from its earliest stages. Several sections of this book were revised, rewritten, and greatly improved by the extensive readings and responses of Jeffrey Haydu, Andrew Gordon, and an anonymous reviewer for the University of California Press. John Griffin, Ellis Krauss, and Martha Lampland read and made important comments on drafts of various chapters. Eiko Tada acted as an invaluable research assistant and critical reader throughout the final preparation of the manuscript. The limitations of the text are far fewer because of their efforts.

Throughout this project, many have offered critical comments, insights, and conversation which have helped form this manuscript. For such help I want to thank Kay and Masumi Abe, Suzanne Cahill, Jane Collier, Steve Cornell, John Dower, David Groth, Mark Handler, Judit Hersko, Kenmochi Hitoshi, Andrea Klimt, Martha Lampland, Catherine Lewis, Richard Madsen, Masao Miyoshi, Kyoko and Hiroko Murofushi, Naoko Obata, T. Pines, Sasaki Aiko, Eiko Tada, Seiichiro Takagi, Sandra Wong, and Sylvia Yanagisako. I am also indebted to the critical thought of an extraordinary gathering of people at the University of California Humanities Institute at the University of California, Irvine for ten weeks in the spring of 1990, including Harry Harootunian, Masao Miyoshi, Oe Kenzaburo, Miriam Silverberg, and Rob Wilson. Finally, I regret that in order to protect the anonymity of the unions and their members I cannot offer my personal gratitude to several individuals at Unikon and Universal who helped me not only to understand their own experience but to formulate the general interpretations of this book as well.

I am grateful for financial support from Fulbright-Hayes, Japan Foundation, the Center for Research in International Studies at Stanford University, the Academic Senate of the University of California, San Diego, the Japanese Studies Institute of the University of California, Berkeley, and the University of California Humanities Research Institute at the University of California, Irvine. In any project of this nature, language is of central importance, and for the training I received both at Stanford and at the Inter-University Center I am forever grateful.

My gratitude is extended to Sheila Levine and Laura Driussi at the University of California Press for their encouragement and skill in helping me prepare this book. I also want to thank Mark Pentecost for careful editing of the entire manuscript, Seiichiro Takagi and Yoko Commiff for copyediting the Japanese language portions, and Kathy Mooney for thorough proofreading and an inspired index.

Finally, I thank John Griffin for day-to-day encouragement and confidence in me and in this project; Chuck Turner for conversation and counsel throughout; Eric Turner for the delight, wit, and wisdom he contributes to my work and to my daily life; and my other family and friends for their personal encouragement and support. My parents were very much present in the earliest stages of this work, providing knowledge and inspiration. Long before graduate school I learned from my dad that people who work with their hands have fascinating and important things to say about the world and from my mom that to understand people's actions one must pay attention to the nuances and complex stories which represent their worlds. It is to their memories that I dedicate this book.

A Note on Names

Throughout this book Japanese names are written in Japanese order, surname first. In recounting conversations I heard or in which I was involved, I have maintained the Japanese form of address *san,* rather than translating it into Mr., Miss, Mrs., or Ms. The usage of *san* has very different connotations and nuances, being neither as formal as the possible English translations nor as optional. I also maintained the customary uses of given names or surnames as they occurred in the workplaces, leading to a greater usage of given names for women than for men.

When I began this fieldwork I promised anonymity to the people with whom I worked. Similarly, I promised to change the names of the unions and companies in which I worked. The two company and union names, Unikon and Universal, are both my inventions. I chose them to sound like English-language names because the real names are taken from English and transliterated into Japanese to sound English.

CHAPTER I

Introduction

On July 17, 1980, Unikon Camera Company workers and their families gathered in a festively decorated hall on the perimeter of the oldest and most beautiful park in Tokyo. Gold screens set across one end of the room reflected soft lighting and gave rich color to speakers and performers on the polished wooden stage. Large tables spread with white linen tablecloths, adorned with flowers, and piled with food were scattered throughout the room. The midsummer heat was suggestively challenged by a six-foot high camera sculpted in ice and placed on the center table, allowing it to tower over the crowd, both celebrating and amusing the workers gathered around it. Nearby was its companion piece, the ice phoenix, only slightly smaller, with wings spread as if to take flight from the beer and deep-fried chicken set underneath. I was one of over six hundred people gathered to celebrate the Unikon union victory in a labor dispute of nearly three years' duration. The red, white, and black victory banner spread over the stage read "We did it! Unikon will reopen!" in large black characters and "Unikon is like the phoenix" in red. Gathered for this event were Socialist Party and Communist Party Diet members, labor union officials of national, regional, and local federations, officers of supporting unions, labor lawyers, and a couple of Japanese researchers interested, as I was, in making sense of this struggle.

Their dispute had ended the previous month with a public announcement of victory. The newspaper *Asahi Shinbun* reported, "Warm spring visited Unikon Camera which went bankrupt three years ago amid the recession. A reconciliation agreement has been signed on the twenty-seventh of June, and the union president will, in August of this year, become the new company president of the reopened Unikon Camera."[1] *Asahi Shinbun* went on to report that "Young union members who endured this time with only 60 percent of their salaries are jubilant!" Their three-year struggle was recalled, their victory applauded, and their jubilation ritually performed at the July party. Large wooden tubs of sake were broken open with wooden mallets, splashing the auspicious wine in all directions and inspiring applause and laughter. Every guest received a fresh wooden cup from which to sip the delicious cold sake. When emptied these became small tokens of this long struggle, on which people inscribed signatures and affectionate messages for one another.

By the end of the evening my little sake cup was covered inside and out, top and bottom with eighteen signatures and greetings. "When you get back to America, start a revolution and a mass movement!" signed one young Unikon man. "Let's meet next time in Los Angeles," wrote one of the national Sōhyō Federation officers who had worked closely with Unikon. "When you are in the neighborhood, please drop by," invited the Unikon union president, soon to be the new Unikon company president. "Now it's our turn to work together with you!" signed the president of Universal Union, the union controlling the company where I was just beginning to work now that the Unikon struggle was finished.

Around the cup, the calligraphy moves in individual styles, capturing memories of the struggle, of my relationships with individuals from so many different locations within it, and of my time studying their lives. At the time it was a precious souvenir of a community I had become familiar and comfortable with and of individuals who had become my friends, coworkers, and teachers. Now, as I write about their experiences and my own, it has taken on new meanings. I look at it now and count the number of women, men, Unikon leaders, Unikon rank and file, national federation officers, and supporting union officers. I see the organization that extended beyond the individual unions and made possible a victory of this nature. I see the advantages of my position within that organization and remember how much I was able to do, how easily I was able to move vertically through layers of hierarchy and then outward, following networks of affiliated organizations. On the other hand, I see the limitations of my situation even more clearly now than at the time, when I often had to choose where and with whom to spend

1. Regarding the anonymity of the unions in this study and the consequent absence of detail in some of the references see below, p. 24. Those seeking further information may contact the author.

my time, thus limiting, grounding, and locating my work, my perspective, and my understanding of these complex struggles.

The two-hour-long party was a buffet reception punctuated by eight speeches, three dance performances, several songs, and innumerable toasts. A lion dance began the party, festively costumed men filling the spotlighted stage with bold movement and bright colors. Children gathered in front to watch the lion, a red, black, and gold masked dancer, fling his long white mane in large circles of dynamic leaps and jumps. Three musicians sang and played flutes, drums, and clappers, setting the stage for a party proclaiming strength, determination, perseverance, and victory. Loud applause followed the rousing dance and brought a Unikon union leader to the stage to begin introducing a series of speakers.

Words flowed around the guests, giving a formal and public meaning both to this event and to the last three years. A labor lawyer who had represented Unikon called theirs a "struggle for democracy" (*minshu-shugi no tatakai*). He complimented Unikon for fighting against the "antilabor policies" of the conservative Liberal Democratic Party government. The Socialist and Communist Diet members echoed these sentiments. Labor's power to challenge management was weakening so rapidly at that time that between 1974 and 1978 disputes had decreased by one-third (Totsuka 1980). The oil shock of 1973 quadrupled the price of crude oil and marked the beginning of a period of slowed growth that has made it increasingly difficult for labor to bargain. The Unikon dispute began in 1977 after the second oil shock. The *Asahi Shinbun* had reported in 1980 that the Unikon victory might be one of the last of a decade of relatively vigorous union struggles. Theirs was a flamboyant struggle, nationally famous for being bold and imaginative in style and clever in strategy. Its successful conclusion was viewed as a boost for the morale of many in the labor movement.

Among the six hundred attending the Unikon celebration were husbands, wives, and children of the workers. Families had come on trips and attended other parties as well. Protracted union management of the work process had changed the daily lives of families in ways that strikes and more conventional dispute actions of the past had not. Workers had been receiving only 60 percent of their prebankruptcy wages, working longer hours, living under the threat of job loss, and coping with the confusing pressures of deciding periodically whether there was enough hope of success to stay with Unikon under these conditions or whether they should quit and try to find other work in more stable companies. Families had experienced conflicts over money and over how long it was reasonable to continue participating in the struggle. All family members were making daily sacrifices in living standards and peace of mind. An official from the Tokyo branch of the All-Japan Metalworkers Federation made his way to the stage, took the microphone, and praised the Unikon families for persevering through three years of a "struggle with no model, with no precedent in Japan." The message of praise for families in victory echoed the slogans on banners under which Unikon workers had marched in protest, messages proclaiming theirs a struggle for families, accusing capitalists of trying to destroy their families. The omnipresence of this oft-spoken and deeply felt meaning of their struggle was matched by the emphasis on its unique and unprecedented nature.

While it was true that there had been no similar cases for nearly thirty years, it was not true that there was no precedent for this kind of struggle in Japan. This claim to newness seemed nevertheless always to accompany the excitement in the labor movement, on the Left, and in academic circles about worker control of production as a strategy for fighting against bankruptcy and loss of jobs, an excitement that far overshadowed any desire to see historical precedent in the worker-control movements of the immediate postwar period. The first instance of worker control in Japan was at the newspaper *Yomiuri Shinbun* in October 1945 (Moore 1983). Ironically, in 1977, when Unikon went bankrupt and the union occupied the factory against legal orders to disband, began worker control of production, and brought legal suit against the owners, *Yomiuri Shinbun's* rival newspaper, the *Asahi*, sought links overseas but called it unprecedented in Japanese experience. *Asahi* coined the term "eastern Lipp," reporting that the French watchmaker, Lipp, had successfully reopened after their union waged a struggle for worker control and that this Japanese case would be the "eastern" version.[2]

Totsuka Hideo characterized the Unikon struggle in a similar but subtler way. "In it I see a new quality of antibankruptcy disputes of small and medium-sized companies. . . . This new type of labor movement may spread to or influence other labor movements" (1980: 3). Perhaps, Totsuka went on to speculate, there is a kernel of change lodged in these struggles which can begin to "crack the traditional stable labor-management relationship and shake the framework of capitalism." With postwar bankruptcies at an all-time high in the late seventies and eighties, workers were increasingly threatened not simply with stagnating wages but with loss of jobs. Labor disputes have decreased overall from 1974

---

2. Lipp went bankrupt in 1968 as a result of increasing rationalization of the production process. After a short period of worker-controlled production the company closed.

until the present, as slowed growth, periodic recession, and the highest rates of bankruptcy in postwar Japanese history gradually changed the nature of economic life for Japanese workers. In this environment the antibankruptcy struggles staked out new tactics and new demands. The fact that they occurred exclusively in small and medium-sized companies emphasizes the greater vulnerability of workers in this sector to slowed growth or recession.

The official from the Tokyo branch of the All-Japan Metalworkers Federation, the trade union federation to which Unikon belonged, was just finishing his speech. "The Unikon victory," he concluded, "will inspire other workers facing bankruptcies in the low-growth times ahead." As I stood and participated in this party, the Unikon experience of protest and protracted struggle was being transformed from a living struggle, with three years of history—formed as often out of contestation as out of consensus—into an inspiring model of unity, determination, and success. I had already begun to study a second worker-control struggle, at Universal Shoes, and it was easy for me to see the impact the Unikon victory was having on them. The leaders from Universal's union who were present at the party were feeling encouraged and inspired by this victory. Their bankruptcy struggle and worker control of production had started several months before Unikon's and they were still very far from settlement. Spirits had sagged at times as they wondered how long they would have to work at this dispute and what the nature of their reward might be. In the end it was to take Universal nearly seven more years to settle. This summer of 1980 was, however, a gratifying and hopeful time for them.

Other sides of the Unikon story appeared in informal conversations, comments, and interactions as we stood chatting between speeches and toasts. One young man walked over to me, offered me some beer, and stood beside me looking toward the stage. "It's all going so smoothly. Everything looks so beautiful. You'd never know how messy things have been, would you?" "No, you wouldn't," I answered. An older woman joined us as I asked why they thought everyone had come to this party, even those who had been angry, frustrated, and hurt by recent conflicts within the union. "All's well that ends well," she quoted in Japanese, adding as a reminder that it was originally from Shakespeare. For those close enough to see the process of the struggle and ultimate settlement, the Unikon model was not an unambiguously positive one. Whether or not theirs was unusually contested is not easy to say because little has been written about the internal dynamics of Japanese union action.

Rank-and-file conversations at Unikon and later at Universal compared the conflicts, debates, and issues they faced to those faced in several other ongoing and recently concluded disputes. Totsuka (1978) writes that there are two types of workers in antibankruptcy disputes, those who want swift financial compensation and those who want company reconstruction. This split existed in both Unikon and Universal, and there were others.[3] Many of the lines of fissure within these unions followed categorical distinctions among workers that are common throughout Japanese industry, differences between part-time, temporary, postretirement, and regular workers, between male and female workers, or between older and younger workers. Inoue Masao, a labor economist who worked on the Unikon dispute, sees these divisions in the work force as obstacles to equal participation in the management of an enterprise and consequently as threats to unity.[4] These and other categories were experienced in daily workplace practice and reinforced and reinterpreted in formal speeches, union publications, and public pronouncements.

A national All-Japan Metalworkers Federation official followed by an official from the General Council of Japanese Trade Unions, or Sōhyō,[5] brought cheers and applause with their compliments to Unikon's women. "Their vitality and strength were of critical importance to this victory," began the All-Japan Metalworkers official. This was, he continued, his voice rising, "a women's struggle [*fujin no tatakai*]." The Sōhyō official repeated that praise, adding that the workers of the Unikon union, nearly half of whom were women, were "workers who have made history [*rekishi o ugokasu rōdōsha*]." With this, all the Unikon workers and their families were asked to the stage.

As children scrambled onto the stage, adults tried with little determination and less success to encourage them to stand straight and look forward. Women dominated. Wives came with their worker husbands to the stage, but husbands did not accompany their worker wives forward. It was generally true that when men came to union events in support of

---

3. Apter and Sawa (1984) and Groth (1986) discuss this same division in other social movements in Japan.

4. Inoue (1991) attributes conflict within the Unikon union during self-management largely to differences in feelings of responsibility between men and women and between union members of different employment status. I address his analysis in chapter 4.

5. This was the most radical of the national federations of labor during most of the postwar period. It was replaced in the late eighties by Rengō, the Japanese Trade Union Confederation, which absorbed all major national federations into a single national-level organization. This is discussed in chapter 8 in relation to the companies I studied, and general treatments are available in Mochizuki 1993, Taira 1988, and Tsujinaka 1993.

their wives they kept lower profiles in public displays of belonging than did women present in support of their husbands. Adding the Unikon women workers to the wives present, the overall picture under the victory banners at the front of the hall put men in a distinct minority. I felt the irony of this picture, since more than a month ago all but two women workers had quit in protest and frustration over leadership decisions to which they were adamantly opposed. On the stage, union leaders stood in the center with their families, and rank-and-file workers crowded around them, spilling onto the floor in all directions. Pictures were taken, toasts were offered, and applause greeted an array of beaming faces and shy smiles. The stories told by the speakers were visually integrated in this picture of unity, family, women workers, and successful struggle.

The remaining hour of the celebration was quieter. Two Unikon women trained in classical Japanese dance performed gracefully, one dressed in simple black and gray, the other in white and embroidered gold. Red fans moved briskly at their fingertips in gestures of festivity, happiness, and the rebirth of spring. Like the image of the phoenix rising from ashes to a new life, images from natural cycles of time danced a musical portrait of renewal. Conversations were subdued during these performances.

Small groups of Unikon workers gathered here and there. Everyone talked about their families, workers who had quit exchanged news about their new jobs, and workers who had stayed talked about working at the new Unikon. One woman was doing office work in a small company where "everything depends on the president. If he's in a good mood everything is fine. There's no union, though, and consequently we sometimes have to work until nine at night. Everything depends on the whim of the president!" Others had found work inspecting stopwatches in a place near the old Unikon site, taking in piecework at home, or working in a small factory doing video cassette assembly. One young man was talking about looking for work at a larger camera company, although he didn't think his prospects were good. "One of the biggest problems in finding new work is that employers don't even want to talk to you once they find out you worked at Unikon!" he said. "It's especially hard at bigger places, because most of them have unions, and that is the worst." Gesturing toward the women standing near us, he continued, "That's why most of the women who quit are finding jobs at places without unions."

The irony of their situations inspired smiles, resigned laughter, and many knowing looks and shaking of heads. In the efforts by Unikon leaders to decrease the work force prior to reopening the new company workers saw the same kind of logic. "We learned too well. Our consciousness was too high," this same young man suggested. One of the former part-time women workers spoke up. "It will be easier for the new Unikon if they can hire new part-timers who don't talk as much as we do, and who don't have our experience." "So, in the end," another woman went on, "we became a little too smart for our own good, and now nobody wants us, not Unikon, not new employers, and certainly not good companies with unions."

As the music faded in the background a national official of the All-Japan Metalworkers Federation took the stage and led all six hundred present in a rhythmic *sanbon jime* clapping, which ended the party on an auspicious note of unity. The Unikon people I had been standing with quickly gathered by the exit doors in a long reception line to smile, say words of gratitude, bow, and bid farewell to the guests. I walked through this line enjoying the familiarity and friendship of the Unikon workers, marking for me an end to my daily routines of work with them.

Process, Protest, and Japanese Workers

This book is about the daily lives, consciousness, and collective actions of about two hundred Japanese blue-collar workers. It is also about protest, conflict, and contestation in private lives, within unions, and between unions and owners. The focus on workers in protest and on conflict is an exploration of social process, one which I hope shows how contemporary Japanese workers conceptualize their own democratic, industrial society and how they think and feel about acts of acquiescence, accommodation, resistance, and protest within it.

There is a deep silence in the literature on Japan, a silence surrounded on the one hand by historical studies of the intellectual and political contests over the shape of modern Japanese industry and on the other by social science work on the institutional structures and practices of contemporary companies. In neither case have there been studies focusing on the intellectual and practical lives of industrial workers. Images of Japanese workers as docile and passive in contexts of efficiently run, highly productive industrial enterprises continue to be pervasive. We seem wedded to an image of intensely modern, even postmodern, high-tech products being designed and manufactured by traditional workers trapped in the social relations and cultural practices of an isolated and feudal past. We know that Japanese labor relations resembled western ones more at the outset of the twentieth century than at present (Gordon 1988), that lengthy and sometimes violent battles were fought over the independence of Japanese workers and management's need to control their labor (Gordon 1987, 1988, 1991; Garon 1987; Moore 1983), and that institutional practices of harmony and cooperation within industry were conceptualized and implemented with the intervention of the state (Kinzley 1991). Modern industrial organizations, democratic institutions, and labor relations were formed through intense debates about the nature of social order and moral value and through political and social conflicts, conflicts and debates in which workers and their organizations have played a significant and defining role.

The starting point for most social science studies of industrial work and industrial workers has been the stability and economic success that has characterized Japan's largest firms in the middle postwar period between the mid-fifties and the early seventies, a time of economic prosperity for the Japanese nation, extremely high growth rates, and the triumph and consolidation of conservative rule. The immediate postwar period in Japan was characterized by radical opposition, rapid rise in rates of unionization, and widespread radical political action. Opposition was systematically suppressed by a coalition of American and Japanese power concerned both with emerging threats from communism in Asia and with the creation of an economically friendly, stable capitalism. The triumph of the conservatives, many of whom were bureaucrats from the prewar period, began a time of stability and growth considered a "Japanese miracle" and which inspired a number of works proclaiming Japan as "number one." The end of this period is marked by most historians as sometime in the early seventies.[6]

The phenomenon of Japan's rapid growth has had a profound effect not only on popular representations of Japan but on research preferences and scholarly writing as well. Koji Taira argues that "this climate discourages a critical examination of events and problems at subnational levels: that is, what has happened to ordinary people in the course of Japan's postwar economic growth and what may happen to them again as Japan continues to use economic growth as a major policy instrument for the glorification and hegemonization of Japan" (1993: 169).

6. For a wide variety of perspectives on developments in social, political, and cultural areas during the postwar period and for a full account of the emerging periodization of the postwar period into early, middle, and late, see Gordon 1993b.

Indeed, most accounts focus on institutions and structures, evaluating them for their strengths and weaknesses, looking for some hints about the miracle of Japanese recovery. They describe the hierarchical structures, participatory practices, and cooperative labor-management relations and generalize from them that "the Japanese firm" is characterized by harmonious work relations and populated with loyal and satisfied workers (Abegglen 1958; Nakane 1970; Clark 1979; Pascal and Athos 1981; Ouchi 1982). These large and most successful firms have employed no more than 20 percent of the Japanese work force throughout this period. While the picture painted may indeed be indicative of attractive models of efficiency and productivity useful to businesses in other advanced industrialized countries, it is not a picture that represents the work structures, practices, or dilemmas of most of the work force. Nor is it a picture which permits more than a glimpse of daily life or critical thought within capitalist and democratic structures of Japanese society. With the notable exceptions of Ronald Dore (1973, 1986, 1987), Robert Cole (1971, 1979), and Thomas Rohlen (1974), analyses of contemporary institutions of work rarely even address such questions. Cultural processes of conceptualization and social processes of accommodation or resistance remain largely in an arena of silence.[7] The people who create both industrial products and industrial structures through daily actions become shadows of these institutional structures, shadows with a traditional cultural shape alluded to whenever structural explanations for economic performance or worker behavior fail.

Revolutionary class consciousness is not a significant factor in Japanese labor relations or politics, any more than it is in most other advanced capitalist societies. This does not prevent workers from taking collective action or entering into relationships that attempt to affect institutional structures and influence their social institutions, nor does it necessarily mean that there is no class consciousness, opposition, or critical thought. Japanese public opinion surveys have been finding that 90 percent of all respondents identify themselves as "middle class" throughout most of the postwar period (Ishida 1993). Other polls report differences in numbers of people identifying with "middle class" depending on the Japanese terms used, with more willing to identify if the term implies status than if it implies economic standing (Odaka 1966). These polls themselves, however, do not escape the political pressures of history. In

7. The recent work of Kondo (1990) and Hamabata (1990) provide lively ethnographic accounts of contested gender, family, and work identities that engage both daily life and struggles over power.

the seventies, as Japan entered a late postwar period with greater needs
to consolidate a national image of consensus and to reassert conservative
power against opposition movements, new categories were added to the
regular national opinion poll reporting on class consciousness. Instead
of "upper," "middle," and "lower," respondents were given a broader
choice of "middles" when the poll was restructured to read "upper,"
"upper middle," "middle middle," "lower middle," and "lower"
(Taira 1993). Results of these kinds of surveys support the observation
of most scholars that class conflict and class consciousness are blurred
(Steven 1983) and fuel the fires of confusion about contradictions within
Japanese society, where labor disputes are fought just as frequently as
elsewhere in the industrialized world (Hanami 1981; Shirai 1983a;
Chalmers 1989). In an ethnographic study of two small unionized
manufacturing firms, Cole (1971) considers class consciousness, collective action, and attitudes toward workplace authority patterns, and he
gives a sense of workers calculating and making choices about speaking
out in opposition, remaining silent, or accommodating themselves to
unpopular management decisions. His ethnography conveys both the
lively mood of the shop floor and a troubled sense of contradiction.
Although workers regularly elected Socialist and Communist Party supporters as union leaders and even supported these parties in local and
national elections, they were reluctant to take collective action and
expressed deep loyalty to their companies. In grappling with this contradiction, Cole suggests that they were not really class conscious but
rather were "symbolically" supporting the political left.

Takeshi Ishida (1984) tries to reconcile such differences with the
concept of "dependent revolt," protest that expresses "ambivalent feelings." The institutional hierarchies so well described by Nakane (1970)
characterize industrial as well as other social organizations in Japan,
including labor unions. Ishida claims that organizations elicit contradictory feelings and allegiances, compelling workers to want at once to
oppose their superiors and fight for their own interests but also to express
their opposition in terms of demands for "better treatment" which
reflect a paternalistic dependency. Thomas Smith (1988) coined the
term "right to benevolence" to describe this conceptual dilemma faced
by prewar Japanese workers in recognizing class interests and taking
collective action. He also points out that workers went to some trouble
to avoid any challenge to the legitimacy of hierarchy within their firms,
thus preserving the "moral claim to hierarchical justice." Ishida and
Smith, working in periods nearly sixty years apart, suggest the impor-

tance of rank-and-file workers' concepts of social relations, justice, and opposition in the particular forms of collective action taken.

The prevalence of hierarchies of power, status, and authority within Japanese industrial organizations has led to many uncritical assumptions about the dependent submissiveness and satisfied passivity in the work force, in its worst manifestation a total invisibility of all but those on the very top of the pyramids of power and decision making. Cole (1979) has bluntly challenged the notion that participation in the context of strong hierarchies of authority is democratic. For both Rohlen (1974) and Dore (1973), questions of paternalism, hierarchy, efficiency, and flexibility are social and cultural questions and involve debates about the nature of work, organizations, and motivation; they take this investigation into daily practices within firms. Hierarchies of power are counterbalanced by horizontal relations within work groups, and training programs synthesize cultural assumptions and social habits necessary for a well-functioning organization.

This work does not reach into smaller firms, only Dore (1986 and 1987) extends beyond the period of high growth, and none has treated the conceptual and practical lives of workers in their efforts to influence the direction of economic adjustments or the restructuring of workplace authority and power. The labor disputes of Unikon and Universal took place during this late postwar period, beginning just after the "big bang" of the 1974 labor offensive in which a total of 10 percent of Japan's workers were engaged in strikes and as a result of which labor negotiated an average wage increase of 4.3 percent in a year when the economy showed no growth at all. Union militancy grew along with inflation following the oil crises. Taira (1993) calls the result a "class struggle," one in which labor actually won a larger share of the total national output and helped to set a national agenda for economic adjustment, one which demanded restructuring without massive unemployment or severe cuts in living standards.

The slowing of economic growth from over 10 percent to under 5 percent in the seventies and the continuing sluggishness of the Japanese economy have inspired labor protest, but that protest has been contained. The Japanese economy has been resilient, conservatives have prevailed over opposition forces, and there has been an increasing, not decreasing, centralization of planning and negotiation. There has been a triumph of what Andrew Gordon (1993a) calls "management culture" within large firms, and many of the structural adjustments have enhanced and been enhanced by the "welfare corporatism" described by Ronald

Dore (1986 and 1987). Worker-control struggles like those at Unikon and Universal, waged in small and medium-sized firms during the seventies and eighties, raised questions about the social forms and cultural conceptualization of capitalism, work, authority, and opposition.[8] In this book I take those questions into the daily social practices, collective actions, debates, confusions, and convictions of rank-and-file workers' lives and into their workplaces, unions, and movements at an important point of transition for Japanese economy and society.

Unikon Camera and Universal Shoes

Unikon was established in 1907 as a family-owned business employing only twenty people. They made tripods at first, but by 1919 were making cameras and winning prizes for technological innovation. They grew rapidly in the postwar years and expanded again to a maximum of fifteen hundred employees in the midst of the Vietnam War. They relied on European markets and, most heavily, on American military sales. The post-Vietnam years saw declining international markets and increasing domestic competition, and threw them into severe financial difficulties. The oil crises of the seventies, revaluation of the yen and consequent slowed economic growth and shrinking international markets led to bankruptcy in October 1977.

Universal Shoes was established in 1946 and at first made only women's shoes. It later started producing both men's and women's shoes and then turned to producing only men's. They were operating as a subcontractor for Custom Shoes, the third-largest shoe manufacturer in Japan, and gradually became more and more dependent upon Custom until in 1967 they became a subsidiary of Custom, completely under their direction. In March 1977, in response to international pressure for the liberalization of imports of leather shoes and the increasing sluggishness of the domestic economy, Custom began a rationalization of

8. Unfortunately there are no reliable statistics for the number of these cases. Totsuka (1978) points out that labor statistics count strikes, slowdowns, and "others" and that as the number of union-managed production disputes increased in the late seventies the number of "others" decreased to zero. The *Asahi Shinbun* (March 24, 1978) reports that as of October 1977 there were fifty-four unions in such struggles. Universal counted ninety-four unions fighting bankruptcies in 1982, thirty-five of which were under self-management, and found that between 1972 and 1982 there were twenty cases of bankruptcy disputes aimed at reopening companies, of which "most" had been successful.

their own company's operations, including a reduction in their own work force and the automation of many operations. At this time Custom had a work force of about eight hundred employees. They proposed 271 "voluntary retirements" and dismissed 12 managers just as Universal was going bankrupt. Some conclude that the Universal bankruptcy was planned to frighten the other Custom employees into accepting the "voluntary retirement" plans. Custom also decided that they no longer needed Universal and attempted to close the subsidiary down by having their owners file bankruptcy.

Both Unikon and Universal were small industries. Firms in Japan are frequently categorized as large or small-medium sized (*chūshō kigyō*). There are several ways to draw this line, one of the most common being by number of employees, in which case firms with three hundred or fewer employees are considered to be small-medium sized firms. There has been considerable criticism of this binary opposition of small and large and of the consequent "dual structure" model of the Japanese economy because of a tendency to hide subtler gradations in the size of firms, the importance of the industrial networks into which many smaller firms fit, and even the relative wealth and economic viability of firms, which are not always perfectly correlated with size. Indeed, the case of Unikon is a good example of the danger of a simple dichotomy of this kind. It is not untypical of a firm to grow and shrink in size over its lifetime, and Unikon moved from fifteen hundred employees down to two hundred as its fortunes waned, moving it from the large to the small-medium category, although in other definitions of these categories the cutoff point comes at one thousand employees, making Unikon a very borderline case even in its heyday.

One of the problems with attempts to define this "sector" of the economy is that it is so diverse, constituting over 90 percent of all firms and about 80 percent of the work force. It is therefore misleading to make very much of its "special" characteristics. It may, however, be useful to compare its characteristics to the 1 percent of companies and 20 percent of employees constituting the "large" sector. Typically there is about a 20 percent wage differential between large and small firms. Prior to their bankruptcies Unikon and Universal paid wages of about $750 per month, plus bonuses which could be as little as one or two months' pay or as high as four or five. This is close to average for workers in smaller firms. With larger Japanese companies, there is a wide range of services and benefits such as housing, low-interest loans for mortgages or education, use of vacation facilities, and large bonuses, often as much as six months' salary. At Unikon and at Universal, as well as at other small companies where I have worked, workers refer to large firms as "big ships" and to their own as "little tiny boats," vulnerable to the ups and downs of choppy economic waters. Related to this is the expectation of movement during a working career. Mobility is on average much lower for regular employees in large firms, where separation rates are 5 percent compared to 30 percent for young men and 15 percent for middle-aged men in smaller companies (Koike 1983: 97). At both Unikon and Universal, workers had had other jobs in similar firms, and younger workers fully expected to move once or twice more during their working career.

Both Unikon and Universal had work forces just under one-third female immediately prior to their bankruptcy. The average age at Unikon for the full-time workers was quite young, around thirty, and for the part-time workers it was about forty-five. Many of the young men and women in full-time positions had been recruited from high school, with large numbers coming from rural areas of northeastern Japan. Part-time workers were, as is the case in most firms, middle-aged women recruited from the immediate vicinity of the factory. These women had all had other jobs prior to bearing their children, had done piecework at home while their children were young, and had returned to jobs outside the home when the children were older. Most had come to Tokyo from rural areas. This rural origin of the majority of workers at Unikon became part of the cultural life of the factory in that it helped fashion the nature of factory festivals, the regional foods which people brought to events, and the kinds of metaphors, references, and stories recalled by people in talking about their lives and experiences at work and in Tokyo. At Universal all but three of the women were part-timers recruited from nearby. The full-time work force was about half postretirement male workers and half middle-aged men. Following retirement at ages ranging from fifty-five to sixty, it is common for men to find jobs in smaller firms for lower wages; at Universal these workers ranged in age from sixty to seventy-five. These profiles are in keeping with smaller firms in Japan, although because this "sector" really includes all but 20 percent of the work force, the primary relevance of this observation is to emphasize that the other 20 percent of the work force in the largest firms is extremely skewed toward full-time males in the peak years of their careers.

Both firms had enterprise unions, the ubiquitous form of union organization in firms of all sizes in Japan. About 34 percent of all workers in manufacturing are unionized, but the rate is 57 percent for firms of over a thousand workers and only 0.8 percent in firms of under thirty (Chalmers 1989: 177–89). Unikon and Universal fit at the lower end of this continuum. Enterprise unions are organized around individual firms and typically include all regular employees, regardless of specific job content, up to and including the rank of foreman. Although it is very rare in Japan for part-time workers to be part of a union, in each of these companies they were. At Unikon they had their own union, which merged with that of the full-time workers at the point of bankruptcy, and at Universal they were members of the same union. Because both Unikon and Universal were so organized, the number of employees at the time of bankruptcy equaled the number of union members. Although these unions were organized around individual firms, they were linked to regional federations and to federations based on type of industry. Unikon and Universal, located in the same part of Tokyo, were both members of the Eastern Tokyo Regional Federation, and the corresponding district organizations beneath that. This network is constituted by unions of firms operating within this area regardless of type of enterprise. Unikon also belonged to the All-Japan Metalworkers Federation and Universal to the All-Japan Leatherworkers Federation. These two are defined by type of industry and both were linked at the national level to Sōhyō, the General Council of Japanese Trade Unions.[9]

In March 1977, when Universal went bankrupt, its union entered into a labor dispute that included court battles, negotiations with the parent company and financial backers, worker control of production, and a variety of collective actions.[10] When Unikon went bankrupt in October of the same year, they copied Universal's actions. They knew each other well through both eastern Tokyo regional networks and through Sōhyō.[11] In each case the unions brought legal charges of unfair labor practices and claimed back wages, severance pay, and other benefits due to them. They also charged that they had not been given the opportunity to bargain collectively, although under law all employers are obliged to

9. Sōhyō was dissolved in 1989 when it joined the new Rengō, the Japanese Trade Union Confederation, a national organization now representing 65 percent of all organized workers in Japan.

10. Hanami 1981 gives some general accounts of worker control as a strategy in the immediate postwar period, and Moore 1983 is an in-depth look at such struggles.

11. Bankruptcies in Japan increased rapidly between 1968 and 1977. In 1977 there was a 400 percent increase in the number of firms with greater than $50 million in liabilities. Smaller firms were even more vulnerable to the recessions and oil shocks that have challenged the Japanese economy. For a full account of trends in bankruptcies see Saxonhouse 1979.

accept recognized union offers to negotiate. In turn they were each sued by their former owners for obstruction of business and for refusing to evacuate the premises.

In organizing these disputes they demanded rights to assets and set as their goal the reopening of their companies under new management to be selected and designed by the unions themselves.[12] As Totsuka points out, these struggles were facilitated by Japanese labor law and arbitration practices which allow that "management-labor relations exist until a company has completed all bankruptcy processes" (1984: 26). This meant that although the unions were defying legal orders to disband and allow assets to be liquidated, their lawsuits and labor disputes were considered by labor arbitrators to be legitimate actions in labor-management relations until some resolution was reached. The other important strategy taken by Universal and copied by Unikon was the writing of a "factory use agreement" that gave the union the temporary right to the use of land, buildings, machines, and other equipment pending resolution of union claims to wages, severance pay, and other appropriate compensation should the bankruptcy be carried out. In each case the unions succeeded, through intense harassment of the company presidents, in forcing signature to these agreements, which were then used to justify their occupation and use of factory premises under worker control.

When these unions entered the dispute process, all their networks were involved. Officers from the regional, industrial, and national organizations were sent to advise, support, and help organize and strategize. Financial and human resources were also made available, as were contacts in extensive regional and national networks of affiliated unions. Because of their relatively small sizes the unions depended on these networks to make their struggles feasible.[13] Both unions ultimately won their disputes, settling in out-of-court arbitration, and reopened under management designed by the unions themselves, but in each case the disputes were long, Unikon taking two and a half years and Universal nearly ten.[14]

12. See Totsuka 1980 for a broad discussion of bankruptcy disputes in small and medium-sized industries and Totsuka 1978 for a discussion of their importance in the wider context of labor disputes in Japan.

13. For more on the role of union networks in labor disputes for small companies in Japan, see Fujita and Takeuchi 1977.

14. See Fujita and Takeuchi 1977 for an account of disputes in smaller companies. They point out that such disputes are generally longer than in large companies and that their duration has been steadily increasing since the 1960s.

Consciousness, Action, and Everyday Life

To understand collective action and the solidarity which must motivate it, the consciousness of the workers involved must be seen in the full complexity of everyday life. Class consciousness and solidarity are built out of experience as much as out of ideology, and the motivation to protest is sustained in anger over threats to unexamined, commonsense assumptions about human dignity as often as in discursively debated issues of workers' rights. I do not mean to underestimate the importance of discursive knowing or heartfelt debates about conviction and social knowledge. On the contrary, the following chapters give accounts of such debates, examined not only by me as an ethnographer but also by the Unikon and Universal workers themselves. In my experience, people analyzed not only their social world and its forms and actions but their own ideas about such things as well. I emphasize the nondiscursive to balance a too-often unbalanced picture of thought and action.

In this book I am preeminently concerned with the interweaving of experience, consciousness, decisive action, improvisation, and serendipity that is the stuff both of daily life and of ultimate meaning. In the current language of postmodernism, the experiences and consciousness of the Unikon and Universal workers "resist closure." In their own language, things "don't quite add up" (*warikirenai*). This points to the importance of process, an old story in anthropology, told and retold by Clifford Geertz, Victor Turner, and their respective scholarly lineages. The significance of Geertz's "thick description" is to contextualize slices of social life so that stories people tell one another about themselves may be interpreted in action—concepts in the context of action, culture in the company of social life. Turner uses metaphors of drama and ritual process, letting thoughts and acts move through time as they are interpreted, claiming that without such movement, society has no life, and culture no time to be experienced.

The recent work of Rick Fantasia grasps for ways to talk about American workers' consciousness within collective actions, settling on "cultures of solidarity" to try to overcome the conflation of consciousness with "workers' conceptions, images, attitudes, and ideational and verbal responses to the social arrangements in which they find themselves" (1988: 4). This conflation is not a new theoretical issue in either anthropology or sociology. Anthony Giddens (1979) has argued from both Weberian and Marxist points of view that "discursive" and "practical" consciousness must be analytically distinguished so that their interactions may be included in analysis of the creation and re-creation of social structure. Michael Taussig differentiates "explicit" and "implicit social knowledge" (1987: 367), and Jean and John Comaroff have used "conversion" for change through argument or image and "reformation" for change in "taken for granted signs and practices" (1989: 289–90).

The choice of sites where people were actively engaged in efforts to transform their social worlds made it easier to see the process of that transformation in both practice and conceptualization, through time and in a rich context. I chose disputes using worker control of production because while they were fought to gain compensation for bankruptcy and to reopen their companies under management designed by their unions, workers within them were working on a daily basis over the course of years under their own management. Workers at Unikon and Universal not only had to think about what sort of work organization was desirable and how best to fight for it, they were also living under new conditions of their own choosing. People at all levels of the unions were living with and reacting to choices about industrial organization even as they were fighting to gain the right to do so on a legal and permanent basis. Questions about capitalism, democracy, power, equality, productivity and about creating a living workplace community were at once issues of daily experience and of political struggle. Words written on banners and marched under were being transformed into daily experience. People were challenged to believe not only in what they strove toward but in what they were living as well.

Under the circumstances, *warikirenai*, the inability to resolve things clearly once and for all, becomes more than the verbal sigh at the end of a long confusing conversation, a frustrating union meeting, or an exhausting and unsuccessful negotiation session. It becomes a theoretical starting point for analysis, suggesting that consciousness and action be seen through a temporal dimension. It is the unfinished, processual nature of social life which constitutes experience for most people most of the time. Pierre Bourdieu (1977) has contrasted this with the point of view of the social scientist, claiming that while social analysis starts with concluded events, the people acting through those events and creating social forms with their own daily decisions and actions see things from the uncertain perspective of the ongoing. They have a past to look to for guidance and a future to imagine, but they act in a present that is always in the process of change. Most decisions about how to act are made in partial knowledge, with partial conviction. The *warikirenai* of

Unikon and Universal workers is the daily life process of conceptualizing one's own social world while creating one's own life in a social space where practices and institutions seem sometimes to be changing and at other times to be permanent.

In the process of trying to change the way things are, Unikon and Universal workers had to grapple constantly with the likelihood that things could change. The permanence of social institutions, power relations, and practices was a matter both of perception and of strategy. For Unikon workers to decide to stay in a dispute for nearly three years required a sustained belief that things might change, that their actions might transform their own lives and the institutions they worked in. For the Unikon workers who quit their company and their union just after their victory to come to the final celebration and engage in rituals of jubilation, unity, and renewal required resignation to what they judged to be inevitable. Both actions were taken by the same workers in the course of the same struggle. Neither indicates docility and neither indicates unbridled activism. Both are evidence of the ongoing struggle to make sense of social life and to act strategically in a social space where capitalism, alternative ideologies of socialism and communism, inequalities of power within unions and between workers and owners, remembered histories of other workers and common peoples, and images of foreign societies all bear weight in social and cultural calculations.

Locating Unikon and Universal

One advantage of using an ethnographic approach to problems of consciousness and collective action is the freedom it offers to see ongoing process, to see social practice and cultural conceptualization interact in daily life. Being in a situation where it was possible to pass time with people, listen to them speak to one another and to me, and taking a participatory role in their lives and organizations gave me an intimacy fraught with practical and ethical problems.

The practical problems involved discovery, introduction, permission, and choice. When I went to Japan I knew nothing of the worker-control struggles, much less of Unikon or Universal. They had not yet appeared in the Japanese academic literature and still have not appeared in the English. My first efforts, motivated by sociological studies of American working-class neighborhoods, were to find communities where I could live and get to know people working in a variety of companies and engaged in a variety of political activities. Neighborhoods in Tokyo, however, tend to be held together by small shop owners, retired persons, and homeowners, not by blue-collar workers, who tend to live dispersed throughout the eastern area of the city in relatively inexpensive, often public, housing. Even the smallest companies have workers commuting from a number of different locations, and in each of those locations workers have relatively little role in local community activities. It is part of the patterning of social life in Tokyo that workers spend most of their time at work or at home—in their homes—with their families. Community is found, to the extent that it is, in workplace-related activities, around school activities for children, or in the habit of returning for special occasions to rural areas or small towns where natal families reside.

After living in eastern Tokyo for a while, I shifted my attention to finding a workplace where I could be with people regularly. This initiated a series of introductions that led me to a Japanese professor specializing in workers' culture and consciousness. The idea of using ethnographic methods of participant observation to study consciousness and collective action seemed unusual but provocative to him, and his enthusiasm led him to open many doors for my project. His unhesitating advice was to study Unikon. "If you are interested in workers' consciousness, that is where you must go. They are the avant-garde of the Japanese labor movement, the most advanced workers in Japan. If there is real workers' consciousness anywhere, it is there!"

With a series of introductions, I began to talk with Unikon labor union leaders. Their situation was ideal for me. They were coping with one of the central issues of late postwar Japan, the threat to full employment. The challenge for them was to formulate an organized opposition to loss of jobs through bankruptcy, raising questions of appropriate and realistic goals for their movement and of appropriate and realistic forms of work organization for their self-managed factory. Fortunately, they understood quickly and sympathetically what I wanted to do, and they liked it. It had taken me six months to find the academic contacts which suggested this location and another three months to work through the university networks to get to Unikon, but three days after my first visit I was welcomed into the factory, given an assigned place to work on the assembly line and a desk in the union offices.[15]

15. Fieldworkers will appreciate the fact that it took me nearly six months to find the right place and the necessary introductions to it, but only three days to get into intensive fieldwork once I arrived on their doorstep.

These first three days at Unikon were a period of mutual exploration. I was asked questions on a wide range of topics, including my own personal history, my parents and extended family background, my political attitudes and activities, American society and politics, and of course about my project, its central concerns, and my motivation. In addition, three union officers, using books, photos, and objects, spent many hours explaining union and company history to me. On the fourth day they put me on their single-lens reflex camera assembly line. Over the next four months I rotated from position to position throughout the line, working with each person in turn, prompting several people to joke that I would be the only one in the company who knew how to assemble the entire camera. I worked a regular shift at Unikon from March through June of 1980 and continued a very close association with them through December 1984, when I returned to the United States. Through visits and correspondence, I continue to keep in touch with the people still working there and with many who have since quit.

My work with them came at the end of their two-and-a-half-year dispute and included the negotiations and disturbances surrounding the final settlement. The party I described at the outset of this chapter marked the end of the dispute, the victory of their union, and the reopening of a new Unikon Camera. When I was about to complete my work there, one of the union leaders came to me and suggested I let them introduce me to Universal Shoes. I did not yet, he politely pointed out, have the "whole picture." This was neither the first nor the last time that my anthropological "informants" informed me of their views not only about their own work, lives, and ideas, but also about how they thought my work, life, and thoughts should be going. I had, he said, only gotten to know their workers, who were young, mostly in their twenties or early thirties, and doing high-tech, mass-production work. My study should, they felt, also include life and work with people who think of themselves as craftsmen (*shokunin*) and who are older. Universal workers fit both these descriptions, and considering them together with the Unikon workers, they urged, would give me a broader and deeper picture.

One of the challenges of fieldwork is making choices with partial knowledge, little forewarning, and less time to ponder. This proposal was offered to me one day and a visit to Universal had been scheduled for two days later. I had been invited to study other union disputes by leaders who explained to me that their situations were as interesting as Unikon's. Most were involved with job security struggles, many with protests of firing due to rationalization. This was the first invitation I had received to work at another company under worker control. I knew that at the time of their bankruptcy Unikon had modeled their own action on Universal's and that the two had been closely aligned, attending each other's demonstrations and sharing strategies and resources over the past three years. I wanted to stay longer in this network of unions, to expand my project to include workers of different ages and in different industries, and to move into a workplace where the struggle was ongoing. The Unikon struggle had ended within a couple of months of my entering the company. I wanted to spend time with workers engaged in the earlier, more uncertain stages, and with Universal there would be sufficient continuities to make their inclusion both interesting and feasible.

Within a day of their suggestion, I accepted the Unikon leaders' advice and let them introduce me to Universal, where I worked from July 1980 through January 1981. At Universal, because of the more complicated nature of the work and the length of time it takes to train people in many of the jobs, I was located permanently in one section, the cutting-and-sewing section, with only short assignments elsewhere. I glued together leather pieces prior to sewing, one of the only jobs simple enough to learn in a short time. I was encouraged to move about the factory freely, talk to those in other sections, and watch their work. As with Unikon, I continued to see Universal workers frequently throughout the next four years, and I still maintain contact with them and their company through letters and visits.

The daily interactions and friendships that grew out of this kind of ethnographic work involved me in people's lives in a very intimate way. Ethical dilemmas greeted me the moment I found these places and stretched throughout my work there and into my writing. Two of them are particularly pertinent to the writing and reading of this book. The most troubling dilemma was whether or not to introduce into my analysis speculation on the role of minority workers in these struggles. Because they occur in small firms where minorities are more likely to be employed, and because of the historical association of leather industries with the *burakumin*, or "outcast" minority, the issue is raised by others even if I do not raise it myself. There are still no laws in Japan protecting individual members of minorities from discrimination by private parties. In addition to the books of names and addresses listing minorities, there is a large and profitable private-investigation industry supported by employers and families of prospective marriage partners, the sole purpose of which is to determine if particular individuals are or are not Chinese, Korean, *burakumin*, or of other minority descent. It is impossible for me to introduce this issue into my writing without engaging in a destructive politics of social identity. Consequently, since these issues were not part of either ordinary conversations or the arguments of protest actions, I will not address them here.[16]

Situated as these unions were in radical protest movements, there were other political issues as well. These two small unions had some visibility in the press, in academic circles, and to the Japanese public. Both advertised their struggles in order to garner support, both engaged in open demonstrations to publicize their grievances, both wrote books about their unions, and Universal commissioned a film to publicize and commemorate their dispute. In all of these activities they used their own names, and some scholars in my position might do the same. Unikon and Universal are, however, not their real names, nor are any of the names of individuals used in this book.[17] It was a condition of my research with each of them that I protect their anonymity. In exchange, I was encouraged by union leaders in both places to be as "truthful" as possible. When I began seeing serious rifts between leadership and the rank and file, I went to the Unikon leaders and asked them if there would be any harm in my writing about such conflicts. That was my job, they said, to be "objective" and write about their situation. At Universal I received similar advice, with one union leader saying that he had never seen a Japanese union where democracy or equality really worked, so it was about time someone wrote about it. In print, however, leaders in both unions wanted the stories associated with their real names to be under their own control.[18] In a political climate where stories told were also political acts, this seemed a reasonable and appropriate request.

Locating Myself within Unikon and Universal

Locating myself within the social worlds of Unikon and Universal was not a matter of settling into a comfortable vantage point from which to observe their workers in daily work and protest activities.

16. For a discussion of these issues see DeVos and Wagatsuma 1966 and Upham 1987 and 1993.

17. Unikon and Universal are both English in sound and derivation as are the actual names. It is common to use English or other western language names for companies which produce objects associated with the West. Such names are written, as were Unikon and Universal's, in the *katakana* alphabet, the alphabet reserved for foreign words.

18. Both unions later published their own accounts.

I had to negotiate an identity within the relationships of their companies, unions, networks, families, and neighborhoods. This identity, the product of my choices and of impressions and decisions of the people I worked with, located me and determined the things I could do, the perspectives I could hear, and the actions I could observe.[19] It is easy to describe the activities I was involved in, but harder to convey a sense of particular location.

I had extensive access to union meetings, shop floor meetings, and many leadership and struggle committee meetings. I commuted to and from work with union members, participated in demonstrations, parties, and trips, joined in after-work socializing, and visited people's homes on weekends. This made it possible to listen to what people said to one another and to see workers interacting socially and politically in a variety of relationships and contexts inside and outside the workplace. I rarely did interviews, relying almost exclusively on these routines of association.

Choosing where to be and with whom to spend time was a daily task. The extensive regional and national networks which supported Unikon and Universal sent representatives who worked on a daily basis in each company and sat on the committees to decide business and political strategy. National officials came as organizers, seeing in these struggles some hope for significant progress for the Japanese labor movement. Regional and industry federation officers were closer to the struggles, seeing in them union efforts to stem the tide of antilabor actions which might hit their own companies next. People from small supporting unions were usually engaged in their own struggles and empathized with the Unikon and Universal situations in a personal way. In addition, all these structural positions were occupied by individuals with their own histories, opinions, and feelings. Some officers were more popular with rank-and-file workers than others. Some rank-and-file workers were more respected by union leaders and outside officers than others.

My presence as an outsider and as an anthropologist made me visible and attracted a lot of attention, with many offers of advice and help. Locating myself in these social situations was an ongoing challenge, presenting me with conflicts, embarrassment, and choices of considerable consequence for my project. An official of a regional federation interrupted one of Universal's Joint Struggle Committee meetings I attended to explain to me that "the root of Japanese workers' con-

19. See Clifford 1986 and Haraway 1988 for discussions of the process of doing fieldwork.

sciousness is rice." He described the frustration of organizers in facing the complacency of rank and file. In Poland, he suggested, workers were more eager to organize and to take collective action because as westerners they want to be able to afford to buy meat, whereas in Japan if workers only have rice they are ready to settle and go along with things.

The situation could become more than simply disruptive or socially awkward. At a factory festival for Universal, a national federation official counseled me, "If you are writing a book about the consciousness of Japanese workers it's going to be a very short one—they don't have any!" This comment, made somewhat tongue-in-cheek to twenty or so people gathered around a table of drinks, was met with laughter by some and with a pained look by others. Several of the rank and file present quietly turned and walked away. These rank-and-file workers were the people with whom I was working on a daily basis. This official, on the other hand, was someone I needed to talk with about the broader labor movement of which Universal was a part.

The nature of my project elicited responses which broadly traced the contours of the struggle for commitment, for consciousness, and for solidarity in these unions, as well as in the Japanese labor movement. It was evident from very early on that the Unikon workers, unambiguously representing the vanguard of the Japanese labor movement to some, were living in a very complex world politically, socially, and conceptually. Unikon union leaders smiled and shook their heads in puzzlement when I asked about class consciousness in their highly visible struggle, and that shaking of heads was just a hint at what became very evident as I did my work, namely, that inside these unions and inside the labor movement generally consciousness was a contested issue, not an accomplished achievement. Furthermore, in the relationship of leaders to rank and file there was potential for great gaps of understanding and feelings of denigration. Efforts by leaders to mobilize action and "raise consciousness" could feel patronizing. Expressions of frustration could sound disparaging.

Activities, as will be evident in the following chapters, almost invariably split leadership from rank and file, not only in terms of consciousness and efforts to affect it but in purely logistic terms as well. They were not doing the same things. While leaders would be entertaining guests, rank and file would be setting up rooms and cooking for the meetings and parties. While rank and file were working on the shop floor and chatting about upcoming demonstrations, leaders were preparing strategies and banners for the marches. I could not do both, and my choice was usually to be where rank and file were. Naturally, the simple fact that I was doing production work on the shop floors put me squarely in the midst of rank-and-file workers and more distant from leaders. Neither company was so large, however, that I was isolated in any way from the union leadership.

In each place there existed a gap between the leaders and the rank-and-file members, although the nature of that gap and its size was quite specific to particular events or issues. Differences in educational background or work experience did not provide sufficient explanation. What distinguished leaders most clearly was their position between regional and national federations on the one hand and their own union's rank and file on the other. I was able to move back and forth across that border much less separated from union and federation leaders than were rank-and-file workers. On several occasions people I worked with requested that I ask their leaders for information to which they had no access. I was clearly liminal in these organizations but leaning heavily to one side, that of rank-and-file workers. In no case could my participation avoid these issues or my interpretations escape the constraints of these relationships.

Beyond the boundaries of my own choices were assumptions others made about me, about the appropriate things to discuss with me or to invite me to do. My identity as an anthropologist interested in their consciousness and actions, as an American, a woman, a person from a working-class family, and as someone working in their daily routine located me in these social spaces in ways which I learned and appreciated gradually and incompletely. I could see quite quickly what advantages flowed from various dimensions of my identity, but I will never be sure what I missed.

When I began this project the worries and warnings of friends, colleagues, and well-meaning university administrators all concerned gender and class—specifically, my gender and their class. My being female had worried others the most, although it was something I had grown accustomed to, and it was something I had grown accustomed to in a working-class environment. There is very clear gender segregation in most situations in Japan and a high consciousness of gendered differences in language and cultural practice. One of the consequences of this situation is that women are less threatening because they are less powerful. Another consequence is that a female researcher has the freedom to speak to women and to men alone or in groups, whereas it is more difficult for men to speak either to a woman alone or even to small groups

of women alone without threatening their reputations.[20] Gender, however, is never an isolated identity. I was not just female, I was a Caucasian
American female. My outsider status released me from constraints which
would no doubt hold for Japanese women researchers.

I had many warnings about the feasibility of any woman studying
blue-collar workers, especially in factories. One colleague suggested that
I couldn't possibly do this work because I don't like to drink, and "you
can't study working-class consciousness in Japan without hanging out
in bars and hearing what people *really* think." In Japan I faced strikingly
similar sets of images. When I chose to live in the northeastern part of
town, a poorer area populated by small businesses, small factories, and
lower-income residences, administrators at the university where I was a
visiting researcher grew alarmed. "Is it safe for you to live there? I've
never even been to that area of town. There are much nicer places in
Tokyo for a young woman to live." People were concerned about my
safety and frankly pessimistic that I could do research there. Japanese
friends whom I had met in the United States or through university ties
in Japan echoed these thoughts, and the more curious made pilgrimages
to my home to visit a part of their own city into which they claimed never
to have ventured.[21]

Fortunately, my personal history made me quite confident that workers and their consciousness were not limited solely to the province of
men, bars, and rough neighborhoods. My family and friends in the
working-class area of San Diego where I grew up had some lively
speculations about my project. "They" might be "just like us" because
"the little guy" is the same anywhere in the world where you find "big
business." Or "they" would be impossibly different because Japan is
such a different place. In all of this there was, however, nothing alarming
about wanting to understand the thoughts and actions of workers and
unions. That part was natural, because the importance of the thoughts
and feelings of the "people who work for a living" was assumed.

Being a young American woman worked for the most part to open
things up to me. I was a very unthreatening presence. During my field-

20. A male colleague doing a fieldwork project at the same time I was had been
convinced of the potential problems of a woman doing work in factories. After several
months in the field we talked about constraints and advantages in being male or female.
To our mutual amusement we discovered that I had greater access to a wider variety of
people than he did. He could not interview, much less "hang out" with women unless
there were many other women present or other men. I could go out with men simply by
having another woman go too.

21. Kondo (1990) discusses her experiences working in the same area of Tokyo.

work at Unikon, Japanese researchers of more senior status were denied permission to interview rank-and-file workers and were accompanied by union leaders when visiting the line. I later asked Unikon leaders why they had given me such a free hand. There were two reasons. The first had to do with my being American. I would publish in English in the United States; what Japanese researchers publish can be picked up by the press and could thus compromise their political negotiations. The second had to do with trust, and involved the Unikon leaders' evaluation of the importance of my own class background, something I had greatly underestimated. Only at the end of my work with them did Unikon leaders reveal to me the other purpose of those first three days of questioning me and presenting their history. Their simple purpose had been to find out if my language was good enough to fit in and allow "natural" life to go on. Beyond that, however, they wanted to know whether or not I was "sincere" and whether or not we would be "comfortable together." Working as they were in a critical time for their union, when solidarity was important and internal politics potentially troubled, it was particularly important that I fit in. They were relieved when they heard that my father, other relatives, and friends were workers and union members. This, they had believed, would make it easier for me to interact with and understand people in their workplace. They shared with my American family and friends the assumption that in some important ways "*hata-raku hitobito*" (an almost literal equivalent of "people who work for a living") and their unions were alike across national boundaries.

At both Unikon and Universal, people were surprised that an anthropologist would be working in a factory. Most people knew anthropology as the study of "primitive" societies or at least of villages. They came to new understandings through our conversations and through my research methods, and in unexpected ways these methods made me very popular and motivated people to help me "get things right." The time I spent doing things with people drew a lot of attention and favorable comment. I told everyone who asked exactly what I wanted to study: the "social consciousness" and political action of their union members. The only way to do that, one man told me, was to "experience daily life with us," because, he went on, "we don't always know exactly what we are doing, we are just doing it." My work, involving as it did doing their work with them, felt most often like a collaborative project. At several points in the chapters to follow it will be obvious how involved people became in trying to help me know them and understand their movement.

The Organization of the Text

The chapters that follow present several events and oc-
currences of everyday life, first at Unikon (chapters 2, 3, and 4) and then
at Universal (chapters 5, 6, and 7). They are presented in each case in
chronological order, at Unikon between March 1980 and July 1980 and
at Universal between July 1980 and January 1981, with some discussion
in chapter 7 of events in 1984. Through December 1984, I continued
extensive contact, visiting the factories and seeing people informally
outside their workplaces, so there are comments and interpretations
throughout this book drawing on those later exchanges, and the material
in the epilogue and conclusion include this plus even later follow-up
visits and contacts through 1993.

In each chapter, people are occupied with their social world both
conceptually and practically. In chapters 2 and 6 workers are involved
in Sōkōdō demonstrations, events that bring thousands of workers into
cooperative protest actions in mutual support of ongoing disputes. In
chapter 2 I put this demonstration in the context of other collective
actions and other labor disputes for the Unikon union. In chapter 6 I
follow the Universal workers through their first such action to explore
its effects on their evolving consciousness and familiarity with social acts
of protest. Chapter 3 follows Unikon workers and guests on a union trip
to the mountain resort of Nikkō where the internal and external relations
of the Unikon union are experienced outside the workplace in a period
defined as play. Chapter 4 considers a crisis which develops at Unikon
at the point of the settlement, spanning six weeks of time during which
the company concludes its negotiations, moves to a new site, and makes
final preparations for reopening. Chapter 5 focuses a discussion of meetings and democratic process on the Twenty-Fifth Annual Meeting of
Universal's union, looking at democratic process, hierarchy, and equality. Chapter 7 looks at the meaning of daily life routine and work itself.

In this introduction, in the concluding discussion of chapter 8, and
wherever relevant to the discussion in other chapters, I treat Unikon and
Universal together. Chapter 8 considers some of the implications of
these struggles for understanding Japanese workers and for appreciating
the relationship between consciousness and experience.

PART ONE

Unikon Camera

Learning to Protest

*Class Consciousness, Solidarity,
and Political Action*

By the time I came to Unikon, the union had been through three major labor disputes with their management and had struggled for sixteen years against strong opposition to form their union. The demonstration which I discuss in this chapter was for them a familiar action. That familiarity itself was a purposefully achieved goal of the leaders of Unikon and an accomplishment of some pride for the rank and file. It had evolved through a combination of explicit education and argument on the one hand and experiential learning on the other. Demonstrations and other acts of open protest are not ordinary in the lives of most workers. While the existence of such actions is known from the press or from union news or even from friends, they are not part of most people's personal experience. Consequently, when faced with a need to organize collective actions, the leaders of Unikon's union needed a strategy to build solidarity and to teach their rank and file to protest. That strategy included both plans for organizing collective action and plans for raising the consciousness of the membership so that their commitment would be deep enough to withstand a lengthy dispute. Moreover, the rank and file had to have personal strategies, including reasons for staying and fighting rather than quitting in favor of other employment. The collective history of the union and its disputes and protests is a history of several different strands of action, strategy, reason, and sensibility that together formed a series of unified struggles. Unity was a carefully and imperfectly constructed social form with divergent internal threads, formed as much from the sense people had of personal experiences as of arguments, analysis, or conversation.

History of Unikon's Major Disputes

There are two influential strands of history in Unikon's struggle: the history which had been shared by most of the workers still present and the history prior to their employment at the firm, providing stories which were a source of lessons, legends, and examples. At the end of the dispute there were 102 persons still working at Unikon. Of these between 80 and 90 had been with Unikon from the beginning of the organization of the labor union, about eleven years before. There were four major disputes in Unikon's history. The first three all involved struggles to form the union organization. In each case workers organized a union and in each case the company took action against it. Only in the third did a union survive, and that is the present Unikon union. The final and fourth dispute was the bankruptcy dispute which was ongoing when I worked there.

UNIKON'S FIRST
AND SECOND DISPUTES

Unikon Camera was established in 1907 and operated without a union until 1956. After World War II, business expanded rapidly as the camera was sold to the U.S. military, and the work force of 150 increased by 1961 to 1500. It was during this period of growth that, in December 1956, an effort to organize a union was made. The new Japanese constitution and postwar labor laws guaranteed rights to organize, and the early postwar period saw an extraordinary rise in union organization and membership from just over 3 percent in 1945 to nearly 56 percent in 1949. From the mid-1950s rates dropped to about 35 percent, where they have remained ever since (Shirai 1983b). This first attempt at Unikon included about two hundred workers. The response by the owners was opposition. They formed a second union to divide workers, enlisted the help of police by charging union members with violence, and mobilized managers to threaten workers with dismissal if they joined the new organization. The union was dissolved within six months, and soon after the management-formed second union was also disbanded.

The company continued to grow, in particular with the expansion of the war in Vietnam and consequent increase in U.S. military personnel, the primary market for their cameras. The second Unikon dispute began in 1966 when five workers were dismissed. These two men and three women were preparing to organize a union once again, and they charged that their dismissal was for that reason. After their dismissal they organized a union anyway and carried on a struggle against unfair discharge and interference in their rights to organize. They brought suit on these charges and picketed outside the factory. The owners of Unikon responded with an uncompromising opposition, refusing to negotiate, and sending company employees to harass them. There were frequent incidents of minor violence. Workers reported being kicked, having lit cigarettes put to their skin, and being threatened with worse violence. Their homes were visited and their families embarrassed and intimidated, and anticommunist leaflets were distributed in their neighborhoods. After three years and nine months the workers were granted reinstatement by Labor Relations Commission mediators and the dispute ended.

These first two disputes continued to live in the minds of union members and were often cited as evidence of some basic characteristics of the Unikon union. They were seen, for instance, as early examples of the importance of women, the experience of victimization of workers trying to exercise legal rights to organize and bargain, and the persistence and determination of Unikon workers to overcome this opposition.

THE THIRD DISPUTE

In February 1969, while the second dispute was still ongoing, five workers came together to try again to form a labor union. To avoid detection and further dismissals the five devised a strategy for recruitment of new members, which centered around the following rules: (1) union members should not interact with one another in the workplace; (2) new members are to be known only to the chairman and the secretary; (3) the existence of the union is to remain secret at the time of recruitment, so each individual is recruited as one of just two employees interested in the formation of a union; and (4) use of strict precautions when going to and from a meeting. This effort proceeded with great caution, and by December they had twenty members and began publication of a newsletter called *Phoenix*. In Japanese and Chinese mythology, this is a bird that cannot be killed, because it revives after each death to fly again. It seemed an apt image for their union's third attempt to become an official representative organization. The secrecy continued, and in fact instructions were given to burn this newsletter after reading it. By 1970 there were fifty members and by 1971 one hundred. In the fall of 1971 they made a flag and began preparations for going public, which they did on April 24, 1972. By this time they had 250 members; they joined the All-Japan Metalworkers Labor Union Federation and flew their red flag at the factory.

In May 1972 the union officers were dismissed from their jobs, and with this began the third dispute. Also in May, the owners formed a second union and sent letters to each of their employees introducing it, an act perceived as intimidation directed against all those who might join the union organized by the workers. There followed a variety of measures by management designed to discourage people from joining this union, including interruption of meetings, confinement of leaders, job transfers for workers, reduction in pay for members, visits to families of members, and forced discussions with members encouraging them to quit or join the other, company-approved union. This struggle continued through August 21, 1973, when the court rejected the dismissal of the union officials and ordered their reinstatement.

THE PART-TIMERS UNION

By 1974 the union had 102 members, the second breakaway union had 80, 70 employees were nonmembers, and there were 200 part-time workers. In the context of a company proposed reduction in employment, part-time workers, under the influence of the Unikon union, formed their own union and in May 1975 announced its existence publicly. Furthermore, this union decided to join the All-Japan Metalworkers Federation of which Unikon's union was a member, and with that decision, the balance of power between the original Unikon union and the breakaway union was won. The second union was dissolved, and the joint strength of the Unikon union and the part-timers union totaled just over 300 members. By 1977 a union shop agreement had been won, and the Unikon union became the representative of all workers within the company.

THE FOURTH DISPUTE

The fourth dispute is the bankruptcy struggle which Unikon was fighting at the time of my research there. This struggle began with three goals: (1) reconstruction of the company, (2) payment of unpaid wages, and (3) payment of debts to workers, including severance pay. Later a fourth was added, the recovery of rights to the Unikon brand, which were sold away during this time. It was only this final demand which was still entirely unmet at the time of the demonstration described below. The others were in the process of final resolution. This dispute took two and a half years to settle.

The Organizational Practices of Struggle

It is of the period of the third dispute that most workers at Unikon have personal memories and experiences, and it is from this time that organizational practices of particular significance for nurturing solidarity became institutionalized. Of enduring importance were (1) formal study groups and educational activities, (2) individual participation in external union activities, (3) emphasis on strong personal ties between union members, (4) frequent meetings and communication among all members, (5) strong centralized leadership, and (6) cultivation of external labor movement networks of support. By the time of the fourth dispute nearly all workers, rank and file and leadership alike, were accustomed to participating in such an organization, and their own consciousness had been formed through such experiences.

FORMAL STUDY GROUPS

The Unikon union was a secret union for nearly three years. During that time, leaders decided that the long-term strength of their organization would be determined by the knowledge and education of each individual member. In particular, it was important to convince people that there were legal and constitutional guarantees for labor unions and collective bargaining, and that historically such action was justifiable. They formed five study groups: for history, literature, labor laws, economics, and U.S.-Japan Security Treaty issues. Each member was to belong to at least one, and they each met once a week. In addition there were training camps held in nearby resort areas once every four months. Here papers and lectures could be presented and members could study and have discussions together.

Since there was to be no socializing at work, due to the continuing secrecy of the union, these study groups and camps were the primary focus of energy and the primary form of the organization. They represent the most direct effort to affect the consciousness of the union members, stemming from a belief that workers had too little information about their own rights to be willing to fight for them and too little information about labor laws and the history of the labor movement in Japan to have confidence in their ability to have at least some success. The coincidence of this education effort with the origins of the union as an organization doubled the effectiveness of the groups in teaching new members about collective action, strength, and solidarity, because these workers were simultaneously participating in a new structure and explicitly learning a way to comprehend its utility and importance.

INDIVIDUAL PARTICIPATION IN
EXTERNAL UNION ACTIVITIES

From the early days of the union, rank-and-file members were sent to other unions, to local organizations, and to the neighborhood associations to explain their struggle, to seek support from these groups, and to represent their union. Leaders of the Unikon union wanted all their members to be so identified with and knowledgeable about their union that any one of them could speak for the whole. Furthermore, they wanted each member to be fully conscious of the place of the union in the community and in the wider network of unions. Some of these concerns stemmed from a small company / small union consciousness on the part of the union leaders. Strength had to come from something other than great resources or large numbers; it had to be built through cultivating individual determination and external support. The explicit strategy was to cultivate these through the practice of having rank-and-file members do much of the external relations work which might otherwise be done as part of a leadership responsibility.

This practice, of course, reinforced the education efforts of the study groups. Workers later recounted how they had to study hard in order to answer questions and defend their union's position when they went out to other groups. In effect, they needed particular knowledge for particular ongoing practice. They also spoke with animation about the expansion of their own worldviews, talking about how much more of the world they understood after these experiences.

EMPHASIS ON STRONG PERSONAL TIES
BETWEEN MEMBERS

Having ties to one another as workers and as union members was not seen to be sufficient for real unity. Leaders of the Unikon union felt that they had to schedule a certain number of opportunities for people to socialize. In the early stages, before the union was public, the study retreats accomplished this by allowing time for drinking, walking, or bathing together. Dormitories also encouraged such socializing, as did various company-sponsored classes and events. At Unikon, however, there were relatively few such events, and as the union became public and larger they began organizing softball games, vacations, and various parties to improve personal ties of friendship and affection between workers.[1] Commitment was believed to be fostered more effectively through such personal ties than through strictly formal ties of work or union membership.

FREQUENT MEETINGS AND COMMUNICATION AMONG MEMBERS

In the early months of union organizing when things were still secret, there were study group meetings at least once a week and a newsletter once every month or two. The newsletter was considered so risky that readers were asked to burn it after finishing it. Later, after going public, there gradually developed a regular schedule of meetings at various levels, beginning on the shop floor once a week and culminating in a general meeting once a month. During disputes, however, the general meeting convened once a week, and throughout the week there were informal gatherings on the shop floor with leaders present during lunches and at the end of the day or during breaks.

Constant contact between people was believed to be critical to a sense of unity and solidarity, and leaders of Unikon's union went to great lengths to keep everyone working together, even immediately after bankruptcy when people were not working on the same products or doing similar work. Immediately following the bankruptcy it was impossible to continue making cameras until the union leaders could reestablish smooth operations. Nevertheless, to enable workers to resist the order to vacate and disperse, their livelihood had to be secured. The solution of the Unikon union leaders was to pool unemployment checks and to have people seek piece work at other factories, bring it to the Unikon factory each morning, and do it there in the same room, thus sharing space and time if not work. The money each one earned was then pooled with the checks, and each worker was given a share at about 60 percent of their usual wage.

1. Chapter 3 is an account of one of the Unikon trips.

In hindsight, leaders claimed that had they not maintained the day-to-day contact of workers with one another in this way their struggle would have disintegrated. Rank and file looked back on this time as "inspiring," although harrowing, exhausting, and filled with uncertainties. Many reflected that it was an experience which built their commitment to each other and to their struggle. Organizationally, it built friendship through sharing of adversity and of resources, and it allowed union leaders to mobilize and communicate on an hourly basis with the entire membership.

STRONG CENTRALIZED LEADERSHIP

The combination of strong centralized leadership with decentralized participation is certainly not unique to the Unikon union organization. It is a characteristic noted in many studies of large Japanese companies (Cole 1971 and 1979; Dore 1973, 1986, and 1987; Rohlen 1974). At Unikon it was a tradition from the earliest days of the union, due in part to the circumstances of these early times themselves. Since the union was organized by a handful of people who then became the core of the union's leaders and remained so through the fourth dispute, there was a sense of charisma, skill, and tradition to their leadership. Furthermore, the initial period, when no one but the president and the secretary even knew the names of the members, left its own legacy in the centralization of information, decision making, and control. The leaders of this union were skillful, dynamic, committed, and well respected in the labor union networks and in the community, in part for their success in organizing against what was considered to be an obstinate ownership. Rank and file were similarly proud of and supportive of them.

Frequency of meetings, agendas, strategies for protest, and programs for members were decided by leadership and presented as suggestions to members in meetings. Proposals were discussed, argued, and largely accepted and then implemented. Extensive programs for participation and discussion were implemented but with a strong centralized hand, one with every benefit of legitimacy and the confidence of its members.

CULTIVATION OF EXTERNAL
NETWORKS OF SUPPORT

Because Unikon was such a small union, there was a great effort to cultivate outside support from the Sōhyō federation, from the

All-Japan Metalworkers Federation, from local union networks, and even from community organizations like neighborhood associations. Unikon was self-consciously modeling itself as an inspiration for workers in other largely unorganized small and medium-sized industries, to whom its leaders wanted to demonstrate that unions could be organized, disputes fought and won, and working conditions improved. This objective was part of the education campaigns for rank and file who were inclined to be more motivated by personal objectives than by wider social and political ones. It was also part of the motivation for sending all members out into the community and to other unions' meetings, to impress upon Unikon's membership that they were working for more than themselves and to educate others that even ordinary rank-and-file workers of a small company can get involved in the labor movement.

The negotiations and contacts with the Sōhyō and All-Japan Metalworkers federations were handled by leaders, and again the pattern of centralized leadership and decentralized participation emerges. In the hierarchy of significance and alliance, it was the higher-ranking affiliations that were handled by leaders alone, as were all negotiations about settlement, while lower-ranking network associations were visited by rank-and-file members.

Unikon's Demonstration

Of all the actions taken during their long struggle, the "Sōkōdō" demonstration described here brought workers into contact with the largest and most diverse population of workers. This demonstration was one of several types of demonstrations in which Unikon participated, and it was the largest and arguably the most important. About once every three months thousands of workers representing hundreds of labor unions engaged in disputes march through the financial district of Tokyo, combining their numbers and thus their strength to stage demonstrations in front of the financial institutions against which they are struggling. The event lasts from 7:30 in the morning until 8:00 at night. The organization responsible for these is Tōkyō Sōgidan (Tokyo Labor Dispute Association), and this action itself is called Sōgi Kōdō (Dispute Cooperative Action) and is often abbreviated in conversation as Sōkōdō.

Tōkyō Sōgidan comprises unions in the Tokyo region fighting labor disputes, most of which are from small and medium-sized firms. Their demonstrations have a history of about twenty years, and were initiated because of a need for strength through numbers. Small unions cannot make much of an impression if they demonstrate by themselves, but through Tōkyō Sōgi Kōdō they can muster thousands of people for a real show of strength. The purposes of the demonstration are to force the financial institution in question into negotiation and to maintain pressure on them while they negotiate. Typically, for example, while the demonstration is under way in front of a bank, there is a team of labor union negotiators trying to gain entry, or in some cases already inside negotiating.

My introduction to Sōkōdō was through the Unikon picture albums. One of the first things the union leaders did in familiarizing me with their union and its history was to take me on a tour of important events through these albums. They were carefully put together, and the pictures were shown and explained to me with a great deal of pride as well as enjoyment. The union leader who was describing these, a man named Tajima-san, explained that now that Unikon's own major struggle was coming to a positive conclusion, they would continue to participate in these partly because of their own still unresolved issues but also because they had a real "debt" to this organization for all the help they had received at critical times during their own dispute. In the spirit of reciprocity with affiliated unions, they would continue to participate to repay others who had helped them.

Unikon had been involved in a variety of actions, taking a very aggressive stance toward their owners. Their workers had staged protests on their own at banks, in their company's neighborhood, in front of train stations, and in front of the home of the owners. Because of the broader involvement of other unions and workers in large numbers, however, Sōkōdō demonstrations were particularly critical to raising the consciousness of their workers and to winning their dispute. Tajima-san even suggested that without these demonstrations, without this show of strength, it might have been impossible for them to succeed.

Among the pictures were scenes of brass bands with people assembled and singing, or in other cases Japanese *taiko* drum troops, also with people singing or chanting. I asked what they were singing, and he spoke with animation about the songs written by the Unikon union for each particular dispute, of which they had had four. The music was supplied by Sōhyō, which seemed to have a number of easily sung tunes on file, and the words were written by particular unions to suit their own particular struggle. Then the members learned the songs, and they were printed up to be distributed to nonmembers at demonstrations.

The scenes as he described them and showed them to me through pictures were extremely colorful, almost festive. People were wearing red and white headbands and chest signs painted in various colors, and were walking amid enormous red flags and banners. His description, which was reinforced repeatedly in conversations with other Unikon workers, was overall of a very important and exciting event, at once serious and fun.

PREPARATION

In April 1980, I was in a shop floor meeting where an upcoming demonstration was announced. The representative asked everyone to join, and as she announced the date people noted it in their open notepads or on scraps of paper. There was no more discussion of it at the time or for several weeks after. It seemed to have been taken for granted that everyone would go, and the mood around it was serious and casual. Not until the day before the demonstration was scheduled to take place did it come up again. I had nearly forgotten about it when at lunch people began discussing the time and meeting place. After lunch I noticed people talking about these details with one another and double-checking things with the shop floor steward. I checked with her to see if I might attend, and she discussed it with the union officials, who encouraged me to do so. We agreed that I should march with them but not wear either chest signs or head bands, since my doing so could get me into trouble with the police. As a foreigner my situation was a potentially risky one if I got involved in political activities.

PARTICIPATION

The demonstration began early, with people gathering between 7:30 and 8:00 A.M. and continued until around 8:00 at night. There was a contingent of union leaders present from the morning throughout the day and into the night. Everyone else showed up in the late morning or after lunch, leaving a tiny staff to deal with telephones and necessary work. The assembly section, where I was working, went after lunch. There was some anticipation in the air in the morning. People had brought snack foods like potato chips or homemade pickles to carry along and eat during the course of the demonstration. They were dressed nicely but not dressed up, and some women were talking about having worn comfortable walking shoes and wondering how far we would be walking today. A number of people took my presence as a chance to explain what was to be expected.

Several said that I'd be tired because we would walk several miles. Others asked me if I had ever been to Ginza or to Tsukiyabashi Park, from which the demonstration was to begin.[2] One of the young men talked to me about the thousands of people who would be present. This kind of discussion went on through lunch and while we were walking in small groups scattered along the street on the way to the station. On the train people split up, double-checking with one another as to the correct station in Ginza where we would be assembling again.

When we reached Ginza, we all disembarked and came out of the subway into a very crowded little park, a park from which all kinds of demonstrations frequently begin. People spoke of peace, anti–Security Treaty, and other kinds of demonstrations which traditionally center around this park. Entering, we found the statue which is its center, where a few union leaders were waiting for us with the chest signs and head-bands each person was to wear. People began putting these on, helping each other tie them securely. Small groups were doing the same every-where. It was crowded, and while putting things on people were handing out and being handed leaflets describing the various union struggles represented in the day's demonstrations. Among the leaflets were also ones for other, related causes and for movies shown by the Socialist and Communist parties. When the Unikon people were ready, we all walked to a nearby street, by this time filled with contingents ready to march, each holding red flags with white or black letters naming their union and proclaiming solidarity (*danketsu*), many preceded by a line of people carrying a banner announcing their union's particular grievance. The Unikon chest signs proclaimed support for all affiliated unions' struggles and demanded their brand be returned to them, a still-unresolved issue and a primary reason for their participation this day.

The Unikon workers lined up in their spot, and I separated from them a bit onto the sidelines, where I could take pictures and observe the march. There were police in obvious attendance all along the route and

2. I believed at first that they were asking me this because I was a foreigner and they were curious about my own experiences in Tokyo. As the event unfolded and as I got to know them better, however, it became clear that it was unusual for them and their friends to go to this area of town. Several people later recounted the broadening of their geo-graphical horizons as a positive outcome of their labor union activities.

a number of onlookers standing watching the march go by. The majority of passersby, however, simply walked along minding their own business and showing little interest in the parade of marchers. At intersections there were police to help with the traffic, and of course that is where people gathered waiting to cross the street, becoming a sort of captive audience for the demonstrators. The comments I could hear were exclusively of the "I wonder what this is" variety. There was no leafleting along the march route.

We marched through the center of Ginza and in the direction of the financial district near Tokyo Station. At our first stop I was surprised to see the crowds of people waiting for us in front of the bank in question. There were people on every corner and in front of the bank giving out leaflets describing their grievance with the bank. The demonstrators began arriving by the hundreds. They lined up on the sidewalk, spilling over onto side streets and up and down the sidewalk in both directions. The most unexpected thing for me was that they lined up facing not the public passing by in the street, but facing the bank building, where no one stood facing them. I realized at that point that I had been expecting them to speak to the public, but what they intended was to speak to the bank, and in the absence of bank representatives, they spoke to the bank building itself, as a way of demonstrating quite literally their confrontation and thus communicating with the bank officers inside. The only attention paid directly to the public was the distribution of leaflets, and that was confined to the area immediately surrounding the building.

A truck pulled up, and the leaders of the involved union and a couple of supporting federation persons climbed on top and spoke, outlining their grievances and accusing the bank of being behind the management and not trying to protect the livelihood of the workers in their union. For ten minutes or so there were repeated accusations and chants of various kinds led by the leaders on top of the van and joined in by the hundreds of supporters on the sidewalk, all raising their fists in the direction of the bank as they proclaimed their determination not to give up in their fight.

There were some ten or so stops on our afternoon schedule, and the activities at each stop followed much this same pattern. The length of time spent varied somewhat, according to the stage of negotiation reached in the particular dispute. In the case of unions like Unikon, which had already been negotiating for some time, there was not even a stop at the bank in question. Instead, on this same day, there was a negotiation session under way. At the site of a demonstration against a bank which refused to negotiate, the time spent was longer, since a primary purpose of these demonstrations was to pressure the opposition into discussion and to keep them seriously negotiating. Once that purpose is served, the pressure is taken off.

The chants, which were led from atop the vans at each stop, were sometimes particular ones for the union involved, in which case they would not be repeated at other stops. A common one was "X Bank, Take responsibility for Y Company's bankruptcy!" There were also several chants that were repeated at many stops: "Victory in the 1980 Spring Labor Offensive!" "Oppose price rises! Oppose lay-offs!" "We demand a livable wage!" These themes came up at many stops, and at the end of each chant fists were raised toward the bank in question. The overall effect of hundreds of voices shouting out these statements and raising their fists was deafening for people inside the group and nearby. It created a very impressive show of strength and unity when viewed either from the midst of the demonstrators or from without.

The speeches from atop the trucks were done with microphones and so were very loud, audible for a couple of city blocks in either direction. The content was very specific to the case around which the particular demonstration was focused. Several of the speeches mentioned the Unikon union's recent success as an example for unions that persevere. Many speeches accused banks of conspiring with management to destroy a company in order to get rid of a strong union. Nearly all accused the banks of not taking responsibility for the livelihood of the workers in the companies with whose management they had financial ties. Every speech ended the same way, with a few chants and a final "We'll never give up!" (*Ganbarō!*) followed by applause.

When one demonstration had run its course people reassembled and marched to the next. There were several courses and at some points contingents would split up and join other marchers in another contingent. Only a few leaders seemed to know just how and when everything was to take place. The rest relied on them for instructions at the end of each demonstration. Between chants, while walking, there was a lot of talking. These conversations did not center around what was being done; they were more likely to be about the scenery of the area or how something had changed since last time they were downtown. The mood was relaxed and congenial. We had a break at one point where we were told to wait for a contingent to catch up to our Unikon group. We waited in front of a beautiful new bank, a skyscraper with elaborate landscaping and a modern architectural design. People walked unabashedly up to the side of the building, sat down on the ornamental walls surrounding the neatly trimmed shrubbery and flower beds and pulled out bags of potato chips, packages of homemade pickles, and other snacks to wait and enjoy a restful break. A few took off the head bands and chest signs, put them in their bags, and went into the bank building and downstairs to the bank's shopping and restaurant floor to use the restrooms. People joked about using the bank's facilities while preparing to demonstrate against them. "We have a lot of nerve, don't we [*Zūzūshii desu ne?*]?"

Everyone was tired by now. It was nearly 3:30 and some of the part-time women were planning to go home after the next demonstration. When the rest of the marchers got to this site there was a very large and noisy demonstration. After a couple more stops the women began going home. Part-time women workers were not asked to stay later than their usual quitting time, although many did remain for an extra hour or so. The leaders continued throughout the day, until about 8:00 that night. I went home with three young men and two women from the assembly section about 5:00. We talked about the incredible number of people who had turned up and about the length of the march and how tired everyone was. Again I was impressed that people did not seem to be as emotionally involved as the chanting, singing, and fist raising would have led an observer to suspect. The demonstrations were barely over and they were definitely not keyed up. Conversation centered on related topics, but it was not emotionally charged conversation. During one break young men even dragged out comic books they had brought along and squatted here and there reading them.

When I saw people at work the next day they were not talking about the demonstration very much. Some asked me what I had thought and asked me to compare the Japanese demonstrations to American ones. There was also discussion about how late everyone had gotten home and some comparing of notes about shopping and dinner preparation by the women who were also responsible for their families' evening meals regardless of the day's activities. There was a certain amount of discussion about the other unions' lengthy disputes and the likelihood of them settling in the near future or the long time that had passed without settlement. This discussion was interspersed with comments about how lucky Unikon was to have taken only two and a half years. Although that had seemed to be a very long time, clearly other unions were taking even longer.

The overall tone of conversation was again serious and subdued, involved but with some distance. People seemed very experienced. They had acted the day before and were commenting the following day in a way that showed them to be longtime veterans of labor movement demonstrations. The agility with which they slipped in and out of their chest signs and in and out of their demonstration behavior was something of which they were quite aware and quite proud. While many rank-and-file workers referred to it as part of their life experience (*jinsei keiken*), leaders spoke of it as an achievement, a carefully planned one. The common reference here was historical, to the years they had had together, to the other major disputes they had fought, and to their own personal, individual experiences within that history.

Learning to Protest

Staying throughout this two-and-a-half-year dispute involved making sense of the struggle and deciding to join it oneself, both processes constituted by discursive thought and by experience. The struggle and its meaning were discussed at work and in conversation outside with family and friends as well. There were arguments about it. Not everyone, even those involved, thought it made sense all the time. There was a tacit, commonsensical side to it that was motivated in part by the action itself. As Victor Turner (1967, 1969) notes for rituals, doing something oneself creates a meaning that is experienced as well as thought through. So when the Unikon union leaders had rank and file go out to present their situation to other unions, they were not only convincing them through words but engaging them through their own actions. Consequently, what had to be made sense of was not just an external situation but one which these workers were themselves actively creating and responding to. Whereas the original causes and circumstances of the disputes were part of the work lives of all workers, the collective action that leaders instigated was not. That response, in order to grow out of this situation, had to grow through the actions and experiences of the rank-and-file workers. The Unikon workers in the final phase of their struggle spoke of these actions growing into and through their lives, creating a sensibility at once known and felt.

Why did over two hundred workers stay at Unikon and fight together in this struggle? What motivated them? How did they understand their own action and the meaning of their union's struggle? It is one thing to talk about participation in a demonstration or the history of union actions in which people participated, but the question remains: Why bother? Why not quit and go elsewhere as most workers do when companies go bankrupt, and as the majority of Unikon workers in this case did as well? Learning to protest is not something people go out of their way to do or arrange to do in their free time, and it isn't without risk and cost. The answers are multiple. There were several reasons that motivated commitment at Unikon, and each worker had his or her own combination of priorities and strategies which led them to stay. Furthermore, decisions to stay or quit, to participate or not in particular events or organizational practices were always made in specific institutional contexts which provided experiential constraints and encouragement. In other words, people were acting with particular structures both of thought and of experience. Their decisions, strategies, and ultimately their understandings were all well thought out and affectively compelling. Common sense and ideology, what felt right and what was believed to be right, what couldn't be helped and what were explicit goals—all were equally important in the process of interpreting situations, deciding upon strategies, and taking action.

Sometimes people had determined to stay out of anger. Most talked about this as the critical factor in the very beginning. They were angry at the "inhuman" treatment they received at the hands of the owners. After some time had passed, however, other factors compelled them to stay. Many talked about wanting to stay with their coworkers, saying essentially that because no one had quit once the dispute began, no one felt that they could quit. There were also elements of pride and excitement about being part of a very important labor movement event. Coming from such a small company, it was unusual to get such attention and support from the national networks of unions. Most people talked about the possibility of success, that all along there had been enough hope to sustain their efforts to win. And some workers talked about fear of trouble finding other employment. These factors had a fluid quality, some being more salient in early stages and others in later stages. Individual life courses intersected and pulled factors in and out of significance as well. And the organizational structures and practices were at all times forming a social arena within which people were weighing and balancing priorities and assessing and reassessing their own thoughts about their situation and their own actions. Comprehension and collective action were at all times integrally connected. The demonstration was not, of course, the only act of protest in which Unikon workers were engaged, but it was one of the most dramatic, most public, and politically most significant.

Making Sense of Struggle

The demonstration itself was always a highly symbolic event, an occasion during which the fact of the struggle was brought front and center, made more visible, and its meanings addressed more explicitly. A lengthy dispute, and one carried out in the context of union-managed production like this one, tends to create a very matter-of-fact daily work life for rank and file. While leaders of the union, who are also managing the production of the factory, are still involved regularly with negotiations, labor networks, and strategy, the workers in the factory spend most days simply coming to work at 8:30 and leaving at 5:30 or 6:00, doing their own jobs, chatting with coworkers at breaks, socializing on their way to and from work, and attending meetings. While their situation is not forgotten, it is not primary in day-to-day consciousness at all times either.

Immediately before, particularly during, and then after demonstrations or other collective actions, such awareness of themselves as being involved in a protest is higher. The very symbolic nature of the demonstration itself makes it particularly good at raising such issues. In the lives of the participating workers, the demonstration is set off from everyday life, clearly bounded by numerous symbolically rich actions, elements of dress, and patterns of movement.[3] Virtually everyone who participates experiences this separation and views the involvement as something different, noteworthy, or special in contrast to the day-to-day, routine activities. The Unikon picture albums recording the history of the union, for instance, noted these demonstrations along with other special occasions like trips and festival celebrations, but had no pictures, until I took them, of people doing their everyday jobs or of regularly held union meetings and shop floor get-togethers. The movement between daily life and the demonstration was smooth for Unikon workers, and this agility in slipping into and out of their roles as protesters stands in sharp contrast to Universal workers, for whom the demonstration de-

---

3. For more discussion of these aspects of the Sōkōdō demonstrations, see chapter 6.

scribed in chapter 6 was their first. Unikon workers had learned this agility, and it was an achievement of the union as a whole, planned and guided by leaders and experienced in a variety of ways by rank and file. The transition remains; that is, daily life is not a demonstration or protest when a dispute lasts two and a half years. Nevertheless, the transition, if it is made easily, is a sign that consciousness of collective interests and the sense that collective action is necessary have become strong and pervasive.

A STRUGGLE FOR ALL WORKERS

The demonstration, their struggle, and all the protests in which they engaged reinforced for them the importance of their own dispute for the strength and well-being of workers in general. At Unikon, words like *rōdōsha* (worker) and *rōdō undō* (labor movement) were very generously sprinkled throughout a day's conversation (given, of course, appropriate conversation topics), so there was a frequent linguistic reminder of a certain identity with other workers. By the time I saw them, the Unikon workers were already veterans of demonstrations of various kinds and of other labor movement activities, so they had in fact already learned to think of themselves and their struggle in this way. Both explicit arguments about such links and the structure of many activities influenced this process of learning to see their relationship to other workers. One woman put it this way: "In the beginning, I stayed with the union without a clear reason. Somehow I just didn't get around to quitting. Over the past two and a half years, though, I have been part of so many union activities like demonstrations. At first they were strange to me, but my consciousness as a worker has been strengthened. Now I work with a certain pride in myself as a *rōdōsha*."

Perceiving oneself as a worker and one's actions as important to all workers involves sharing some characteristics with all other workers and identifying in a universalistic sense with them. The existence of the Sōgidan organization itself is a statement of sorts about shared problems, shared conditions, and shared strategies for workers. Its role in promoting the collective action of unions in similar circumstances reinforces such an identity. Participation in these demonstrations rehearses in and of itself a communality of shared identities, interests, and collective action strategies. The negotiations or speeches at each stop are led by Sōkōdō organizers accompanied by the officials of the union specifically involved. The membership watch as the same organizers and negotiators stand up for each of the individual unions involved. This, plus the thousands of demonstrators going from place to place in support of each union, is a very powerful statement arising out of the very structure of the event.

The colorful trappings of the event echo these themes as well. At the very least, for the duration of the demonstration all the participants share the same special attire, consisting of a headband and a chest sign. The exceptions are few, taking the form of substitutions by some contingents of arm bands for chest signs or headbands, for instance. Upon arrival at the demonstration site, everyone ties these on, and they mark them clearly as participants throughout, just as their removal marks clearly the end of the event. More specifically, their removal marks the end of the individual's participation, since if someone leaves in the middle it comes off and if they rejoin it goes back on. The color of the individual attire is echoed in the huge flags, banners, and signs of various sorts carried by members of each marching union and set up outside the institution against which each demonstration is to be held. The colors are primary— red, yellow, and blue—and the linguistic form of Japanese used in the written slogans is the direct command. These conventions are followed by each and every union, and the result is a tremendous feeling of sharing a language of power and struggle with thousands of other participants. The slogans chanted while marching and at each demonstration are, for the most part, designed to appeal to a common denominator for all workers. Slogans in support of the particular year's Spring Labor Offensive or in opposition to rising cost of living or demanding protection of the livelihood of workers are repeated throughout the day in unified chants. Even the chants specific to a particular union's struggle and chanted only at their demonstration are joined in by the thousands of accompanying workers from other unions, and the effect can be quite a strong sensation of solidarity.

Of course there is a powerful network of union affiliations supporting any union in dispute, and the union officials are always aware of these relationships. For the rank-and-file workers, however, the experience of these social relationships, of having some relationship with members of other unions, is not a frequent one. This is the source of a significant difference and sometimes of potential conflict between rank-and-file members and leaders. It was also a site of attention and efforts to educate by Unikon leaders.

In addition to the practice in demonstrations of these relationships of workers to other workers and of workers to particular institutions that structure their workplaces, Unikon workers also had study groups, meetings, the daily experience of work in their particular company and their particular union. The study groups, begun at the earliest stages of the union's history, gave instruction in such basics as labor law and constitutional provisions for worker rights. Many workers learned only through such groups that the constitution guaranteed to all workers their right to organize and that labor laws would protect certain of their interests. Study of the history of the Japanese and international labor movements made young workers aware of what they shared as workers with others. By the time of the demonstration recorded here, the Unikon workers took this identity for granted, just as they had learned to assume that their own struggle was of great inspiration and importance to workers in other firms, especially in smaller ones facing the problems associated with slowed growth. Demonstrations by now served to reinforce symbolically and experientially what Unikon workers already discursively knew. (The power of such demonstrations to create the conditions for knowing will be clearer when we take a look in chapter 6 at Universal's experience with their first such collective action.)

The effectiveness of demonstrations in inspiring this consciousness of solidarity and shared interests varies from union to union. The nature of the struggle and the particular conditions of experience leading to the dispute set a certain social and political field within which the demonstration is enacted. Unikon's bankruptcy dispute began with workers occupying the factory to oppose liquidation and dispersal. They received the support of local residents and of unions in their regional federation. They also initiated a system of selling bonds to supporters to create an even broader network, a practice modeled after a union struggle at a French watchmaker, Lipp.[4] The *Asahi Shinbun* labeled Unikon the "Eastern Lipp." The networks of unions helping them grew rapidly. Their small size and scarce resources made them extremely vulnerable, so the importance of the support of others was critical and more visible than it might otherwise have been. This visibility itself was enhanced for rank-and-file workers by the leadership policy of sending each and every member out to canvass neighbors and other unions for such support.

Once the bankruptcy dispute began, a Joint Struggle Committee was formed to oversee the struggle. That committee consisted of representatives from federation and affiliated unions and only the top leadership

4. Lipp went bankrupt in 1968 as a result of increasing rationalization of the production process. After a short period of worker-controlled production the company closed.

of the Unikon union. Formally, it was an advisory committee, but in practice it planned strategy and took over primary decision-making power. In a larger union the union itself often retains greater authority, but in such a small union the outside support was the core of their strength and became integrated very thoroughly with union activity. Rank and file were aware of this structure at every meeting, since these "outside" members would be present and their opinions valued and given precedence.

In short, the experiences of struggling in concert with other workers and unions and of having Unikon's own struggle managed by a committee of their own leaders and outsiders, combined with the participation in demonstrations of this kind, together forged a very strong sense of solidarity.

CAPITAL, LABOR, INEQUALITY, AND INJUSTICE

The demonstration is both a vehicle for the experience of certain relationships of social inequality and a compelling force pushing many participants to reflect on and discuss their relationships with one another. Staying and fighting in the Unikon dispute meant for most struggling against forms of injustice associated with particular relationships, specifically those between capital and labor—also phrased as owners and workers, "the weaker" and "the stronger," protesters and institutions, and larger and smaller organizations.

The distinction between capital and labor was not in any sense introduced by the demonstration, but it was evoked and given dramatic experiential dimensions. The entire course of events at Sōkōdō demonstrations is designed around labor protesting against capital. This explicit opposition is discussed with a correspondingly explicit terminology in use throughout conversations surrounding the event. "Capitalists" (*shihonka*) and "workers" or "labor" (*rōdōsha*) were not only the common terminology used by leaders to rank and file and in speeches and pamphlets, but also in discussions by Unikon workers over tea, walking to the train after work, and during work-hour conversation having to do with disputes and grievances and events which are part of the demonstration. The identification of oneself and one's own union with *rōdōsha* as discussed above presumes this distinction. It is a distinction, however, that faces clear constraints.

In conversations about the struggle, its personal costs, and the personal sacrifices made, workers more frequently lament the distinction between capitalists on the one hand and common people (*futsū no hito*) or human beings (*ningen*) on the other. This distinction has less of the explicit ideological consciousness of relation to the means of production and more consciousness of a gap of wealth, power, and moral character. It calls to mind a distinction elegantly delineated by Tetsuo Najita between efficient, impersonal structures and an oppositional, idealistic, and caring human spirit. In his analysis of the intellectual foundations of modern Japan, he identifies an "elemental axis that is basic to an understanding of modern Japan" from the earliest formation of the nation and its industrial base into the postwar period, an axis constituted by "bureaucratism" (*kanryōshugi*) on the one hand and "purity of human spirit" (*ningensei* or *kokoro*) on the other (1974: 2). Capital, government, and bureaucracy are taken interchangeably and opposed as a system against "people." Furthermore the excesses of power and its uncaring use are conceptualized as "inhuman" and lacking in the moral character valued in human relations. This distinction is the most common one in conversations not specifically concerned with demonstrations and collective actions per se. It is this relationship of really blatant inequality and inhuman moral lapse which came to people's minds walking through the valleys of beautifully designed skyscraping financial buildings and which prompted comments about the incredible wealth of the "capitalists" who own such buildings.

On the other side of the coin are the "common people" living and working in small and crowded buildings not at all modern in design or convenience, what several Unikon workers liked to joke about as "rabbit hutches," borrowing a disparaging comment from a European journalist about Japanese housing. Unikon people were fond of saying that the capitalists and the Japanese government were anxious to object to that characterization, and to turn the eyes of the world toward their own lovely new urban structures and comfortable "Japanese" houses and gardens, in an attempt to hide the reality of the enormous gap between the average person and the capitalist. Demonstrations, taking place as they must in the territory of the elegant financial district, occasion this kind of observation and conversation about the economic inequality. The importance of buildings, both workplaces and homes, as symbols of both the wealthy and the poor ends of the spectrum shows up repeatedly.

Both the capital-labor and the capital-common folk distinctions represent relationships through which workers make sense of their struggle and structure their thoughts about injustice. Again, specific experience motivated certain feelings which were only later gradually given form and meaning. That process itself is an interesting interaction between consciousness and action in the conversations among coworkers, in organizational structures and incentives, and in explicit efforts to raise consciousness and motivate rank and file to join in collective action.

Most of the issues which made sense of the struggle for people took form later, after the fact. Action preceded carefully discussed and frequently considered thoughts on these issues. People were already fighting, already participating in the activities, had already decided—for the time being—to accept the personal sacrifices required, and of course they had already been working for years in companies structured as capitalist enterprises. As they organized, socialist ideology inspired much of the language and rationale for their struggle, but the great majority of rank and file did not decide to join or stay throughout these years primarily because they wanted to fight for socialism, for the right to own their own shops, or even for the sake of all Japanese workers.

They joined, they say, because they were angry, terribly and intolerably angry. They were being put out of work, without warning, without consultation, without an honest effort on the part of the Unikon owners to protect their jobs. The lack of effort in trying to save their jobs and the lack of enough consideration to at least discuss the situation with the union representatives prior to the bankruptcies left the workers feeling betrayed, feeling that they had been treated as less than human (*ningen to shite atsukawarete inai*). "Less than human," they explained, means that the managers and owners did not see them as human beings with lives to lead, a daily life and livelihood (*seikatsu*) to protect. These workers speak of a right to maintain a peaceful daily life, to a minimum livelihood. These rights are echoed in chants at demonstrations and in speeches at most union gatherings. The responsibility (*sekinin*) of the owners, financiers, and managers toward the workers was, they felt, sadly neglected.

The bankruptcy itself was not sufficient to inspire the anger they described. Bankruptcy may have been unavoidable, and some union members even suggest that the union itself may have gone too far and made bankruptcy inevitable by making too many demands without considering the fortunes of the company. It was more the way in which it was handled that angered people. There is a "responsible" and an "irresponsible" way to handle a crisis like this, a "human" and an "inhuman" way, a way that shows respect for workers' needs and a way that ignores them.[5] At Unikon, people claim that their company was irresponsible, inhuman, and disrespectful, and it was here, in the realm of attitude and manner, that their anger was kindled and intensified.

Here is the nexus of concerns that reappears throughout this book because it reappeared through various activities and innumerable conversations. The content of their demand for "human" dignity and respect was a heartfelt belief that people have a fundamental right to some measure of control over their own livelihood. Livelihood here is not employment per se, but livelihood as employment linked to daily life, to family, to human existence at however modest a level. Control here is not an absolute concept existing outside the social relationships which define the company and the union relationships to rank-and-file workers. It includes the debate over the nature of control of labor which was ongoing at both Unikon and Universal. Union leaders were making concerted efforts to mobilize people around the idea that workers should control their own labor.[6] Socialist and Communist Party resources and ideology reinforced this message. Rank-and-file workers were more convinced that they should have some measure of control than that they should have full control, and here the distinction between being managed and being controlled emerges and marks the unsettled issue for Unikon, Universal, and other worker-controlled struggles as well.[7] Within this collective action were workers fighting for control of their own company and workers fighting for a stronger position within a structure of control which included managers.

The Unikon case involved fierce and even violent demonstrations in addition to the Sōkōdō events. The Unikon workers went to the home of the owner and harassed him and his family. They went to the local branch of the bank involved and stopped business for hours at a time by lining up single file and opening and closing accounts all day. These actions and others, like occupying their factory against court orders to

5. See chapter 7 for a discussion of notions of responsibility in these labor protests.
6. At the point of settlement this becomes ironic as leaders calculate that to be a viable company they must settle for ordinary labor-management relations, whereas by then the majority of rank and file have become committed to a more radical notion of control. See chapters 4 and 8 for more discussion.
7. Totsuka (1980) discusses this problem for these late postwar struggles and Moore (1983) discusses it for early postwar worker-control struggles. A related discussion of appropriate points of compromise in struggles over employment security is made in Gordon 1987 and more generally in Gordon 1988 and 1991 as well.

evacuate, kept the workers constantly on the verge of illegality and in a state of uproar, not to mention financial sacrifice. The reason that the leadership was able to mobilize over two hundred rank and file to participate in this was explained to me by a union official:

We were lucky, I suppose. It wasn't so hard to get people to do even the most outrageous things to fight against our owners and the bank. It's because of the way they [the owners] did it. If they had talked to us, made a sincere effort to maintain the solvency of the company, encouraged our cooperation or even insured our back wages and severance pay, we could never have enlisted enough support from the rank and file to fight against it.

But they just deserted! They deserted the company, our contracts, and the workers. They didn't even think about the consequences their actions would have on us, about our lives and our families. It made everyone angry and they were ready to fight.

The Unikon workers and their leadership talked of their owners as having been militaristic and feudalistic, saying that their behavior had always been shocking and uncommonly lacking in compassion and respect for workers. Clearly, notions of inequality between capital and labor are involved here, but it is a particular dimension to that relationship which inspires a sense of injustice. For both Unikon and Universal workers, the injustice of the social structure which creates classes with unequal wealth and power was less moving personally than was the breach of basic human consideration appropriate to the treatment of workers by those with economic and political power.

People acted first on their implicit assumptions and a sense of outrage at offenses against those assumptions. The skill of the leadership at Unikon was in their ability to transform that highly emotional and largely unexamined action and outrage into a formulated collective act and a sensible struggle that would hold its rank-and-file participants together for two and a half years of sacrifice and extraordinary activities. That was accomplished with a combination of union organizing experience and education.

Deciding to Join, Deciding to Stay

Even given the anger and the sensibility of this struggle, not everyone stayed. Personal choices to stay or quit were based also on strategies for individual lives. The critical mass of workers who stayed and fought had in common a decision that it was worth it to them to do so. There are a cluster of factors which determined final decisions, a cluster from which each person pulled at least two or three factors to make a choice. These choices were made in the context of outsiders, with family and friends putting pressure on workers to stay or to quit. That pressure itself often became an important and sometimes determining force. Nearly everyone reported uncertainty about the decision to stay through this dispute. It was different from previous ones in that it concerned the total elimination of employment for all workers and the dissolution of the company itself. The odds of success were much harder to gauge and the risk of a lengthy and finally futile fight seemed high. Many workers talked frankly about their own decision as comprising a series of smaller decisions, reevaluations, and calculated risks. The reasons people stayed in the beginning were generally different from reasons for persevering a year or two later. Reasons also flowed in and out of importance over this long time, and for all but a very few certainty was uncommon.

There were three kinds of concerns people could voice: affective ties and feelings, political purposes, and personal lifetime goals and con-straints. In making the decision to join and stay through this struggle, individual workers had to feel that it was personally sensible and worth-while. For them the solidarity which their own time and efforts con-stituted was a complex, changing, and uncertain phenomenon, and one upon which their own decisions could have a profound effect.

AFFECTIVE TIES AND FEELINGS

The two most important affective dimensions in workers' decisions were anger and closeness, anger at their owners and managers and feelings of closeness with coworkers. The notions of injustice which inspired this anger were discussed above. Here it is important to take note of its role in decision making for individual workers. The anger they felt upon initial news of the bankruptcy was a deciding motivation for many in joining, although no one recognized it as important in their staying beyond the first few weeks.

Closeness to other workers, ties of friendship and history were critical. People talked about working together through three previous disputes, about working at this factory with these same coworkers for ten or twelve years, and about sharing the extremely rough days and weeks immediately after the bankruptcy. Just as anger was the most commonly mentioned reason for joining, ties of closeness to other workers was the most common reason for staying through the two and a half years of the dispute. The sharing of demonstrations of all kinds, of building the union, of working day by day with one another, of trips, study-group retreats, year-end parties, spring cherry blossom viewing parties, and a host of other special occasions and daily life experiences came up over and over again in conversations about the effort and energy put into the struggle by the Unikon workers. Clearly one of the critical components of the union's political solidarity was this affective closeness, which was both explicitly cultivated by leadership and stumbled upon through routine practices as well. In the end, however, it was the remarkable solidarity of this union that prompted journalists and scholars in Japan to label them "advanced" and even the "avant-garde" of the labor movement.

This attention and these characterizations provided endless amusement for rank and file. The idea that they had "high class consciousness" or were at the cutting edge of the labor movement made people smile and laugh. It seemed distant and unfamiliar, as though the authors of such phrases were depicting some other group of people in some distant place. People insisted that they were "ordinary" and that ideology and labor movement goals had little to do with their own involvement in the struggle.

POLITICAL PURPOSES

While people did not talk in abstract terms about the politics of the labor movement when discussing personal decisions to quit or to stay, there were two political factors that came up frequently: the inspiration of their leaders and the defense of their own rights. The Unikon leadership was held in very high regard by rank and file. This too was contextualized in conversation by the proud recounting of history, the lengthy struggle of these men to form and sustain the union from its inception and through three other disputes. In essence, the respect for these individuals became one way of expressing a pride in the accomplishments of their union over the preceding ten years. People would say that they didn't want to "pull the rug out from under" their leaders by giving up. Once these leaders started a fight, many workers felt a strong sense of personal commitment to support them. Rank and file would also speak of the advances in working conditions under these leaders, which itself inspired a kind of obligation grounded in gratitude.

In comparison, defending workers' rights was infrequently mentioned, but nonetheless there were occasions when some people would talk about the feeling that they had to fight this battle to prove that workers could defend themselves against injustice. They related this to the anger they felt toward their owners and wanted to prove to them and to the public that workers couldn't be taken advantage of and dismissed in such a disrespectful way. The anger, which seemed to abate after a few weeks, appeared to have transformed itself into this commitment to stand up for a kind of justice for workers. This transformation itself showed the skill of the popular leaders in guiding the individual feelings and motivations of the workers into a more lasting solidarity. Practices like study groups, sending people out to speak on their own behalf to related groups, and frequent communication and education, especially in early stages, were extremely effective in accomplishing this transition.

PERSONAL CIRCUMSTANCES

The factors people felt were most important to their own decisions were quite personal, having to do with their own desire to learn, to be part of something "larger," the difficulty of finding another job in the same kind of industry, or another job at all, and their own particular family circumstances, which determined whether or not they could afford to accept less pay for the duration of this struggle. I didn't have the opportunity to talk with people who had quit in the beginning, but those who stayed defended their decisions, saying that they were mostly men in their mid-thirties with children in school and higher expenses, thus unable to take the risk either of losing the dispute or of weathering many months of lowered income. Only younger men in their twenties and women with employed husbands could afford to stay. As the struggle wore on, it was this factor which most frequently caused people to reassess their own decisions and wonder if maybe they were being too optimistic. Many considered quitting, some did and then returned after a certain amount of encouragement from union leaders and coworkers.

Learning about the world, broadening horizons, and making this struggle into their own life experience were the attractive aspects of staying for many. Workers talked about seeing all parts of Tokyo, going places for demonstrations where they had never been and becoming familiar with the trains and subways that traverse the huge city and with its parks and downtown districts. The factory itself was located in the northeast section and most people lived farther east on the borders of

Tokyo, whereas the owners' residences were in the wealthier western districts and the demonstrations against financial institutions were downtown in the financial district.

The long history of political protest in Japan was a factor for many. Some linked the Unikon struggle to struggles over the U.S.-Japan Security Treaty and other progressive causes supported by the labor movement. One young man laughed about learning to protest as a child playing in public housing playgrounds, where kids would dress up with handkerchiefs as headbands and handwritten signs pinned to their shirts and play "*anpo gokko*," or "pretend anti–U.S.-Japan Security Treaty demonstration." They would wind through the walkways between the apartment complex buildings, hands linked and chanting in playful imitation of the "snake dances" characteristic of the political demonstrations of the sixties. Many had parents in unions affiliated with Sōhyō and which had therefore been drawn into a variety of radical political actions through that federation. It was not unusual then or now for parents to take their children with them to peaceful demonstrations, and many of these Unikon workers recalled such experiences.

The larger social and political world experienced through Unikon and its federations broadened people's experience immeasurably. Since their small union was affiliated with many others and now actively utilizing those ties, each of them had visited other unions, some had gone to affiliated organizations' conventions or meetings, and they had Diet members and union federation officials at every one of their own general meetings. They were represented in the Sōkōdō demonstrations by Sōhyō officials and began to feel "larger," as many put it, that is, tied into something bigger and more important than just their own life or work with their limited boundaries. This expansion was in and of itself attractive. Many used the expression "life experience" (*jinsei keiken*) to describe the satisfaction of being involved in this fight, saying that the union's struggle had become their own life experience.

The very practical necessity of having a job was of utmost importance, and many were reluctant to quit because they were uncertain about their prospects for finding another job at all, or because they wanted to work in high technology and particularly in camera production and were afraid that they wouldn't be able to find such a job elsewhere. For virtually all the regular employees who stayed, this was their first full-time job. Most of these workers—nearly all men—came to Tokyo from the rural areas of northeast Japan to work at Unikon, and they were not eager to quit and look for other work. For the part-time women, a different factor was at work, the proximity to their own homes and the virtual nonexistence of labor unions for part-time workers. Unikon was one of the first anywhere in Japan to consider including part-time workers in their union, so finding another job with working conditions as good as this company, or with even a voice in the formation of working conditions was quite unlikely. Again history became important, in that these part-time workers had formed the union here and had a particular pride in its existence as well as in its strength. Several of these workers spoke of the impossibility of finding a job where there would be a union and admitted that while they could be active in one, they didn't feel they knew how to organize one from scratch by themselves.

Consciousness and Action

The experience of the Unikon workers suggests several lessons: there is a very strong dialectical relationship between experience and consciousness; it is necessary to create a personal sensibility conducive to struggle; and learning and process are critical to taking and analyzing action. The bankruptcy of their company, their union activities, and their collective actions like the demonstrations were, as experience, part of their consciousness. Workers' thoughts, feelings, and actions are not segregated or compartmentalized, but rather contextualized and interdependent. The bankruptcy made them angry, but their anger had its own history; it was shaped and cultivated through previous experiences. Every individual had been through weekly meetings of study groups which taught them about legal and moral rights, discussed labor history, and promoted a sense of identity with organized unions and workers throughout Japan and the world. Each of these workers had also been through three labor disputes and all the collective actions and successes these had entailed.

Consequently, when their owners declared them bankrupt and neglected to consult with their union and to follow cautious legal procedures, they were angry. They felt angry, they knew why they were angry, and they took actions that expressed that anger. Their dignity as human beings was offended and their legal rights as organized workers were ignored. The organizational skill of Unikon leaders lay in weaving the threads of heartfelt offense against human dignity and ideological protest into collective actions which integrated goals of worker control and goals of worker participation into a single powerful movement.

Knowing that a struggle is for the benefit of all workers, finding it sensible to protest inequality and injustice, is still not enough to build motivations for action. A personal sensibility must develop, such that struggle seems reasonable, feels right, and matters to the individual worker. Such sensibility cannot be cultivated outside the experiences of social life and political action. For that, demonstrations and other organized union activities were critical. It was here that the merging of experience and thought were most obvious, and most reminiscent of the kind of ritual process discussed by Victor Turner. It is not necessary to have a ritual, however, to have a profoundly transformative experience. What is necessary is that an individual be personally participating in a socially constructed action while ideas about what those actions mean are presented in a coherent and convincing way. The reasons for this struggle, for instance, must become significant in explaining one's own behavior and action, not just the actions of others or of the union. While workers were angry and confused about what to do, the union sent them to explain and justify their cause. It sent them into demonstrations of various kinds. Within a few weeks efforts to understand the struggle of the Unikon union were efforts to understand their own personal experience and action. Their own participation created a personally felt sense of struggle, which shaped their motivation and commitment. Furthermore, this process had to be repeated. In the early stages it might be characterized as transformative. Later it was reinforcing. Throughout the two and a half years it was critical in rehearsing the personal importance of the meaning of their collective action.

The link between personal experience and purposeful political action is through a web of significance and feasibility. Decisions to take certain actions or stay in such a struggle were not made once and then left alone. They were themselves part of a process of learning that is just as concerned with experience and common sense, or implicit knowledge, as it is with ideas, interests, and explicit knowledge.

Both leaders and rank and file were involved in a fluid process of learning, teaching, experimenting, inquiring, explaining, reassessing, and deciding. Decisions, however, were not one-time events, taken and then followed through. They were sometimes actions taken with little thought, which just seemed natural, right, or inevitable. And sometimes they were agonized over and regretted and even resented. But always they were just points on a trajectory through the two-and-a-half-year period of time during which the 150 people who remained learned from one another and in each other's company how to construct both a convincing argument and a successful collective action to cope with the threat bankruptcy posed to their livelihoods.

CHAPTER 3

Playing with Social Relations

Hierarchy, Organization,
and Affect on a Union Trip

Japanese organizations are known for their liberal use of parties, drinking outings, sporting events, and other recreational activities in the interest of building community. Unikon and Universal are no exceptions. There was a recognized need for such events, not to mention a recording of them in photograph albums. Why all this emphasis on relaxing, fooling around, even getting raucously drunk in the company of coworkers? Creating the opportunities for such behavior is neither easy nor cheap. Yet even in these two small companies, operating as they were under severe financial constraints, with workers receiving only 60 percent of their wages, union leaders, acting both as such and as company managers as well, felt that not only were factory festivals, parties, softball outings, and celebrations necessary, but that every year a minimum of two overnight trips to resorts was essential for maintaining solidarity in their union and the commitment of their workers.

The importance of these events reflects the importance of juxtaposing organization and affect, collective and individual identities, formal structures and informal interactions, and of playing with as well as recalling the elasticity of boundaries that define not only the company and union but the various levels of organization within them. It is through this process of playing with their organization, with the social relations within it, that workers achieve a degree of alignment between their feelings of closeness to one another as people, their sense of belonging to various levels of their organization, and the purposes which their organization pursues. It is also here that the dissonance, problems, and frustrations of organizational hierarchy, relations of unequal power and status, and feelings of inclusion within it are experienced and even dramatized through particular events and practices. Playing with, within, and through their organizations was always participation in a complex drama of institutional social life.

In this chapter Unikon workers travel to Nikkō for a two-day trip. If the story of that trip is a story of this playful juxtaposition of activities and images of closeness, belonging, and purpose, the interpretive process for these workers is a process of aligning, with varying degrees of success, their own notions of work as a material livelihood, deep emotional attachment to coworkers, a sense of identity with their organization, and commitment to certain union and company goals. The ideal state of workers' consciousness from the standpoint of Unikon leadership was, of course, a smooth interlocking of these motivations, and for many workers this was realized some of the time. One worker with some fifteen years' experience in the assembly section told me, for example, "I can't separate my work from Unikon, or from the union. It all gets wound up together. I work hard because I need money, and because I want to do my job well. But I also want to make this company a success and to be part of a strong union." For most workers this kind of integration was realized at some times but not at all. Perfect and consistent commitment is not easily achieved nor easily maintained. Solidarity was one of the most critical goals for the union leaders in organizing union actions, and commitment to work one of the most important in managing Unikon as a company. From the perspective of rank-and-file workers, feeling at one with others in their union and feeling like part of a comfortable community were very important assets and motivations in their struggle as union members and in their work. The trip to Nikkō was, like the ongoing operation of Unikon, both a company and a union event, had both workplace and collective action goals, and dramatized the social relations of both their union and their company in all their complexity. Both the explicit messages of speeches and toasts and the implicit structuring of events expressed goals, organizational structure, social relations, and important meanings attached to effort and action for Unikon workers as workers and as union members and activists as well.

It is common for Japanese parties, after-work drinking, company trips, and other work- and organization-linked festivities to be associated with—indeed, to be interpreted exclusively as activities for—expressing and building harmony, for overcoming and counterbalancing hierarchy, and for providing spaces where true thoughts and feelings can be aired.

In my experience these activities were never so one-sided, were in fact not even significantly more harmonious or equal or honest in feeling than daily life activities, demonstrations, or other events and actions. These activities were institutionally structured, and people participating did so in the same social relationships within which they worked and engaged in political action. What was special about trips and other more playful occasions was just that—they were playful, informal, special. And what was particular to the organized banquets and formal elements of such a trip and of parties and meetings as well, was their formal, performance-oriented dramatizations of social relationships and themes that would otherwise be lived as part of daily life and mundane actions. In this trip to Nikkō, union solidarity, the solidarity both of an interest group and of a community, was expressed, performed, and rehearsed with all the elements of harmony and dissonance present in daily life. Just as these coexisted in the demonstration, in other collective actions, and in daily work routines, they coexisted here in the trip as well.

The enthusiasm, commitment, and motivation workers felt toward their company or their union had a certain fluidity through time. There were real ups and downs such that, for instance, a sense of consistency between personal self-interest and company or union goals was felt at some times and not at others. Similarly, a sense of identity with other workers or with a real community in their workplace or union was stronger one time than another. These experiences of social relationships through time followed certain patterns in response to both personal and public events. Success or failure in pursuing their dispute might inspire optimism or doubt. The gentle dampening of spirits by routine, exhaustion, or malaise—always a recurring factor in a very lengthy labor dispute—could create a heavy inertia of feeling. The trip was designed and envisioned to counteract just this kind of dampening, to rejuvenate people, community, and solidarity. Beyond this characterization neither union leaders nor rank-and-file workers could go in analyzing the very commonsensical structure of the event and the "natural" way in which it progressed. The event tapped into a very interesting mixture of implicit and explicit knowledge about organizations, unions, work, hierarchy, closeness, solidarity, commitment, and belonging.

"We have to go away, forget about everything, and relax together," said the union leaders about their trips. What they traveled some distance to forget was not, however, "everything," but some very particular things, the most obvious and notable of which were their daily routines of work, of meetings, and of efforts in their dispute. They emphasized release of tension and recovery from exhaustion, but in fact everyone knew that a trip like this was always very strenuous. In this chapter the Unikon workers travel to a mountain resort a few hours' drive from Tokyo in search of fun, relaxation, and time with their coworkers.

The Nikkō Trip

Nikkō is a popular resort in the mountains just east of Tokyo. The Unikon trip to Nikkō was announced in a shop floor meeting about a month in advance, and workers volunteered to be on the committee to make arrangements and plans. The volunteering was done mostly in a passive way, that is, by volunteering someone else's services until several people who could not say no had been recruited to do the job.

The job, everyone agreed, was a very big one. Unikon had some 150 workers, and most were likely to go, as were members of their families. Buses had to be chartered, hotel reservations made, meals ordered, and itineraries planned. For the following weeks those on this committee were periodically teased about doing a good job. "We're all counting on you to make this the most memorable trip ever!" or "Don't forget that what I really like to eat is sukiyaki, so order the best for our dinner." As it got closer to time for the trip, those planning the trip started showing signs of wear and tear. They sighed about the scale of the task and remarked that it was going to be hard to relax and enjoy the trip itself with so much responsibility for organizing it on their shoulders. But they did their job, and by May 11 everything was ready.

FROM TOKYO TO NIKKŌ

I was late. We were to assemble at 8:00 A.M. in front of the factory for a departure at 8:30 A.M. Getting into the vacation spirit, I was not worrying too much about time, and when at 8:20 I turned the corner and came into sight of the assembling group I was greeted with "Oh, there you are," "We were getting worried," and "We telephoned your house." This was only the first of several surprises for me, generated by very different expectations of what constituted a vacation.

The next surprise was visual. The daily attire of the Unikon workers was quite casual, and since people were looking forward to hiking and sightseeing around waterfalls at Nikkō, I came dressed in jeans and casual, comfortable shoes, and I expected that others would be dressed the same. A few of the younger women were in jeans, but not so much casual as fashionable ones. All the other women wore dresses, high-heeled shoes, and nylons. They had on more makeup and more jewelry than usual, were complimenting each other on their looks, and generally enjoying the special opportunity to dress up with their friends. Men were in slacks and sport coats for the most part, and the whole assembly felt very much like a somewhat dressy party.

When I came up to the gate I said good morning to Tajima-san, one of the union leaders in charge, and he introduced me to the tourist agent who had helped them organize the trip and charter the buses. He was a short man and always seemed to be smiling, mostly by virtue of his facial composition, irrespective of his feeling. He was flushed and busy and began worrying about my being able to understand him, but Tajima-san put him at ease and he seemed relieved.

To get things moving, our names were read out and we were assigned to buses according to the departments we worked for. I was with the assembly department on Bus 2, which we shared with the parts man-ufacturing department. These workers were almost all older women and were affectionately called by everyone, including women of the same age in different departments, the "aunties of the parts department" (*buhin no obasantachi*). This title expressed a certain affection toward these women and at the same time reflected the lower status associated with their work. Theirs was considered to be the simplest work in the factory and was done almost exclusively by part-time workers. These women were less dressed up than the assembly department people, and their laughter was louder and more uninhibited. The assignment putting us on the same bus with this division pleased everyone, and people settled down to joking and anticipating a good time.

Attendance was taken, and at almost exactly 8:30 the buses pulled away as we waved good-bye to the young men from affiliated labor unions who were left to act as security guards until we got back. We had just left the curb when the tour guide assigned to our bus stood up and introduced herself to us. Suzuki-san was young, pretty, dressed in a perky hat and red, white, and blue suit. She had her hair tied back and looked altogether bright and cheerful. She spoke quickly and kept up a continual banter not only about the trip but also an ad-libbed dialogue with those who made it their pastime to needle her. Not having expected a tour guide, at least until we arrived at Nikkō, I was amazed to see her take charge of the entire group, acting as a sort of master of ceremonies, getting things going, nudging people to relax and have a good time.

She in fact kept telling us all to relax and get rid of our self-restraint (*enryo*), and she gave us a glimpse of what was to happen in the next forty-eight hours. She had been very well briefed. She congratulated the union on its proximate victory, talked about the auspicious nature of the trip, including the good weather, and urged everyone to pitch in and make it a happy affair. Suzuki-san introduced the bus driver and then started joking about all of us. "The seating arrangements," she said, "tell me a great deal. There is a generation gap starting about the middle of the bus. You guys up here all look pretty old—and married. You back there look young and single. Since both the driver and I are still single, please don't hesitate to introduce yourselves or your friends to us." All of this and her subsequent joking, however risqué, took place in formal and impersonal linguistic forms, adding still further to the incongruity and humor of her performance. The mood was loosening quickly as her talents had their desired effects.

At 8:45, just fifteen minutes out, she asked who was in charge of refreshments and suggested that they be passed around, "just in case some had come without breakfast." This brought beer, whiskey, sake, and soft drinks to everyone, followed by sweets, dried squid, peanuts, rice crackers, and oranges. Everyone took some of these, and several of the women brought out additional snacks they had brought from home and these too were offered to those nearby. The array of snacks brought from home added very personal touches to the gathering with people complimenting and commenting on one another's pickles—all home-made. Since most came from a variety of rural areas famous for slightly different recipes for pickle making, this was always a way of starting discussion not only of cooking skill but also about memories of past gatherings in distant family and village settings.

At 9:30 we had our first rest stop. It seemed as though we had barely gotten going, but it turned out that we stopped about once an hour for a twenty-minute break. Everyone got off the buses, used rest rooms, played with the kids who were along, and hung around in the sunshine munching on snacks. Nikkō is only a couple of hours' drive from Tokyo, but this schedule with all its stops made it seem that you were going a very long way, when in fact you were just proceeding very slowly to a relatively close place.

After the second rest stop, just after 11:00 A.M., the guide again took charge of our activities, brought out cordless microphones, and told us it was time to liven up the trip with some singing. The bus was equipped with recorded music and lyric books. This style of singing to recorded music, karaoke, is ubiquitous at company and union gatherings and is popular at the small bars and coffee shops frequented for after-work stops as well. Some people are exceptionally good at it, others quite bad, but everyone has to take a turn. The guide sang the first song and then the rest of us took turns.

The variety of music covered quite a spectrum. There were standard Japanese folk songs (*minyō*), longing for return to native villages or lamenting the hardships of working in the fields or at sea. There were contemporary ballads (*enka*), mostly sad songs about lost love or love triangles. Then, particularly from the younger generation, were popular rock-and-roll songs, and finally from the kids came cartoon theme songs. There were ten children on our bus, all between the ages of four and eight. Between the singing and the alcohol the mood on the bus was growing increasingly uninhibited, and people were moving around more, talking more loudly and to those sitting farther away. People started interacting more as a group rather than simply with the person sitting closest to them.

As we got closer to the mountains into which we were headed and as people loosened up, songs got more entertaining, some bluntly risqué. Popular children's songs were sung in their jesting versions, such as:

> Why does the crow caw?
> That's the crow's business, isn't it!

And one song, which in the original went

> Mr. Elephant! Mr. Elephant!
> You have such a long nose!
> Your mother's is long too!

on the bus came out as

> Mr. Elephant! Mr. Elephant!
> You have such a long nose!
> Oh, yes! And my penis is long too!

Adults and children alike were laughing in delight at these modified versions of the classic children's lyrics, and we were all getting dizzy on laughter, joking, and altitude as the bus climbed higher and higher into the mountains.

The next step upward in the collective goofiness came on the Iroha Slope, a famous series of forty-eight hairpin turns on the narrow winding road leading up to Lake Chūzenji from the town of Nikkō. As you ascend through these turns, the bus and all those in it lean to the right, then lean to the left, sandwiching everyone close together. This was a natural excuse for yet another kind of playing around. The leaning was exaggerated and encouraged above and beyond necessity by the men, going so far as to leap across the aisles and into the next seat during the leaning, and accompanied by grabbing and putting arms around the women nearest them in the direction of the lean. At first, the women giggled and fell out of seats and tried in vain to escape, but after ten or fifteen of the forty-eight turns they started grabbing back and talking loudly about how much fun this was after all. Meanwhile, the guide added to the hilarity by continuing her now precise and well-rehearsed narrative on the historic and scenic importance of the sights which were passing on both sides of the bus all the way up the hill. She discussed flowers, seasons, when the trees were expected to blossom, the history of the area, and exaggerated her own inattention to the frolicking.

SIGHTSEEING

We arrived at Lake Chūzenji about noon and stopped at a restaurant near the lake. The lake was lovely, the restaurant was not. It was on the second floor of a souvenir shop, and people began mumbling apprehensions as we went up the stairs. When we got into the large tatami room, there were rows of tables already set up with our by now thoroughly cold lunches. The food was very unsatisfactory, but in respect to those who had organized the trip people kept their complaints to a minimum and spoke them softly. After lunch there was boating, picture taking and baby watching, and some visited a small museum of history nearby.

After lunch and "free time" were over we began boarding our buses for the short drive to the first waterfall we were to visit. Tajima-san came by and told us that some union officials, guests of the Unikon union, would be shifted to our bus for the remainder of the trip. This announcement was met with pleas to Tajima-san to reverse that decision. "Oh, can't you do something to get them into the other bus?" Others chimed in, "That will change the whole mood," "We don't want big shots [*erai hito*] on our bus!" and the simple, "This is just awful [*Iya na no!* or *Iya da!*]!" When everyone realized that they were going to have to give in to the inevitable, they started cleaning the bus. Things were neatened up, seats brushed off, and aisles cleared. Things quieted down considerably, and there was a lot of sighing. The "big shots" sat quietly in their seats and smoked nervously.

In a few minutes we arrived at the waterfall, Ryūzu no Taki. We got out, walked down to it and took pictures, ate Japanese sweets, and had some tea. We boarded the buses again after about an hour and stopped at another famous waterfall. The area was very crowded with school children on outings and other tourists. People hiked down to it on winding paths through beautiful trees and walked along the river. There was more picture taking and playing with children.

Our final stop was the inn where we were to stay. As we pulled up in front, we noticed that they had "Welcome to Unikon" painted on a sign sitting by the entrance. There were three similar signs for other groups, as this was one of several inns in the area which cater to large group affairs. We found our rooms and settled in, then most went off for a walk, downstairs for some video games, or just sat and talked during the couple of hours of free time we had before the evening banquet and parties began.

The area around our inn was very beautiful, being near one of the sources of the Nikkō hot springs. There were reeds, forests, and a small shrine nearby, and bridges of wood were laid all across the swampy hot springs area, enabling us to walk across and climb part way up a hillside.

THE BANQUET

There were three parties that night, a main banquet (*en-kai*), a second party (*nijikai*), and an informal third gathering (*sanjikai*) which lasted until 3:30 A.M. Beyond that there were more, but I went to bed and those who remained claim to have lost count. Many, mostly men, did not even go to bed at all but stayed up all night talking, singing, drinking, and dancing.

The main banquet began at 6:00 P.M. in the inn's banquet hall and was attended by everyone. Formality of the sequence of events mixed with an informality of dress and performance. The inn provided *yukata* (cotton kimonos), all the same pattern and size. All the men and most of the women came dressed in these, although many of the women had brought their own colorful belts from home. The younger single women wore their street clothes. These same *yukata* are also worn to sleep and represent a very casual informality. This plus the group bathing add to the slumber-party mood.

The room was very large and had a stage facing six rectangular tables, around which people sat on pillows. Each table seated about thirty people, and the one in the middle closest to the stage was designated for guests. People sat at these tables by department and within departments by shop floor groups, although aside from the table reserved for guests there was no clearly obvious guide to seating arrangements.

Food was laid out before we entered, and other dishes were added throughout the evening. Most ardently consumed were the sake and the beer, not the food. Again people complained a bit about the quality of the food and about how bad banquet food usually is, but not enough to dampen the mood. The atmosphere was one of anticipating a good time; people were playfully enjoying each other's company, and because of the distance from their tables to the stage or the table for the guests of honor, they were very uninhibited in their joking.

There was a series of addresses to the entire group, the first five of which preceded any eating or drinking. First came the bus guides, thanking us for inviting them and saying they looked forward to seeing us all again the next day. The second address was from the head of Unikon's Joint Struggle Committee (Kyōtōkaigi), the committee formed of representatives of affiliated unions and Unikon union leaders to plan and manage the labor dispute. He spoke of how hard everyone had worked and how much they had overcome, and he reiterated that it was important for people to continue working together until all their problems have been solved. His messages and all the others similarly emphasized in a very explicit way the necessity of solidarity, its benefits and successes.

The next address was by an All-Japan Metalworkers Federation official who talked about the injustice of the Unikon owners, who just fled from the bankruptcy without taking responsibility for the livelihood of the Unikon workers. He congratulated the Unikon workers for their success in fighting this and talked about how indebted he and all Japanese workers were to them. "President Sasaki and all of you are to be congratulated for what you have done for all of us, for all Japanese workers. It will be harder for owners to take such unjust and irresponsible actions in the future because you have set an important precedent."

The large room was quiet through these speeches, with polite applause following each one. The next speaker introduced was Unikon's

President Sasaki. He spoke very briefly, thanking everyone for their efforts and congratulating them on their success. He concluded with, "Drink as much as you like, let's really enjoy our sake tonight. Let's forget everything else [literally, other places: *yoso o wasurete*] and drink!" His choice of words echoed those of other leaders speaking to the group, urging people not just to enjoy and relax but to forget other things, "other places."

Following the still subdued applause after the president's address, an official from an affiliated union offered the toast. He complimented the perseverance of the Unikon union. "You have all struggled for over two years. There are many who have been involved with you, who have worked side by side with you. Let's have a round of applause for those to whom we owe a great debt of gratitude [*osewa ni natta hito*]." He introduced, in turn, the lawyers, the officials from cooperating unions, and Universal leaders, whose union was still in the middle of a similar struggle. As he did so these people stood up, and at the end he raised his voice and his glass, and everyone in the banquet hall stood and raised theirs as he shouted, "Please drink a lot! *Kanpai*! [Cheers!]"

After these speeches we all started to eat, and the tour guide from our bus started off the singing, which was next on the agenda. Following this, she and other guides from the bus company left the banquet and did not join in the subsequent activities that evening. Tajima-san continued to be master of ceremonies through the lengthy and structured program of entertainment and clowning that followed. Spirits rose as the drinking, singing, dancing, and general fooling around brought everyone in the room to the stage to take their turn at being the center of attention.

There was a lot of poking fun at the entertainment provided by everyone for everyone. The union officials—with the exception of the president—joined in a mimic of a popular comic dance from TV, called the *hige dansu* (the beard dance). The assembly, parts, and lens divisions each did songs. Then all the young men did a song and another version of the "beard dance." Tajima-san called up each division in turn to do something. In every instance it required cajoling, applause, and insistence to get the people up to the stage, and the performances were given with displays of embarrassment and fluster gradually growing into uninhibited play.

Those on stage fell into each other and onto the floor laughing and giggling, grabbing each other and the microphones. Meanwhile, toward the back of the banquet hall an unscheduled game of catch the rice ball was going on with real enthusiasm. It eventually caught the attention of most of us, and real cheerleading got started as rice landed here and there between the folks playing catch with it. The less gregarious would stand back through all these antics toward the edges when on the stage or sitting in their places when not, laughing and looking a little embarrassed.

Throughout the banquet and the performances people were getting up and pouring sake for their shop floor group leaders, division leaders, union officials, and guests. The women were particularly attentive and also poured for men of relatively equal rank. As the party went on, the union leaders started going around to all the tables pouring for the rank and file. Having sake poured for you makes it very hard, and for men almost impossible, to refuse to drink it. Consequently, by the time the one hundred fifty or so guests had poured for all those they either were working for or had working for them, nearly everyone was happily intoxicated.

After all the speeches and after each division and then each shop floor group had performed, it was nearly 9:00 P.M. To bring this formal party to an end, we all stood in a giant circle around the perimeter of the room, a tape of a Japanese folk dance was played, and we twice moved in a circle around the room dancing to the music in the *bon odori* folk dance style, using a lot of arm and hand movements. When that ended we all joined arms, again forming this huge circle around the room, and swayed back and forth as we sang a union song about unity and strength. The final closing of the party was the *sanbon jime* hand clap, a signifier of good fortune and unity.

THE SECOND PARTY

After the banquet broke up, everyone wandered into the halls and up toward the rooms still talking and joking, some linking arms. There was an unorchestrated, "natural" dispersion of people into smaller groups, in each case around shop floor groupings. The rooms in the inn were all Japanese-style, that is to say, beds were in the closet until time to sleep, leaving the tatami mat room open and free for entertaining. There was a low table and stacks of floor pillows in each room, so as many as twenty or thirty people could fit comfortably into some of the larger guest rooms. The notion of comfort, of course, is dependent on the degree of enjoyment of closeness, and in this case people were trying to be as close as possible, and enjoyed having to squeeze in extra people around a table or even to share a floor pillow.

I went to the assembly section party, which was one of the larger gatherings. Several of the drunker men just took a couple of floor pillows and lay down along the edges of the room, while others gathered around the table pouring more beer, sake, and soft drinks. There was another toast, this time to the assembly section and the future of Unikon. People moved freely around the table, singing, chatting, and joking. The men continued to make overtures toward the women, putting arms around them and suggesting they "close dance." People came and went, some checking in on other parties in neighboring rooms.

After a while, one of the women from the front office came to recruit some of us for the "big shots' party," that is, the room where the guests and union officials were having their "second party." They were "lonely" she said, and needed some perking up. Four or five of us went with her from the assembly section, and she gathered others from other rooms.

This party, after we all gathered, began with another toast, more informal this time, and more rapid drinking. The dancing here was western social dancing, instead of the Japanese folk dance of the banquet. Men and women were dancing very close and joking about the sexual significance of it, saying things like "Ooo this feels good, I never do this with my husband," or "Well, I know the Unikon women have a reputation for being special, and now I know what that means." This playfulness grew into kissing and hugging accompanied by giggling on the part of the women and further restrained assertiveness on the part of the men. Single women were not, for the most part, involved in this particular fun. They were invited, they refused, and they remained seated, looking embarrassed.

The singing was varied and joined in by everyone. There was solo karaoke singing which all listened to and encouraged by clapping, and there was group singing as well, in which everyone joined. Those who didn't want to sing were persuaded, sometimes with really amazing persistence until they gave in. Voice quality was no excuse, and in fact everyone did end up singing something. In addition to the kinds of songs sung on the bus and at the banquet, the typical popular ballads, folk songs, and union songs, there were peace movement songs, some American and Russian workers' songs, and a Hebrew song. For the ballads, one about a wife who had run away, sung by a young man with exaggerated sadness, people laughed and fell left and right in amusement around the small table. For the peace songs they sat straight up in formal *seiza* style, and then with the "Oh Suzanna," "Yesterday," and "Hava

Nagila" they clowned around again. One of the union federation officials there sang us a Russian song, in Russian, and reminisced a bit about his trips there. The young Unikon men present then sang a Unikon favorite, *Seishun Jidai* (Youth), and were teased about this song not including young women as well. The popular songs were led or sung by the Unikon rank and file, the union songs by the labor federation officers, and the lewd songs by the Unikon leadership. Women joined in all but the lewd ones but led none of them.

As the hours wore on more and more men began laying pillows out and drifting in and out of sleep. Gradually the numbers resting began to convince those of us still partying that another break was in order, and this party began to disintegrate. As we left this room the group reformed and found itself downstairs in a lounge for yet a third gathering, this time of the young people of the Unikon union, with only one or two outsiders.

THE THIRD PARTY

This party became very political, recalling a student activist gathering of the late sixties or early seventies. We discussed Iran, Afghanistan, the U.S.-Japan Security Treaty, and labor issues. The late hour—it was past midnight already—and the amount of alcohol already consumed plus the continued drinking gave a certain fervor to this discussion not matched by continuity of topic or resolution of debate. This was a smaller group of about fifteen or twenty, and several side conversations competed with the main one. Some near me decided to practice their English a little. Others gossiped about possible couples who seemed to be spending a lot of time together. About 3:00 in the morning I finally left and went to bed, as did about half the others.

While this third party had been going on, there were others elsewhere, and still other groups of people taking baths together and drinking quietly in their rooms. We were about six to ten per room, so even after returning to the room there was socializing, and of course the large communal baths encouraged people to bathe together as well.

THE MORNING AFTER

At breakfast I was very tired from lack of sleep, and others seemed quiet and even groggy. I had gotten more sleep than most, as it turned out, and had consumed relatively little alcohol. The general mood was hung over, and yet a determination still reigned to continue the partying until the last moment. There was beer on all the tables and the men, especially at the table of honor for guests and officials, were drinking beer with their soy bean soup, seaweed, and fish breakfasts. Some of this looked a bit forced, as though upholding an image was a stronger motivation than desire to actually start the day with a beer, but nonetheless there was a lot of drinking still going on. There was no question, however, that these men were enjoying blustering about their drinking.

After breakfast a group of us from my shop floor area took a walk out to a small lake and talked about the previous night's parties, how late people went to bed, and how much people had drunk. It was a lazy and relaxed mood with people worrying about each other's stamina in light of the night's activities.

As soon as we got back, we boarded our buses and headed out of the area. On the bus people were sick and/or sleeping. There was no more frolicking of the kind coming up to Nikkō. The bus's movements seemed to be making many people feel very uncomfortable. The humor in the situation was provided again by the tour guide. Having left the parties early, having had a good night's sleep, and having arisen early, she was as bright and cheerful as ever. Her impeccable Japanese and formal, well-rehearsed commentary on Nikkō continued, with occasional teasing about people's lethargic moods.

THE SHINTO CEREMONY

The buses stopped at Nikkō's famous Tōshōgū, a mausoleum compound housing a Buddhist temple and a Shinto shrine, and we all lined up for a guided tour of the grounds. We filed through various areas and had a number of historical spots pointed out to us. We then found ourselves being led into the inside of a Shinto shrine on the temple grounds. This stop had not been announced, and people didn't seem to know we were planning to make it. Someone near the front of the line remarked that since it cost three hundred yen to go in, he was not going, and he got out of line and said he would wait for us to come back out. A handful of others followed his lead, but the majority of us went on in. We all lined up sitting in the formal *seiza* seating position at the back of the shrine, facing the altar. The union president, who was to become the president of the new company, stood at the front, and we began to realize that this was going to be a ceremony. The priest and two shrine maidens came up and they bowed to Sasaki-san and he to them. The priest clapped once and we all bowed again. The young women danced and assisted in the ritual, with another young girl playing a drum and the priest a flute. His chant asked for the business success of the soon-to-be-established Unikon Camera Company. The priest worked "Unikon Camera" and "business success" into a droning chant. As we left we each received a small charm and walked out through an intricate shrine garden. People commented that they had not expected this ceremony, and that it had been very beautiful.

After this we proceeded straight home. A few young people got seriously sick, threw up, and were cared for by the older women. Most read, slept, and rested. Even the tour guide was quiet for most of the return trip.

Creating Distance

This trip, which was both a company and a union trip, had several purposes. The stated goals for Unikon leaders were to build and renew solidarity and community and to treat both union members and representatives of supporting unions to a relaxing good time as reward for their hard work. The specific goals around which leaders wanted to reinforce solidarity were the continuation of the struggle to use their brand name and the cooperative efforts it would require to open the new company. For rank-and-file workers the stated goals of the trip were relaxation, fun, and a chance to enjoy their workplace friends while traveling at union expense to a lovely spot. They also expressed a need to convey their gratitude to the representatives of supporting unions for their help.

The question of interest for me was, of course, why a trip? This was a question of no particular interest to leaders or to rank-and-file workers, all of whom assumed its appropriateness and necessity. Why did leaders feel that a trip was essential to building commitment and solidarity? What made it the appropriate vehicle for persuading people to make union and company goals their own? My questions were not answered with confusion or an inability to respond discursively. They were answered with sensibly linked circles of assumptions. You go on a trip because you want to reward people, you want to relax, you want to build solidarity and community. Because you want to do these things you go on a trip. And so on. This kind of explanation through unexamined assumptions makes reference to examples of "successful" trips and to other organizations in Japanese society that also use them, ultimately giving such trips a sense of appropriateness based on an historical and social record of shared common sense in the cultural field of Japan. In short, everyone does it because it is the "natural" thing to do, dropping the trip squarely into the realm of implicit social knowledge as a "taken-for-granted practice" that "makes the normal normal" (Taussig 1987: 366).

One of the most obvious characteristics of a trip is its ability, through travel, to create distance. This is important not only in this union or this company, but in schools, clubs, and companies and unions of all sizes and character all over Japan. In the cultural field of Japan, the trip provides an opportunity for people and practices common in other organizational settings to be put into a new and distant environment and thus into a new and different context for feeling and thinking about the important relationships, goals, and activities of the organization. In this case work, workplace relationships, union activities, and union relationships were central. What is unique to the trip as different from parties, factory festivals and celebrations, and union gatherings is that all this takes place at a distance.

The search for strangers is one obvious aspect of these trips that helps forge a common identity. By virtue of being someplace where others are strangers and where the place too is relatively unknown, those within the group reinforce their own group boundaries vis-à-vis these unfamiliar people and places. The exaggeration of relatively minor regional differences within Japan supports this search for the unusual; on this trip there were frequent references to the unique character of Nikkō, and each of the major scenic spots was given attention.

Members of Japanese organizations usually use the terms *uchi* and *soto* to refer to those within and those outside their boundaries. *Soto* can be replaced with *yoso*, which has a nuance of slightly more distance. The distance between the destination of the trip and people's homes, families, neighborhoods, and the other companies and organizations with which they are affiliated serves to isolate them and emphasize, for the duration of the trip, the strength and importance of their own ties to each other within this organization.

Forgetting and Remembering

The stated goal of trips, as everyone agrees and leaders remind at every opportunity, is to "forget everything," or literally, to "forget all other places." Physical distance is hoped to encourage a much-needed mental distance as well, and thus the list of previously visited resorts is a list of some of the most scenic spots surrounding Tokyo. The emphasis is always on relaxation and forgetting, to refresh the spirits. As one union leader put it, "We all get into the hot springs together and forget about everything."

Many things, however, are not included in "everything." While daily work routines, production quotas, the stress of commuting, and difficult union or company problems or issues are left behind, some aspects of the organization, of daily work and daily union issues are taken along and even reemphasized in this new and distant environment. This reemphasis serves to bind them in some inseparable way to the group and its identity.

Not left behind are, first of all, people. No one stays home. Even the ongoing necessities of basic company operation, like security, were delegated to volunteers from affiliated unions. So if we assume that everything taken along is implicitly considered indispensable, every person in the union and in the company is considered, in this context, equally indispensable.

In addition, the structure of the organization is maintained in a variety of ways. The Unikon community that was being renewed, reemphasized, and enjoyed was structured around departments, sections, teams, and other workplace groupings, all of which were related as a whole to other unions and integrated into federations and political parties with a clear sense of relative status and power. Everything from bus and room assignments to seating at the banquet was done according to sections and work groups. Even the entertaining was organized so that different sections took turns and in some sense even competed with one another. The atmosphere was one of joviality, but even then people were commenting that their section or division was "not about to lose out to others" (*makenai zo*). Most of the external networks within which the company and the union operated were represented by the "guests" who were invited to come along. These included leaders from affiliated unions, federations, and from local associations, as well as some from unions which Unikon was helping in their own struggles.

Accomplishments and goals of the union—without any hint of difficult or divisive issues—are also remembered, although in a very abbreviated way compared to their treatment in routine meetings at home. They are brought into the partying by way of greetings and addresses given by the guests and union leaders. Not only are these remarks much briefer, but they are also largely encouraging in form, avoiding issues that are complex, divisive, or require decisions. There is no hint of decision making or discussion of any kind in this distanced context.

What people do forget, or at least get away from for a while, are just such decisions, complex issues, and problems within their organization. They also get away from the exhaustion and routine of daily workplace life. This is not to say, however, that people really come home rested or relaxed. Most workers complained beginning several days before about the grueling schedule, anticipating late nights and lengthy and thoroughly predictable banquet and after-banquet partying. And for several days after returning people talked about "recovering" from the vacation. It is, however, a very different kind of exhaustion from that of daily life, and nearly everyone participated in and enjoyed the sharing of snapshots during the first week or so back. Similarly, before the event there was much gay anticipation of getting out of Tokyo, out of the daily routine, and having fun with workplace friends. In the context of the Unikon dispute there was the additional element of financial difficulties and the benefit enjoyed by rank-and-file workers of having a short vacation paid for by their union at a time when they had more than the usual trouble affording extras.

Closeness, Belonging, and Purpose

The trip to Nikkō provided an opportunity for everyone to "get away from it all," but without getting away from each other, or even from the particular institutional and social relationships of their workplace. They left the workplace behind but took the people, the social organization, and the goals and purposes of their union and their company with them. And here is the most telling characteristic of these events. The trip provides structured opportunities for unstructured interaction among workers, and through these it fosters the building of "natural" and affectionate bonds of friendship and commitment, which then can become the basis for a sense of workplace community. This sense of community in turn is given a goal, a sense of purpose, so that commitment to one another, to the organization, and finally to the organization's goals may be mutually reinforcing. Without analyzing the event as such, participants are aware of the importance of trips taken together to build community, solidarity, and a sense of purpose.

They are also of more than one mind about both the success and the inherent pleasure of the event itself. What was shared by all with whom

I spoke was a clear sense of the importance of this common practice. What was shared only partially were responses, opinions, feelings, and enthusiasm about it. In this case, as well as in talking with people about their meetings and festivals, it was true that a variety of evaluations and personal responses coexisted quite comfortably with an unquestioned assumption of appropriateness and significance about certain practices. What I think I encountered in the trip was one of the organizational practices assumed to be centrally constitutive of community. It is important not to confuse that assumption of centrality and significance with a unity of consciousness among all participants. The experience of this event was not totally different for each individual nor was it totally the same. It neither created a single collective consciousness nor did it fail to deliver some convincing messages. Through their participation in this dramatization of their community, people lived, in their own experience and in a clearly bounded and separated special space, some of the central realities and images of themselves and their organization. The differences in their responses entailed the differences between them as individual people with particular histories and identities and as workers in particular locations in their organization.

The trip is an event assumed as part of organizational community and creating an atmosphere reminiscent of the atmosphere of a village festival. Just as in such a festival, most participants are quite conscious of both the cooperative, enjoyable, and harmonious aspects of the community and of the divisive, difficult, and painful side. Mature participants in this cultural field know that the festival in the village and the trip in the urban organization are times to emphasize one and set the other aside.

CLOSENESS

What constitutes closeness for Unikon workers? They often used expressions like "*sumigokochi ga ii*" (a comfortable place to live) when referring to their workplace, or "*koko wa minna issho desu*" (everyone is together here). I followed up on these comments by asking what made them feel this way. The answers were inevitably about mutual understanding, ties of affection and caring, and a sense of mutual respect. The most common expressions used were *ninjō* (human feeling) and *aijō* (love). What, then, I would persist, constitutes *ninjō*? And what, in the context of the workplace and the union, constitutes *aijō*?

While I realized that I was touching on one of the basic affective constructions of community, I was not prepared for the degree to which *ninjō* was also explained and expressed in terms of respect, understanding, and enjoyment of individuality. "Everyone has his or her own feelings [*minna sore zore kimochi ga chigaimasu*], but we understand each other." This is not considered to be easy, because "everybody is living in unique and particular circumstances [*minna hitori hitori jijō ga chigaimasu*]." *Ninjō*, however, means that you try, as one human being to another, to understand and appreciate everyone else's situation and feelings. It also forms a substantial moral basis for mutual aid based on understood need rather than measured reciprocity of specific action. Knowing that one of the part-time women had an ill mother-in-law at home to care for brought both leaders and coworkers to drop by, seek to help her, and reassure her that her job was waiting for her when she could return. It also meant that workers who quit at the point of bankruptcy were understood not as less committed to the struggle so much as in individual situations where it was impossible for them to survive economically if they stayed. *Ninjō*, in other words, was used as an explanation of morally valued behavior motivated by deep and sincere human feeling that makes it possible to put oneself in the very different shoes of another person. Thus both the individual differences in circumstance and the shared human commonalities of feeling and understanding are emphasized. In the trip, as well as in meetings and parties, these are both brought forth as central to the constitution of community and solidarity.

The particular ways in which this is accomplished are examples of the ways companies and unions structure informality into their organizations, counting on this to facilitate a closeness among members. The general craziness in the buses and in the banquets and parties was, in each case, released by two things, sake and karaoke. Karaoke is omnipresent not just here but in Japanese parties of all kinds. It stems, workers would repeatedly tell me, from the village festivals, where the centerpiece of the festival fun was the *nodo jiman* or singing contest. In "the old days" there were no electronic microphones or music to accompany the singing, but people took turns singing to their friends and neighbors nonetheless. "The important thing," said one young man, "is that you know each other, that you know the people who are singing and can appreciate their individuality [*kosei*] and can understand their feelings. Japanese people," he continued, "don't know how to express themselves, but they can sing, and that lets them communicate their feelings and their spirits to one another." Another worker told me simply that "singing is a person's heart," so there is no "good" or "bad" singing, there are only different hearts. "Sometimes, in fact," he laughed, "the ones that sound the worst are really the most moving or the most fun, because you can hear that person's spirit most clearly since they aren't really performing."

Like karaoke, sake is a way to tap into and release the expressions of an individuality commonly held in reserve in daily social life, where certain restraints are necessary. Sake invites self-expression; karaoke suggests its form. The two together provide the contours of an affective dialogue through which informal and spontaneous ties of friendship and closeness can grow.

BELONGING

Because this process is an informal and unstructured one, with elements like sake and karaoke suggesting a form for interaction without determining any specific outcome, the feeling of closeness that results is not uniform throughout the group. Individual workers feel closer to some of their coworkers than to others, from personal friendships and personal inclinations. In addition, the line between drinking enough to loosen inhibitions and participate in the party and drinking "too much" and becoming a nuisance is a fine one. Certain individuals have a reputation for "drinking well," others for being "unable to drink." In the context of this kind of social drinking the distinction is between harmonious and disruptive behavior at the earlier banquet and parties. By the middle of the night, as the gatherings become less structured, the distinction becomes less important. Singing too, in its encouragement of individual performance, opens the door to a host of particular behaviors, including hogging the microphone, "showing off," or even making fun of others. Since the purpose of this trip was to build ties of closeness, not in fact between personal friends along lines of personal allegiance, but between workers in this company and members of this union, the organizers of the parties made efforts to balance the structured and the unstructured activities. It is important to even out these feelings and bring people into some degree of emotional alignment with one another as members of the same organization, to balance feelings of personal closeness with feelings of collective closeness. Ties of friendship should serve ties of belonging.

Where karaoke suggests an opportunity for self-expression and enjoyment of individuality, the group goofiness that typifies the banquet and, along with karaoke, the parties afterward, is an opportunity for the shop floor groups and sections to express something of their own individual characters. The competitive comments that surround these shows, like "We know the assembly people can't do anything, there's never been any talent there!" or "It's just like the office staff to do that silly dance!" all serve to underscore the sense of identity and character that each group within the company cultivates for itself.

The organization of these expressive opportunities by work groups and sections is followed, of course, by songs and dances that the entire union joins, and finally even the guests are asked to join in. The levels and boundaries, the linkages in the networks, are all reemphasized, performed, and dramatized by this entertaining inclusion and exclusion of members of various units and levels within the organization. The sequence is also important. Everything begins on the buses, where it is your closest workplace friends whom you are sitting near, and where it is individual karaoke and sake that open the trip and get people relaxed and informal. The banquet comes next, at which entertainment never goes down to the individual level, but operates at the levels of shop floor, work group, section, and whole company. Finally even the greater network of affiliated unions and companies is suggested by inclusion of these guests in a final song and dance. Following these, however, there is a return to the individual and more unstructured level of interaction in the second and third parties, only loosely organized in several rooms. And in this special, distanced location, what Taussig refers to as the "sensation" of the social relationships is emphasized, legitimated, and reinforced.

The structure of the trip suggests integration of these different levels of experience, and it balances the structured and the unstructured interactions carefully enough to allow participants to feel both close as individuals and connected as members, both emotionally involved and socially defined.

PURPOSE

The daily interactions and routines of workplace life, the experience in union activities, and other collective events and actions like demonstrations, meetings, and festivals, are all part of this process of encouraging ties of closeness and purpose. The distance of the destination allows the introduction of karaoke and sake over an extended period of time into the workplace social organization. It is an explicit and performed version of the organization and its goals, and it allows several levels of organization to participate in the affective practices sequentially and repeatedly for a couple of days. Not only does this extended experience motivate individual closeness, it also suggests that the ties between people are the ties binding the organization together. The relationships are formally marked and defined while being informally encouraged to develop affective dimensions. This affective dimension is, however, not left to chance or allowed to dissipate but is again formally integrated back into the organization. And it is here, in the integration of informal ties of closeness and belonging, that the affective dimension is introduced into the organization.

This emotional commitment to one another or to Unikon is, however, not meant to be a simple commitment to the group per se. It is a commitment to the organization's goals and purposes as well. In the case of Unikon there were two sets of purposes. On the one hand Unikon was their workplace, where they expected to participate in producing a camera they could be proud of, where they were trying to make a product capable of competing in a very competitive market, and where they wanted to be able to make a living and feel comfortable during their working hours. On the other hand, Unikon was also their union, and they were committed to its "struggle." "This union's struggle," one woman told me, "became my own [*jibun no tatakai ni natta*]." Ideally most workers would emerge with feelings like these reinforced.

On the trip there was time to remind people about their goals and time for spontaneous and informal interactions. The particular character and strength of this event was time to do both and furthermore to superimpose the two so that the community could remind itself of its purpose. While speeches were considerably abbreviated, and unlike those at meetings were given by "big shots" dressed in casual cotton kimonos, they did reiterate the common themes that represented Unikon's various aims and goals. Similarly, the visit to the Shinto shrine to pray for the future success of the union's battle to regain its brand and the new company's struggle to retain a place in a competitive economy involved participants in a serious ritual reminder of the organization's goals.

The decision at the shrine of many workers not to pay the fee and join the ceremony served as a reminder, however, that while the language of the trip is "everyone is one" and the practices of the event emphasize community, solidarity, and commonality of purpose, the participants were responding as members of their organization, as people in particular locations within it, and as individuals with their own interpretations as well.

Organization, Inequality, and Affect

Several aspects of this trip were obviously meant to emphasize equality of belonging and a sense of camaraderie between leaders and rank and file, between guests and Unikon members, and between different sections within the organization. The nature of the trip put this dramatization of equality in the context of play, fun, and pleasant feelings of relaxation. As a whole, the event juxtaposed equality, pleasant feelings, and organization with the hope of building just such a connection.

All male participants regardless of status dressed in the same *yukata* provided by the inn. All single women and many married women as well dressed in casual clothes. Everyone sang and performed on stage. Everyone used the same big baths, and they all joined hands in several songs toward the end of the banquet. Everyone poured sake for everyone else, a gesture of deference and respect, and most engaged in great frolicking. Men were much freer to frolic, drank more, and dressed alike. Women were more reserved, drank much less, and dressed in three different ways: unmarried women dressed in their own clothes, not in the *yukata*; most married women brought their own colorful belts to wear on the inn's *yukata*; and others brought their own clothes. The most obvious difference between higher-ranking and lower-ranking participants was that higher-ranking men, the guests from other unions and federations, drank the most obviously and displayed even more exaggerated drunkenness than those in lower ranks.

While all the explicit messages of speeches and addresses were of unity, equality, and commonality of purpose, the implicit structuring of events and the practices of the trip rehearsed both these elements and the differentiation, inequality, and even some dissonance. In this context the emphasis was successfully placed on the former, but the latter were not missing.

Behavior on buses changed when guests, "big shots," came aboard. Eating and drinking did not begin until they had given their short speeches. Members scurried to pour more sake for them than they poured for rank and file and tried in general to take care of them. Unikon leaders were also given this kind of treatment, although to a lesser degree. Language differences never varied. Regardless of sake intake, deference in linguistic forms remained.

The sequence of addresses and of frolicking on stage and the arrangement of tables were more formal reminders of status differences.

In a very subtle way the efforts made by leaders and guests to pour sake for rank and file, to display more drunkenness, to be even more lewd, and to be all part of the same group reminded people—by virtue of the break with usual custom—ever more clearly that they were not. Thus the scurrying around to reverse this gesture and make sure that even though they made the efforts to level the relationship ritually, in fact they were cared for and treated with deference. Paradoxically, the efforts at this kind of leveling created even more dramatized practices of deference to higher status than would be common in other contexts.

In addition to such performance reminders of organizational structure, there were other aspects of the trip that served the same purpose. Union leaders provided the money to finance the trip and planned much of the itinerary in cooperation with a committee of rank and file. Rank-and-file workers, for instance, did not know about the Shinto ceremony, planned by leaders and not announced. The money came from the union treasury, collected of course from members but managed and dispensed largely at the discretion of union leaders. Similarly, it was the leaders who decided who would be on which buses and even during the event could and did make without consultation decisions that were unchallenged in their legitimacy. These actions were assumed to be natural and appropriate, corresponding to ordinary daily life. The point for the understanding of consciousness, however, is that it is precisely because these ordinary structures and practices were patterned so closely to daily life that the trip was experienced by workers as not so much a break from daily life as a playful and purposeful extension of it.

Organization and Community at Unikon

When I asked how the union's struggle became their own, the responses of Unikon workers indicated that in addition to ideological commitment to the purposes of the union struggle—and for most people this was even more true—they had a commitment mediated through affective ties of fondness, mutual respect, and caring for other members of the workplace community. "Everyone else was doing their best to help, so I just had to stick with them." These ties motivated actions that were collectively taken and purposefully aimed at political goals. However, the uncollected thoughts and motivations of participants were often coming together in part through a kind of sharing of affective ties cultivated in common experiences over several years, some of them like this special trip.

The nature of community at Unikon had to do with closeness, belonging, and purpose. The images most frequently cited by these workers were the urban neighborhood (*machi*) and the rural village (*mura*). It is common in the literature on Japanese companies to evoke images of family to describe workplace community, an approach with a specific political history in prewar and postwar Japan. Efforts to create a harmonious workplace included state-sponsored and industry-sponsored attempts to use the metaphor of family, household (*ie*), and the close, inclusive, and stable ties that these imply to secure labor within enterprises.[1] At Unikon the firm-as-family metaphor was not part of company or even union identity. The coexistence of hierarchy, authority, and power with assumptions about cooperation, community, and mutual aid seemed not so much like a family as like an idealized rural community. Closeness was compared to neighborliness, not kinship, and belonging to the union to being part of an organization in a neighborhood where each person has an important role. Inevitably each person's social and economic livelihood and well-being were tied to their membership, and that recalled villages and farmers. Dissonance rather than harmony was expected and accepted, and it was cited as a primary reason why so many events were organized to harmonize and familiarize people with one another. Familiarity was not assumed; it was cultivated. Harmony was a goal, not an assumption, and some conflict was considered inevitable but tolerable and manageable.

Leaders will sometimes use the image of the family to refer to their union and to imply a sense of unity, to characterize the organization as close, committed, and of a single purpose. Rank and file do not use this imagery for their organization, but they do use kinship terms like "auntie" or "uncle" for particular relationships with coworkers. This practice is common in Japanese neighborhoods, villages, and most organizations. Its importance lies in the association of familiarity and intimacy with social relations in organizations, and at Unikon its use was not ubiquitous but rather selective. Favored bosses would be referred to as "older brother" by middle-aged women. These would be affectionately referred to as "aunties" by younger men and women. This usage

---

1. Cole 1979, Gordon 1988, and Kinzley 1991 explore this subject. Kondo 1990 presents some of the contested meanings around this issue in a small, family-owned firm, and Hamabata 1990 looks at family-firm relations among owners of larger and very successful firms.

was, however, highly contextual. It was never used as a direct form of address, but only as a reference. It was used only in praising or speaking with warmth, never when criticizing or expressing frustration or other more problematic feelings.

At both Unikon and Universal, the use of familial terms did not so much define the relationship as being just like a family or define as familial the structure or relationships of the institutions. It did not even define the character or interpretive processes of social consciousness at work. The critical factor for understanding these forms of address and reference is the social context within which they take place. Using them in a nuclear family and using them in a workplace are not equivalent acts and they do not have equivalent meanings or consequences. Interpretive processes and consciousness cannot exist outside institutional and social structuring processes. When a worker says that her boss is "just like a father," it references some important affective and cognitive similarities in her experience of these social relationships. It does not mean, however, to preclude her knowledge and experience of her boss as a person of power and authority or of her workplace as an economic institution.

In such a context, what is assumed and unspoken may be the more dominant elements of consciousness. In other words, her understanding of herself as a worker, working for wages under a certain system of authority and power in a particular institution, may well be so obvious that it is in no particular need of emphasis or comment. In a daily life world of work, routine, and special events like a trip or a party, it is not the deeply felt structuring of life around such defining relationships that is in need of comment but the less obvious and more uncommon. When one of the women at Universal, for instance, commented that her foreman was "carrying the whole section on his shoulders," the term she used, *onbu suru*, implied a father carrying a child. Her coworkers understood, however, that this was about his particular and laudable character, not about the nature of foremen and subordinates in the company as a whole.

Workers in Unikon experienced and discussed their institutions of work both as comfortable, with some relationships reminiscent of good family relationships, and also as hierarchically organized, with relations of power being dominant structuring forces. The pattern of the use of familial terms at Unikon suggests them as compliments to the character of certain people or terms of endearment for certain groups of people. It also suggests, when used by leaders, the importance of family as an image of unity and closeness, significant in building the solidarity of the union. In all of these forms of usage, however, what seemed consistent was the contextualizing of images of family relationships within a social organization most frequently imagined to be like a village or neighborhood.

What is so often missed in discussion of community in Japan, especially workplace community, is the coexistence of dissonance and harmony, of often frustrating relationships of unequal power and other relationships of equality, and of feelings of being isolated or taken advantage of with feelings of comfort and caring. What the trip dramatizes is the positive. What participants experience is the positive, but in the context of their ongoing work life. The trip is an argument for seeing relationships in their work and union organizations as harmonious, caring, unifying, and above all necessary and inevitable. The argument is not made, however, in a vacuum. It is made to people living these relationships in all their complexity, willing to consider the smooth and comfortable side of their organizational life, but fully cognizant of the problematic as well. The trip, with its emphasis on community and harmony on the one hand and its relationships of inequality still present on the other, may in fact be more effective because it is a special event that represents many dimensions of a complex institutional setting. These dimensions are experienced in daily life as complex, and thus the trip may be more appreciated and seem more "real" when it represents and dramatizes social relations as such.

CHAPTER 4

The Phoenix Falters
Solidarity, Community, and Conflict

The Unikon union newsletter was called *Phoenix.* In mythology and popular culture the phoenix is a bird which can be killed, but will not die. It always revives, ready for another life. For Unikon this was a powerful image of their union and its struggle. From the very beginning, when they were forming their union, these workers had faced obstacles and since then had been through three separate disputes before this, their fourth one. All but a handful of the workers who were there at the end had been present when the union began and throughout its history. The *Phoenix* had been around since the very beginning of the union and was their earliest attempt to communicate with one another as an organization. It had been one of the earliest symbols of unity, one of the central forms for creating solidarity and for raising consciousness.

Ten years had passed since these first attempts, and now just as the "phoenix" was reborn, it began to falter. Its faltering stemmed from disagreements about the form of the new company and a failure in internal processes to cope with that. The turmoil that followed was all the more painful because of the degree of solidarity and the heightened consciousness that the union had succeeded in creating. Instead of a smooth transition from victory in their dispute to a reopened Unikon Camera, people in this organization faced, along with a sense of success and pride, a series of conflicts, dilemmas, and disappointments.

Although the signing of the official reconciliation agreement by the union would not occur until June 27, 1980, the arbitrated settlement of the dispute was being negotiated and the basic terms had already been worked out. By March, following months of negotiations between the

95

union, Unikon's creditors, and the owners, the owners had agreed to release an asset worth 750 million yen and to sell the Tokyo property. Unikon's creditors, the court bankruptcy administrator, the union representatives, and the owners signed an agreement assuring the Unikon workers about 100 million yen, which was to go to back pay and severance pay, for reconstruction, machines, facilities, and for the official purchase of both the smaller Unikon property located just outside Tokyo and land adjacent to the large Tokyo site. From early May the union had been celebrating their victory as details of the settlement continued to be worked out.

The decision to sell the Tokyo property and reopen Unikon under union-selected management meant that the factory operations had to be moved, that decisions had to be made about the organizational structure, working conditions, and personnel of the new company. In addition there continued to be union action to recover the rights to the Unikon brand name, which had been sold by the owners during the course of the bankruptcy. It was around these decisions, the communication about them, and the procedures to handle disagreement that conflicts arose, rank-and-file disillusionment grew, and a very intense period of reappraisal, reflection, and struggle to make sense of their experiences took place.

Rank-and-file members experienced this process as things "falling apart." One woman predicted to me, "We have been one for the past two and a half years but now you will see things unravel. It is all going to fall apart. We will all be separate, the unity gone. And it is starting now." By "things" people referred to their sense of unity, of "being one," and to the particular images they held of what they collectively, as an organization, were like.

This chapter is about rank-and-file union members changing their minds and about their efforts to make sense of particular actions taken by their leaders just as they won their lengthy struggle. These actions challenged in a variety of ways the various images around which understanding, solidarity, and commitment had been formed, and what unfolded in the next six weeks was a process of assessment, reassessment, social negotiation of understandings, and a very intense period of wondering how to make sense of their present, their past, and their future commitments and actions. People had to make immediate decisions about responding to policies with which many, even the vast majority of the rank and file, were in sharp disagreement. In so doing, they explored with one another options and interpretations, making sense of various notions and interpretations of democracy, conflict resolution, fairness, and compassion. Discussions arose about inequalities of power, gender, and class, even about exploitation. Both ideas subject to discursive conversation and argument and tacit assumptions implicit in commonsense ideas about appropriate behavior were involved in their attempts to understand their organization's internal dynamics and their own action. It became common for workers to ask who was in charge of social relations in their union, who was responsible for maintaining the good human relations they had enjoyed, who was in charge ultimately of their union and the new company it was creating. They began to talk about who was making and carrying out decisions, and who was maintaining the unity they had valued so greatly.

While all this struggle for meaning was evident in this time of conflict in a way that it was not at other times, I would emphasize that it took a very particular form. Efforts to make sense occurred in specific contexts of actions taken or needing to be taken. That is, what most people were striving for was not a wholly coherent view of the world, or a system of well-integrated beliefs and values per se. It was more likely to be a set of understandings clustered around certain experiences or events and related in a coherent way to their own actions and decisions. When the Unikon leaders stopped consulting rank-and-file workers about decisions, it mattered less whether or not workers had, individually or collectively, a clear image of democracy than that they could figure out why their leaders took these actions. What motivated the search for meaning was their frustration about those actions and the uneasy feeling that they should perhaps—no one was sure quite how—respond. What got conversation going and what kept it going and what fueled intense and continuous reflection without satisfactory resolution for months afterwards, was this uneasy feeling.

When people said that things didn't quite add up, didn't quite make sense (*warikirenai*), they meant not that they were without any understanding of the situation, but that they were wandering the uneven and rough terrain where understanding, experience, and decisive action run at cross-purposes. In their efforts to make sense of their experiences during this time they drew on whatever knowledge they had; they shared and compared stories, metaphors, and reasoned arguments which might shed light on things; and they considered with anger, frustration, humor, seriousness, and sometimes weariness all the possible options for their own actions. In this process the sense of what felt right in that implicit, commonsense way and the sense of what could be argued to be right were often at odds with each other.

Extending My Stay

Were it not for the considered advice of several workers I would not have been around during these six weeks. Following the settlement of the Unikon dispute I was scheduled to move on to another company, and as the Unikon workers prepared to pack and move to the site of their new factory I was preparing to leave them. I discovered once again how perceptive these workers were and how helpful they could be to me and to my research. Many rank-and-file workers had suggested that I stay through the move because it would give us more unstructured time to talk. I had been reluctant, however, because I was already scheduled to begin at Universal immediately. I was, consequently, wishing I could stay but feeling that I had no choice but to go.

The day before my scheduled departure, I was working with Aoki-san, a woman I had grown to appreciate as insightful and analytical in her understanding and feelings toward the union, its struggle, and the human relations within it. As I came up to my work station next to hers she challenged me:

"Are you really quitting after tomorrow?"

I replied, "I'm not really 'quitting,' but I will finish up my research here and go on to Universal after tomorrow."

"You shouldn't do that," she went on, "it is just now starting. You may think that it is over because the dispute is settled, and they [union leadership] will tell you that since the dispute is settled you may as well move on to another company. But in fact it is really just beginning around here!"

I wasn't sure what she was getting at, and I asked her, "But you have just won a major victory. What remains is moving and cleaning up. What do you mean that *it* is just starting? What is starting?"

She smiled as one might when appreciating the naive and explained, "You came here to study the thoughts and feelings of workers, didn't you."

"Yes, of course I did," I replied.

"Then you must not leave now no matter what. It is now that you have a chance to see just what is going on under the surface. You are going to see what Japanese workers are really up against and how they feel about it. Things aren't always as they seem."

I was intrigued. "I would love to stay, but I have already been introduced to Universal and am expected to begin there after tomorrow. I don't know if I can stay at Unikon any longer."

She interrupted, "You are a scholar, aren't you? It's your job to do good research. That makes it your job to find a way. Do it! You aren't here to be nice and get people to like you. You are here to do a job, even if it isn't easy. Find a way."

I laughed at her lectures and asked how she thought I might manage to stay.

"Oh, it isn't so hard. Just go in and tell them [union leaders] you'd like to stay a while longer. They can't say no. It would look bad for them now that you are already one of us."

After work that day I went in and talked to the union leaders about staying to help out with the moving and cleaning and about postponing my entry into Universal for a while. They worried that I would get tired and dirty doing all that work, but I told them I did not mind that and that it might even be fun as a change of pace. They laughed and teased me about doing so much sedentary academic work that even a dirty and exhausting job like cleaning and moving a factory seemed a pleasant change. They warned me not to overdo it and reminded me that I was free to rest anytime I liked and to drop into the office for tea and a snack when I felt like it. Their attitude was, as it had always been, completely helpful and encouraging. They told me I was welcome to stay with them as long as I liked. These union leaders had made all of my research plans remarkably easy to carry out. I left the office happy to be staying with this company through their move because it would give me access to informal situations and discussions and because I had grown to be friends with these people. My curiosity was engaged, and I wondered what if anything was behind Aoki-san's determined advice.

Moving

It was the middle of May, and production was winding down. Moving was the primary task of the next six weeks, the period between cessation of production at the Tokyo site and the reopening of Unikon at the new Saitama site. People were beginning to complain of the heat and humidity of the rainy season as they started packing up. Everything had to be moved and all areas cleared out. The present factory was very large and had once housed over fifteen hundred workers. The new factory was an hour's drive or an hour and a half by train. It had previously been the site of the Unikon dormitories. What we were all helping to do during this time was to clear out a four-story factory building covering a full city block of Tokyo and set up a factory in a two-story building covering about one-fourth of an acre in the neighboring prefecture of Saitama. Equipment not needed in the new building would be sold or thrown away. The old buildings were to be destroyed, the land sold, and an apartment complex erected.

Activity during this time was casual and relatively unstructured. The normal constraints and conventions of the everyday work routines were absent, and the mood was relaxed, intimate, and talkative. There were innumerable unscheduled breaks and a lot of ice-cream eating appropriate to the hot and muggy weather. There was also a great deal of nostalgia accompanying the packing and a constant interweaving of joking and prank-playing, much of which was tinged with cynicism. The playful familiarity of the Unikon workers with each other and their evident enjoyment of working together and being together continued, an atmosphere with which I had become familiar and which I had grown to enjoy tremendously myself. Things were changing though, and gradually I felt and then began to understand that this atmosphere was not simple or inclusive of all the attitudes and feelings of these people. There were serious discussions during breaks, and some emotional expressions of personal sadness, anger, and frustration. People were feeling foolish, betrayed, and hurt and were finding no simple or direct way of expressing these feelings, of challenging or changing the situations they faced, or even of understanding why things were evolving as they were.

I had sensed some of these concerns emerging, but had incorrectly attributed them entirely to the unfortunate distance of the new factory site from the present one, a distance that made it untenable for many of the workers, over half, to continue working at Unikon. After ten or twelve years working with the same people and doing work they liked, and after nearly three years in a very committed fight to gain control over their own company, these workers were, I thought, feeling the unhappiness and frustration of having to quit. It became clear, however, that this was only a minor element in the problems people were experiencing. As many told me later, if the only issue had been sadness of leaving Unikon due to increased commuting distances, they would have felt at most a wistful nostalgia, but even that would have been colored with the positive tone of their long experience in a union that had achieved not only victory, but unity, or as they expressed it, "singleness of feeling" (*kimochi ga hitotsu ni natta*).

Unity, Solidarity, and Community

Unity, solidarity, and community are each relevant in their own ways to the Unikon union organization and workplace and to the various images held by its members. The only one of these words used with any frequency in daily conversation of rank-and-file union members, however, was "unity." Workers expressed their feelings of commonality, motivation, commitment, identity, and meaning most often and most simply as "being one," or "feeling the same." This was true whether the reference was to their own motivation and comfort with the organization or to the strength of the union in its political struggles. "Solidarity" was a word used almost exclusively by leadership and in the context of formal events or for slogans and speeches at collective actions. It stood for something like the unity discussed by rank and file but carried with it an explicitly politicized, organizational, and goal-oriented connotation. Community was referred to without a particular noun to represent the thought, by mentioning how "comfortable it is to live here" and using expressions evoking metaphors of village and neighborhood. The nature of their workplace was like a community where compassion and understanding flourished. These three different ways of expressing the nature of organizational life and the character of the union flourished side by side throughout much of the life of the Unikon union and certainly through most of their struggle. What workers now felt to be "unraveling" was not just the ties that bound together their workplace community but also the fabric of their image and understanding of themselves and their sense of pride and satisfaction in their work, their efforts, and their achievements over the past several years.

The Unikon experience, its struggles and its victories, had been an extremely unusual and positive one for most workers. Pride and satisfaction set the tone for their organization and for their characterization of themselves as workers, as union members, and as individuals involved in an important political struggle. Unikon workers had grown accustomed to seeing themselves as members of an "advanced" union and as workers with "advanced consciousness" within the labor movement nationally. Their achievement of organizational solidarity was held as an example for other unions, and was considered to be the key to their success and to their strength. While many expressed amusement at the thought, for the most part workers did feel that they and their organization were "different" and "special" and that they were achieving something of great importance to the Japanese labor movement and to Japanese society as well.

The process of making sense of their lives, their work, and their political action took place in the context of these images of their organization. The Unikon leaders, regional and national federation leaders, journalists, and academics reinforced these interpretations. Just as important, the Unikon workers had seen change in their own daily lives and had lived the experience of their union and workplace as different. Conditions under which they worked had changed, the ways in which people treated one another had changed, and the ways in which their small union was treated by outsiders, the press, and the academic world had changed. They did not just hope for, imagine, or believe in alternative ways to organize social relations in the workplace; they had lived the transformation of their factory from one run under authoritarian management to one run by their own union with consultation and consent from all workers. Their ideas about political action and about workplace social relations evolved as interdependent with their experiences, and largely because of this experiential validation of particular ideas they had become wholly committed, convinced participants in their union's political activities.

Staying and fighting in the bankruptcy dispute had been an even more earnest commitment than staying through the previous three struggles. This time they had already lost their jobs as they formerly knew them, were working for the duration of the dispute at only 60 percent of their prebankruptcy wages, and were by no means certain of victory. It was clear from the beginning that whatever solution would be reached would take months or, more likely still, years. Many had quit. Those who stayed reevaluated their decisions many times over the course of the struggle. When I asked about their decisions to participate and, as months and then years passed, to continue to fight, rank and file told me that what motivated their commitment changed as they went along. "Of course when we are interviewed by the press or by academics, we all say essentially the same thing—that we are fighting for the rights of Japanese workers and to protect our livelihood. This is part of the truth. But it was never so easy. In the beginning people had one motivation, and as time went on and as our experiences taught us things, there were other reasons to stay or to quit." Reasons for staying or quitting were varied. For those who stayed, their understanding of their struggle, their motivation to continue—or not—and their own sense of what their union

and their personal and collective actions meant were subjects of reflection and reevaluation. Images of themselves, their union, and their
experience were embedded in everyday social interaction at work and
when people gathered away from work. They wondered aloud to each
other and to me, sometimes asking for my opinion as an outsider or an
American, about the real nature of their union and its actions. They were
aware of and had grappled with problems both external and internal to
the union organization itself. Social conversation, implicit modeling of
actions and orientations for one another, union and federation leadership efforts to educate and mobilize, and the day-to-day experience of
events were all forms through which consciousness evolved in a continuing process of making decisions and making sense.

The conflicts and dissatisfactions that emerged during the final settlement challenged rank-and-file sensibilities. The images of themselves,
their actions, and their organization were all challenged. Feelings of
unity, of "being one," were shattered. The solidarity of the organization
was threatened, and the various aspects of their workplace and union
which made Unikon a community were reevaluated. What most Unikon
workers had come to expect was that the important things at Unikon,
namely the social relations of their organization, would remain essentially unchanged. For the rank-and-file workers, much of what had
inspired a serious emotional commitment to the struggle was the transformation of the workplace into one which served the workers and
created a community while manufacturing high quality products. At the
same time their union's character, proudly asserted to be unique, and its
political successes were a great source of motivation to stay and be part
of the struggle. Motivation and commitment stemmed as much from
these factors as from the specific goals of their dispute. People stayed and
fought not only because they shared certain ideas, but because they
shared certain experiences, feelings, relationships, and orientations. The
strength of the Unikon union was in part its weaving of these related but
distinct strands of experience, consciousness, and commitment. The
dilemma of this faltering victory was in their unraveling.

Commitment, Sensibility, and Images of Strength

One of the practical difficulties for a fieldworker is that
"singleness of feeling" and other such images of collective identity are

so easy to see. In this union solidarity was a goal, a proud symbol of strength, and an achievement. It was hard to miss. Working in this union as an anthropologist, I had become aware of a variety of conflicts, sources of dissonance, and differences in the motivations and consciousness of its members. I already knew, for instance, that theirs was a collective action with imperfectly collected thoughts and feelings. I saw contradictions between union ideology and union practice, between thoughts about unity and concerns about inequality. The strength of their sense of oneness and solidarity was, however, so strong and people so willing to present it to others that I was unprepared at first to see clearly the more tentative, contested, and uncertain dimensions of the images and understandings held by these workers.

Part of the problem of interpretation for me was in the uses made of consciousness. The context of my study was ideal for seeing consciousness as a process because people were in an unusually intense situation demanding decisions, reflections, and conversation. The context was, however, a labor dispute where solidarity was a critical tool for success. Presenting unity was itself a learned skill and rank and file were nearly as adept at this as leaders. Solidarity was almost synonymous with consciousness for leaders when they worked out their strategies for "raising consciousness," meaning, for them, building solidarity to ensure the critical mass and motivation to win the dispute. I was consequently in a context where "consciousness" had strategic value and where solidarity, unity, and images of strength had political importance in a very immediate sense.

What follows is a selection of characteristics deemed by Unikon workers to be central to the character of their union and, in the context of their struggle, to its strength and success as well. It is useful to start here, with the consciousness of strength, unity, and solidarity, before considering in detail the process through which these images were challenged and reassessed and different understandings reached.

YOUTH

Both from within the union and from without, youth was seen to be a primary reason for the energetic tone of Unikon's activities and consequently an important factor in its relatively swift success. The Unikon strategies were active and bold and were carried through with a certain flair that made them famous in union networks and in the press.

The union seemed willing to try anything. Their harassment of the owners at their residence, creating a very embarrassing situation in that upscale neighborhood, stayed just on the border between the legal and the illegal. They tried strategies that were unusual and new, like demonstrating at local branches of the financial institution backing their owners. They also demonstrated in the usual way in front of its main office in downtown Tokyo, but the impact on business and on the reputation of the bank in the local area where the community was already sympathetic to the Unikon workers was greater and may have been more powerful in forcing negotiation. In fact, the union was so active and mobilized their workers so intensely and in so many different actions that it was impossible in the end to know which act had how much impact. This intense, whirlwind approach to fighting was associated with the energy and daring of youth.

In the cultural field of Japan there is very significant grading of appropriate behavior according to age. I will address this again, as it worked to slow things down at Universal, where workers were on average much older and consequently had some trouble feeling politically bold acts to be appropriate for themselves. Here at Unikon, the leadership was drawn entirely from the ranks of the younger workers, all in their twenties and early thirties, and the actual age of most of the workers put them in a stage of life where boldness is considered appropriate and where their responsibilities—and consequently what they stood to lose—were fewer. In fact, the words for youth, *wakasa* and *wakai*, are used in popular culture as synonymous with or evocative of strength, vitality, naiveté, and boldness. From such metaphors the Unikon workers built an appreciation for their youthful acts into their image of their own strength, an image that was central to their understanding of themselves, to their representation of themselves to others, and to the ways others viewed them.

The older workers, nearly all part-time women workers in their late forties and fifties, were proud of "our young people," and enjoyed being with and supporting them. There was a distinctly protective, admiring tone to their remarks along these lines. These younger workers, on the other hand, complimented the part-time aunties (*pāto no obachantachi*) for being so young at heart (*ki ga wakai*).

In conversation, the image of youth was also connected to the Unikon ability to incorporate new ideas and practices into their workplace. During the period of union management Unikon had less inequality and better working conditions than most companies, and that was often attributed to the youth of its members and their willingness to try new things.

EQUALITY

Equality was a very important ideal for Unikon and one which leaders and rank and file proudly claimed to have realized to a very unusual degree. The language used to talk about equality was like the language of unity, emphasizing being the same (*minna onaji da*). Equality of men and women, of leaders and rank and file, and of part-time and full-time workers was boasted about with considerable pride. It was often said that Unikon women outnumbered men and that there could not exist the traditional and customary superiority of men over women. Leaders emphasized the importance of the women in their union and put them on the cover of the widely distributed handbook publicizing their struggle. One leader told me, on my first visit to the company, "The women are our strength. It is they who have been totally committed and involved, and it is their support and persistence which has both inspired the rest of us and led to our victory."

Workers, especially men, spoke often of the absence of traditional "Japanese male dominance." Men illustrated this characterization by discussing the political determination of women, describing their single-mindedness and aggressive participation in union action as frightening (*kowai*). This comment was generally accompanied by a broad smile, a tilt of the head, and a certain jesting tone, but it was repeated very commonly nonetheless. It became clear that the men of Unikon were at once proud of the women and of the equality they had achieved within the organization and at the same time slightly wary and uncertain of its implications and consequences.

Women generally coupled remarks about this relative equality with comments about excellent working conditions and their ability to participate fully in the union. "Working conditions for women are terrible in Japan," one woman explained, "but they are better here, better than anywhere else." Comments like this were made more often to me than to one another. One of the challenges in listening to people speak to one another about their own concerns and images of themselves and others is that they are often silent about what is most obvious. It was not necessary for women to talk to one another about how bad they thought employment opportunities were for women in Japan, nor was it necessary for them to say at every turn that things at Unikon were not really "good" but "relatively good." They knew that already. When they spoke to me, however, they would look at me with an effort to see in my eyes whether or not I understood their thoughts and then, as if to confirm, they would add a phrase or two. These were the phrases which expressed the more general knowledge, seemingly held in common and unnecessary to express to one another but critical to communicate to me.

At Unikon, women, both full-time workers and part-time workers, were encouraged to work and reminded that theirs was the sort of industry in which women and men really could do the same work. Provisions for special needs of women were made. A day-care center was set up on the premises which accepted even nursing babies. It was accredited and became a source of public interest and worker pride. Because of the large number of young mothers working there it was seen as a significant improvement in working conditions. Women were allowed breast-feeding breaks whenever necessary, and during scheduled breaks women and men would congregate around the play yard and enjoy time with the children. Older women were "part-time" workers— that is, they worked six or seven hours a day—and in most companies would not have been included in the union at all. Even before the bankruptcy dispute, however, these women had been welcomed into the Unikon union and were reminded at every opportunity that they were equal union members (*onaji kumiaiin*).

The equality of all workers, regardless of sex or status, was important, and it was linked not only to formal equality in workplace and union practices but to the experience of sharing difficulties and sacrifices as well. All these workers, and their union leaders as well, had gone through the hard times following bankruptcy together, staying at the shop, losing sleep, wondering how to make ends meet, and later fighting and risking their peace of mind and personal security to continue the struggle together. People recounted memories of taking a 40 percent cut in wages—all of them equally—when money was scarce, and they had vivid stories to tell about the hardship and the fun of bringing all different kinds of piecework to their factory, doing it together, then pooling that and unemployment insurance money to distribute an equal share to each worker. These and countless other anecdotes about their experience always culminated with the same sort of expression, that at Unikon "everyone is the same," "everyone has been through the same hardships," "everyone faces the same harsh conditions."

The equality between leaders and rank and file was asserted by leaders and in many ways accepted and felt by rank and file. Because the leaders of this union had shared the same history and experiences and had faced these same conditions, there was a strong feeling of closeness between them and the rank-and-file members. Since most workers had been in the union from its inception, they could recall these young workers in the days before there was a union, when they worked side by side without this distinction. People had seen them struggle to organize their union in a hostile environment, fighting a very hostile antiunion management. Consequently there was "no gap" between workers and leaders—or as many would more carefully put it when talking to me, "relatively little gap." In fact, in the conversations of rank and file, words like "above" or "below," "superior" or "subordinate," or even "big shots" were not used in referring to their own leadership. I learned in hindsight that this was "relatively" unusual after further experience at Universal and with other unions. Thus for most people, equality, viewed within the context of a society with predominant patterns of inequality, was an achievement of some pride and importance. In an imperfect world, theirs was a little better, an improved version of what most workers were living with.

DEMOCRACY

Another important component of being "the same" was democratic process within their organization. Words like "equality" and "democracy" were present in discussions among workers but much less common than expressions like "the same as," not being "above" or "below" someone else, being able to "say what you think" and being "listened to and taken seriously." A major concern was participation in discussion and decision making. This overlapped ideas about equality: being able to "say what you want to say" was usually associated with everyone being able to do this equally, regardless of sex or position in the union or workplace. Like remarks about equality, remarks about participation took a different form when workers talked to me than when they chatted with one another. What was added for my benefit was that in the world of small firms, and even in the world of unionized workers, it is very unusual to find a "place where you can speak freely with no bad consequences and where you can be taken seriously and can feel a part of decisions." Unikon workers felt that, from the beginning of their union, they had been involved in the planning and implementation of strategies, that their leaders were listening and responding to them, and that overall they were part of a democratic union where things were not decided without their prior knowledge and discussion.

Worker participation at Unikon, during the time of union management, extended not only to political or union issues but also to management issues. Production statistics and plans were discussed at meetings and although leaders played a greater role in making final decisions and sketching out plans, people felt involved. One young man told me, "Before union management began everyone just did their job and went home and thought about their own personal situation. Now, we are all used to worrying about sales, productivity, quality control, making ends meet—essentially management issues."

Democratic practices were instituted by Unikon leaders with the specific intention of creating solidarity, and their success was a source of pride for them. They had scheduled daily meetings when they first began self-management, only gradually going to weekly ones. There were, in addition to these, monthly meetings and shop floor meetings and then large general meetings several times a year. All this was an attempt to work together, to build a solidarity based on "mutual understanding" and "commitment," which leaders felt could best be accomplished through deeper participation and involvement by each and every worker.

RESPECT FOR INDIVIDUALS

Along with talk of unity, equal participation, and being able to speak out, a sense of being respected as an individual with particular needs and characteristics was also common and important in the discussions at Unikon about commitment and motivation.

Workers expressed pride in the organization's ability to respect individual feelings and thoughts (*hitori hitori no kimochi*) and the uniqueness of each person's particular life conditions (*hitori hitori jijō ga chigau*). These two dimensions to a person's individuality were closely intertwined, in that the conditions of one's life were seen to motivate certain feelings, and the uniqueness of the one implied the specialness of the other. This personal recognition and respect coming not only from other rank-and-file members but from leaders as well was proudly recounted as an important factor in making Unikon a place where it was good to work and good to be.

Memories of being called or visited by union leaders when their spirits sagged or when they considered quitting were treasured by many. Stories of concern expressed by coworkers or union representatives when members were ill or nursing relatives were retold frequently. This sense of personal "significance" was also deepened by union efforts to meet the needs of the variety of "unique individuals" that made up the union, not only through excursions, trips, and special events, but through things like the day-care center, free visits by acupuncturists, and a general flexibility in responding to workers' needs on a daily basis as well.

WORKPLACE AND UNION COMMUNITY

One of workers' most common characterizations of Unikon was as a comfortable place to live (*sumigokochi ga ii*), referring to location, time spent physically together, experiences shared, and a whole set of social relationships strongly felt to be significant and largely felt with affection, respect, and comfort. Images evoked along these lines were of villages and neighborhoods.

The sharing of experiences built one of the most critical components of the Unikon image and inspired a central factor in worker commitment, motivation, and perseverance, namely, the sense of what they described as "sameness or singleness of feeling." Some people talked of the pleasure of "everyone working together for the same goals" and told stories of working together through the night preparing for demonstrations or of suffering the same hardships, even of losing their jobs suddenly at the whim of their owners. One young man told me that those hardships, because they were shared by everyone alike, were "almost fun." The expressions used to describe this feeling of community and compassion were "everyone is together" (*minna issho da*) or "everyone's feelings are one" (*minna no kimochi ga hitotsu ni natteru*) and "everyone is one" (*minna hitotsu*).

The sharing of physical space was explicitly seen as critically important, both by leaders and by rank and file. The simple "here" (*koko*) is omnipresent in expressions of commonality like "everyone is the same here" or "everyone is together here." Even more literally, people refer to their many years working together as "having lived with everyone for so long" (*minna to issho ni nagai aida seikatsu shite kita*). The comfort of being in this community was expressed as "Unikon is a comfortable place to live." Conversational metaphors compared Unikon to villages and closely knit Tokyo neighborhoods, and workers would frequently invoke the traditional association of the union's yearly festivals and parties with those held in urban neighborhoods or rural villages. Months after this struggle ended and some members had quit, former coworkers continued to celebrate such occasions with get-togethers.

The importance of the physical sharing of space, the accompanying face-to-face interaction that it implies, and the sense of community that it inspires were seen clearly by leaders of the Unikon union to have a strategic dimension. It was stated as the primary reason for the in-factory piecework that was done in the earliest days following bankruptcy. Workers could have done that work at home in the usual way and then pooled their money, in which case they might have met once a week, but this would have hurt their solidarity, leaders explained to me. It was important that all 150 workers shared space on a daily basis, that although doing different tasks, they would be "together," in the same place. One leader explained, "If we had all gone off working separately, we would have seen each other only at meetings, and nothing would have come of our struggle. We had to see each other and work together to build a sense of unity."

PRIDE

Pride in their product was very important for the Unikon workers. Other unions had been successful in manufacturing under their own management, but none had produced such a complex product, nor such a "modern western" one. A Unikon leader told me, "Nobody thought workers could produce such a complex thing as a camera. But we did it. And we did it even more efficiently than before."

People boasted about the increase in productivity that came with their reduction of "silly" shop floor regulations. There was much joking about the previous owners' ridiculous and childish rules of conduct. People were free now to move about and talk if they liked, and the result, they boasted, was higher productivity and better quality. Their worry was not about these aspects of their production, but about the research and development challenges of the camera industry.

During my first months with them, this pride in their product, in their union's flair for strategically smart political action, and in the type of social relations and working conditions they had created under their own management was, for me and for other observers, their most striking and distinctive characteristic. Combined with their sincere enjoyment of the company of their coworkers, this created an extremely positive, satisfying, and committed atmosphere whenever Unikon workers gathered, either for work, for union business, or for play. It was quite common for this pride and its sources to appear in responses to my questions about their motivation to join and remain in a two-and-a-half-year struggle. There was a very evident inspiration and commitment stemming from being in an organization experienced to be good in these various ways. In significant measure, the solidarity required to continue the dispute over this extended period was grounded in these experiences and was conceptualized through the stories, metaphors, and associations they created.

"Falling Apart"

A series of events had triggered the "falling apart" (*bara bara ni naru*) which people began to feel deeply around the time of the move and which consisted of surprises, unexpected events, and acts that were hard for rank and file to understand. Leaders were not in conversation with workers about these issues, and when I would approach the subject they would refer to "necessities," look embarrassed, and try to change the subject. It was only much later, after the company had reopened and things had resolved themselves, that several leaders described to me what they had been experiencing at this time. The following account is predominantly one of rank-and-file feelings, perspectives, and experiences at the time.

The first thing rank-and-file workers recalled that struck them as strange (*hen* or *okashii*) was the "rumor" at their winter trip that the company might be moving out of Tokyo when it reopened following the settlement. The rumor was started by a very well-respected federation official who apparently did not realize that the rank and file did not already know about the possibility. He was a person who had been helping Unikon all through their fight and was considered a highly credible source. The fact that the workers heard this first from an outsider rather than from their own leadership was described as painful and confusing. The fact that information about the future of their new company after settlement should become a rumor rather than a simple statement at a union meeting, open for discussion, was called "unprecedented." Furthermore, an unpleasant sense that things were moving without their own involvement began to grow. The response to this incident was disbelief, suspicion, hurt feelings, and a wait-and-see attitude. Rank and file talked about it among themselves and would sometimes bring it up in an offhand way around their leaders, hoping to inspire the casual confidence to which they had grown accustomed. That did not work, and no one felt comfortable bringing it up openly, so they settled back into their daily work routines, albeit with a shadow of doubt in their minds, and waited.

The next step was an announcement in May that the company would reopen outside Tokyo at a new and smaller site. This time people had to face and try to make sense of the fact that a very important decision had been made without so much as a consultation with them. Workers would later see this as the most serious problem they faced. "Only after everything was set were we told about it. By then it was too late to change anything. There was no discussion at all, and that is the worst part of it." This announcement was followed by another, about working conditions for the new company. These plans hinted, people felt, that part-time workers in particular and women in general were being invited to quit.

Following these announcements came what on the surface might seem a simple and unobjectionable move by union leadership. A questionnaire was passed around asking who planned to continue working at the new company and who to quit, and what their plans were if they were going to quit. This questionnaire itself followed a meeting at which the new policies had been discussed, disagreements expressed, and no resolution found. This was a meeting—the only one during my study—that I was asked not to attend. For the workers, the questionnaire was leadership's response to their expressed disagreements and need to discuss other options, and in its inadequacy it was taken as the final assault on their perception of their union as a community and a democratic organization and on their sensibilities and commitments. One of the part-time women told me with indignation, "Then they passed around a questionnaire! They wanted to know if people were going to stay or not. 'Are you going [to the new Unikon site], yes or no.' So people who still hadn't quite decided just said no. They [leadership] asked us what our plan was if we were quitting. [She laughed.] Aoki-san wrote, 'I'm going to pull a quilt over my head and go to sleep.'"

The impersonality of the means of collecting this information and the lack of any encouragement to those who said they were planning to quit stood in extreme contrast to the personal attention given each member who had considered quitting during the years of the struggle. People were stunned, then hurt, then angry. As one young man explained to me, "Those who weren't sure if they wanted to quit were told abruptly to decide right now, because if they waited too long there would be managers and if they aren't liked by the new management it will cause trouble. And the ones who said they planned to quit weren't given any kind of encouragement to stay on."

People felt that all this indicated that the union leadership, now the new company management, was anxious to get some members to stay and others to quit. That all but men and young women without children quit was seen as the indirect but intended consequence of the leadership's decisions and the form of their communication.

What the Unikon workers struggled with in the course of the packing and cleaning operations in the old plant and the setting up of the new one was essentially this dilemma. The union and its successful self-managed production of cameras and its victory in a very important labor dispute had been a tremendous source of pride. Each individual had felt important in these accomplishments. People described their feelings about the struggle and the victory saying "the struggle became my own struggle [*jibun no tatakai ni natta*]" and called it "an experience of great importance in my own life [*jibun jishin no jinsei no naka de no totemo jūyō na keiken*]." They had grown accustomed to thinking of and experiencing themselves as equal union members, as involved in decision making, and as members of a compassionate and caring community. They had also come to think of themselves as young, bold, good at their jobs, and in many ways special.

Now, however, in the events that unfolded after victory, they were confused about why things were happening as they were, about what they could or should do, and even about how sensible their commitment had been. Many began to see themselves as powerless, unable to participate in decision making about the organization of the company that their own efforts had secured. What had seemed to be bold, new, and young began to look tricky (*zurui*) and shameless (*zūzūshii*) and very much the stuff of the past. The most extreme exasperation made some feel that there was really nothing at all special about Unikon, and the language of class emerged. One worker put it to me this way: "You can see what things are like for Japanese workers. Everywhere it is the same. It isn't just the capitalists you have to watch out for, it's your own union leaders too."

Unikon workers also felt foolish (*baka mitai*), tricked (*damasareta*), sad (*kanashii*), lonely (*sabishii*), fed up (*mō iya!*), and insignificant (*chiisai*, literally "small"). They criticized themselves for not having been more careful, wiser, for having been "too lazy" and for having "trusted too much." A clear split between themselves and their leaders emerged on their horizon.

Faced with these feelings and these uncomfortable and confusing thoughts about themselves and their union, two workers quit and the rest began a lengthy, six-week process of socially renegotiating individual commitments and the meaning of their own and their union's actions.

The Discussions

People talked, made cynical or sarcastic remarks, and even joked about the situation while they worked, ate, walked to and from the station, or sat on the train together. At after-work get-togethers there were opportunities for more involved discussions, but the majority were sandwiched between other topics and interrupted incessantly by practical concerns of work or commuting. The same issues were repeated in various conversations. At stake were two things. First, a decision had to be made about what if any action would be taken. There were several possibilities, including open protest at the meeting already scheduled for June 20, quitting immediately and/or collectively, or some other open display of discontent and request for negotiation. Second, workers wanted to understand how things had come to this conclusion, and they wanted to do what was "right" and to feel that they had made the right decision. These issues—what collective or individual action should be taken and how to make sense of the situation—were intermingled in a continuous conversation that in fact spent much more time identifying issues and reassessing images than talking about specific decisions, strategies, or actions.

The discussions were emotional, with men expressing more anger than hurt and women doing the reverse. For me it was a rare opportunity to hear people dip into the realm of silent assumption and express some of the thoughts resting there as their intense exasperation, anger, and hurt inspired their reiterated articulation of the "natural," the "obvious," and the "reasonable." This happened with some frequency during these six weeks, as people worked on understanding the unreasonable and confusing actions taken by the leaders they had learned to trust. The following were the most frequently discussed topics of frustration and confusion during these weeks' conversations.

INEQUALITY

The Unikon leaders' actions had made everyone think about the inequality of power within the union, something they had not had to remember before. It raised certain suspicions that the head of the union was using them to gain political and economic power and prestige. At a social occasion during this time, an older man, the husband of one of the part-time women and himself a worker in a small print shop, compared the Unikon situation to a serialized historical television drama being broadcast at the time depicting the transition from Tokugawa to Meiji: "They are just like all the rest of the Japanese unions, and just like what is going on in *Shishi no Jidai* [The Time of the Patriots]. Those on top use the people under them to get power and then dump them."

One of the reasons the union president took the risk of everybody quitting in disgust, explained a young Unikon man, was that the worst that could happen if every single person quit was that he would be left with significant resources, probably enough to begin a new company himself. As the new company president he would be in a position of some power. Furthermore, mobility up the hierarchy of union federation offices was also a way for their president and other leaders to improve their own status and economic position. What happened internally to the Unikon union would be less important than the distinct success of their union in its struggle, and the credit for that success would go to the Unikon leaders, enhancing their status and reputation among the federation officials with whom they were associated.

In these conversations, rank and file offered three interpretations of the way these decisions were taken without their consent and outside of the democratic process they had expected in their union. One was an interpretation of the way in which position in a structure of unequal class and power relations might determine human action. "Japanese people," a young man remarked, "don't have a certain way of thinking; they don't integrate things." An older man, the husband of one of the part-time workers, explained, "One problem is that when a person changes his position in the structure, his way of thinking changes too. You can't trust anyone to stick to what they believe. Their position is what speaks, and only their position can be believed." His wife completed this train of thought. "When the president of the union became the president of the company, his position [*tachiba*] changed, and we are back now where we started from, back to where we were before we even had a union at Unikon. And this," she concluded, "is the situation of Japanese workers in general." Many workers accused themselves of being too naive precisely because they had not seen clearly that it is the position of a person, not his or her words, which should be believed, and many thought that they had not taken active enough roles in defending their own positions in that structure and thus considered themselves partly responsible for what eventually came to pass.

The Unikon workers had by this time developed a very strong identification as workers in a capitalist Japanese economy. Terms like worker and capitalist were used regularly in ordinary conversation. In the face of the dilemma they were now facing, they talked about the "weakness" and "powerlessness" broadly characteristic of the position of Japanese workers. One woman even moved smoothly from a discussion of her own situation at Unikon to a description of her mother-in-law's experiences in prewar Japan as a textile worker, relating tales of locked and barred gates preventing workers from returning to their homes and families, of contracts under which they were sold into their jobs for a set period of time, and conditions of work that involved beatings and other physical as well as mental abuse. "Things have improved quite a bit since then," she concluded, "but there are still a lot of similarities." Another reiterated that historically Japanese workers have always been weak and powerless against capitalists. "It can't be helped. After all this is still a capitalist economy." Many of the women had husbands who saw the similarities between the Unikon union's behavior and management action in their own nonunionized shops.

Both those who were to stay and those who were going to quit came to speak of the whole incident as "not so surprising when you come to think of it, given the nature of capitalist society." This sometimes lent an almost forgiving tone to the evaluations. One young man spoke of how, in order to keep a small company solvent in the contemporary competitive world of camera production, it was necessary to imagine that you will go broke the next day and to operate on that assumption. "This kind of mentality is harsh and unbending, but it can't be helped. When the company is reconstituted as a regular company in a capitalist economy, the leadership doesn't have much choice but to behave as capitalists. They are good people, but their position has changed." Some scholars studying Unikon and other union-managed firms fighting struggles have pointed out the contradiction between the administrative needs of a capitalist enterprise and the "spirit of labor" typical of the union (Inoue 1981a: 79).

The second interpretation was also linked to class, but in a more historical sense. People spoke of the similarity of their own situation to that of other Japanese workers, both contemporary and historical, and of the "commoners" of feudal Japan, and they told stories, some legendary and some from popular TV or movies, of the powerless and weak in general. This reflection on their lack of participation in decision making was an occasion for sarcasm and jokes comparing themselves to feudal subjects and for play-acting as obsequious peasants. As we were cleaning up in a little-used room one day, a strange item was found whose resemblance to a whip was enough to prompt one young woman to wave it about and start off a series of comedies by claiming that it was the whip that the original Unikon owners had wielded to keep the workers in line. That was followed by quieter comments and slightly stifled giggles suggesting that maybe it should be cleaned up and set aside for the union president's use when he became head of the new company.

This perception of themselves as having much in common with the weak and powerless of Japanese society was further revealed by the way they described my research to their family and friends. I told them I was there to study to the consciousness of workers in small firms. They sometimes introduced me this way, but just as often they would say I was there to study the consciousness of the lower class (*teihen no hito no kangaekata*, literally, "those on the bottom").

Many of the Unikon workers came from rural areas, and the similarities in the positions of workers and farmers made for an easy analogy. When they were faced with feelings of weakness or exploitation, as they were during these weeks, analogies built around tenant farmers struggling to make ends meet and stories from the past about landlords pushing farmers into poverty or the political impotence of commoners in feudal times came to mind nearly as often as stories about contemporary fellow workers.

The third interpretation was about gender. Men as often as women complained bitterly about the transparent attempt to dismiss the women once they were no longer needed. During the struggle, they began to understand, it was important to have as many people as possible, for demonstrations and production and also for credibility. The fewer people who quit the more determined Unikon looked to the courts and financial institutions with whom they were fighting. In the beginning, the women had been skeptical. One woman recalled for me their initial fears:

We had seen other companies win disputes and then all the women with kids and the part-timers would have to quit, because all of a sudden they weren't needed anymore. When we were encouraged to stay on and join in the struggle we came right out and asked them if that would happen to us, too. And they said of course not! Then in the end they decided they didn't need us anymore and without any discussion or chance to voice opinions or objections, they just forced us to quit.

"After all," explained another woman, "the situation for Japanese workers as a whole is dreadful, and the situation for women workers is even worse." The women had been "tricked" and "used" (*riyō sareta*), said Unikon men and the husbands of many of the women. The equality that had been emphasized between men and women and between regular and part-time workers had suddenly disappeared, as all the part-time women and full-time younger women with children quit, leaving just two women at the new company, both young and single.

Interestingly, the reason for this treatment of the women was seen, even by those who condemned it, to be the "lower productivity" of women in the factory. When I asked what "lower productivity" meant, people would cite greater needs for flexible hours and for services like day-care and acupuncture, all things which would no longer be possible under the more severe conditions of the "ordinary company" soon to be reopened. Behind the concern with reducing low-productivity workers, assumed to be women, was that the new company required fewer employees and could afford only those who were most productive. This explanation was never given publicly by union leaders, but it was commonly understood by workers, as well as by social scientists studying the case, to be the truth about what had happened, and in private affiliated union and federation officers would admit this as well.

DEMOCRATIC PROCESS

Closely related to the issues of newly recognized inequalities were issues of democracy. "Only after everything was settled were we told anything about it. The people below didn't know anything about it. The people above just decided everything!" The use of terms like "above" and "below" within their own union was new, as was the frustration of having decisions simply announced. Paradoxically, the critical turning point was their victory. "Until the end of the dispute, everything could be discussed and openly decided upon. After it ended and the union president became the company president, they [the leadership] clammed up and we haven't known anything since." The fact that Unikon had been a place where people had been able to speak out, be listened to, and participate in decisions made the loss of this opportunity all the more keenly felt. And it was in fact this break that was of greatest concern. "Working conditions and the move were just *announced!* No discussion. And they aren't very encouraging. The major complaint, however, is the way things were handled, especially toward the end. If it was necessary to have these conditions and to move the company out of Tokyo, it should have been discussed and the leaders should have gotten everyone's cooperation."

The move out of Tokyo, harsh working conditions, and the elimination of services were all understood and had even been anticipated as possibilities. People had been prepared for things to get even more difficult after victory in the dispute because the reorganization of their company as an ordinary company (*futsū no kaisha*) in the extremely competitive contemporary economy would dictate severe measures within. The greater distance from Tokyo, for example, while economically sensible because it reduced the cost of their land and allowed them to agree to sell their Tokyo property, meant between forty-five minutes and an hour additional commuting time each way. The new commute was, of course, the reason given by leaders for people quitting, especially the part-time women and women with children. The women, though, had been planning ways of allowing for that time in their schedules, had been talking with their families and trying to work things out. Most wanted to continue at Unikon even though the distance was greater. An example of another company which had won a similar dispute and had moved out of Tokyo was brought up. "They provided people with a minibus that would meet them at the station and take them to and from the plant. The federation helped them pay for it. Why couldn't we have done that?" Whatever their ideas about what constituted reasonable working conditions or how things like distance might be overcome, the rank-and-file members had only one chance to express them, and that came after things had already been decided. The resulting realization that there were real disagreements was met with a closing down of discussion by the leadership, and the workers had no subsequent chance to express them.

A second, related issue which drew much attention was the control of information on the part of leadership. To go from regular meetings, newsletters, and shop floor discussions to announcements and sometimes just "leaks" from outsiders was a shocking change. Leaders from other unions, however, seem to have known and wondered about this for some time. One official commented, "In some cases Unikon members knew nothing. I as an outsider knew more. I wondered what was going on. I guess Unikon members trusted their leaders." Exemplary of this now explicit and recognized control of information was the fact that the results of the hated questionnaire were not even made public. People felt insulted and outraged. "We don't even have any way of knowing who is quitting and who is staying or who is planning to do what. We have to go around asking each other one by one!"

COMMUNITY AND RESPECT
FOR INDIVIDUALS

The Unikon workers' sense of belonging to a united group of people, to a community comfortable to be in, was threatened, as were ideas about respect for individual feelings and circumstances. In large part the threat came from the disintegration of a sense of equality and participation, but there was an additional element, a loss of the sense of individual dignity within the organization.

People talked of feeling insignificant or "small." As we gathered for a break one day one of the women broke into tears as she talked. "Now I will have to start all over again, get small again. Here we could finally speak up and be taken seriously." The impersonality of leaders' actions hurt and angered rank and file. It was exemplified by the lack of assistance in securing new jobs for those who were quitting. After participation in such a highly visible and radical labor dispute, the Unikon workers were going to find it very hard to get hired. "Saying you worked for Unikon means you aren't going to get hired! And the union isn't helping us either." Nonunion shops posed an obvious problem, and union shops were worse in that owners and managers would worry about radicalization of their own unions. The network which had helped Unikon win could have been mobilized to relocate workers, but it was not. Everyone was just asked, "Yes or no," are you staying or not, and if not, "what are your plans?"

Sometimes this loss of personal dignity was expressed in terms of the loss of uniqueness, the loss of individual significance as workers. At the final party one young man spoke with discouragement about the situation of Japanese workers. "We are really just interchangeable parts of a big machine." People agreed and met the remark with sharply drawn jokes about which part of what machine they each might have been. At Unikon this kind of interpretation of assembly-line work, for example, had been tempered, even screened out, by a sense of mutual caring and shared experience and by a strong sense of the importance of each individual within the union.

The actions of the leaders were received by rank and file as insensitive and a breach of trust. They broke the collective ties which had held the whole together as a cohesive and extensively committed organization. What remained might be seen either as a community of workers without leaders or as a factionalized organization polarized around the issues of how best to reconstruct a new company. In their reassessment of their union experience and in their discussion of possible actions they might take, people fluctuated between these two models of their new situation. What was clear—and what they were mourning—was the loss of unity in their organization. They had not lost their sense of community with one another as rank-and-file workers but that community no longer fully contained their leaders. Their organization contained both, but it was now seriously troubled and its solidarity splintered. Their community and their organization were now disjoined. The problem, of course, was that without the organization, collective action was extremely difficult, thus paralyzing the community, and without the community, commitment was unattainable, thus emptying the organization of its strength.

What People Did

In the end, Unikon workers did three things: they persuaded one young woman who quit in disgust to return for the remainder of the time; they agreed to stay on and help the union move the factory, which meant commuting to the new and more distant plant for about two of the six weeks; and they threw a very big party at which they sang, danced, and feasted until the wee hours of the morning.

The Unikon workers were immobilized in the face of leadership control of information and decision making. They did not accept the situation as inevitable, but they could not organize themselves to take any particular action. They began using the passive voice in speaking about what they were to do for the last few weeks. The union arranged that everyone, whether staying or quitting, would commute to the new company for a while and help set up the new shops. This meant that even those who were quitting "because of the distance" would be commuting to the new company to help unpack and clean and set up production areas. This was extremely dirty and hard work, made worse by the summer heat. When I asked if everyone would actually do this, I was told, "Yeah, it has been arranged that we will go," and "It is said that we are going," or "We've been told that we are all to go through the twentieth of June, and there's nothing we can do about it now." In fact two people did quit in outright protest, one young man and one young woman. The young man was pursued by leadership and asked to come back, but he refused. The young woman was convinced by the rank and file to come back and stick it out with them to the end.

No formal action was taken, no formal complaints were made. There were constant informal threats about what they were going to do, about how frightened of rank-and-file outrage the leaders were, and how the final summary meeting scheduled for June 20 would "really be something!" In fact that meeting ended early, with no one having spoken up about their grievances, and people adjourned to bowl and take walks in nearby parks until it was time for the huge party they threw that night.

Unikon workers experienced this series of events as a loss, an emotional loss and a loss of meaning. As we moved into the new company, people polished their conveyor belt, joking about its symbolic meaning to them. They had never really used it, and when they did it moved very slowly. There were frequent jokes about "the line," which they essentially worked around rather than from. Once it was set up, however, and the work stations set up on each side of it in the newly cleaned shop, people started sitting at different stations and wondering to each other what it would be like if they could stay and work there. Those who were staying talked of how empty the place would be and wondered what sort of atmosphere it would have with less than half the present employees. They had wanted to work together in the shop they set up, to help organize and staff the new company, and to be a part of the union in whose history they had all participated.

When they saw the changes in their union and felt discouraged, their response was resignation. There was no sense of satisfaction in this response. Indeed, people spent much of their time analyzing themselves, questioning not only their leaders but their own actions as well. In the end, though, it was felt that it was "too late" to do anything about the situation. The union leaders were praised cynically for their skill in timing the whole series of events, thus effectively preventing rank-and-file response. Aside from talking and partying, there was only resentful and restless acquiescence.

This acquiescence, several people explained to me at the party, is not easy to achieve, but is worth striving for. It is "what is Japanese about the consciousness of Japanese workers." One woman compared Japanese workers' response to what she thought American workers would probably do in similar circumstances. "American workers would never give up. They would fight if this kind of thing happened to them. Wouldn't they? They wouldn't just keep quiet, complain to each other and throw a party. But Japanese workers aren't like that. Once a thing is done, it's done. Everyone just tries to deal with their own feelings by themselves. Essentially you give up, thinking there isn't anything you can do anyway." The party, those at my table explained to me, was really a way of helping people express and handle their feelings and, hopefully, help each other feel better when it is over. "Giving up [*akirameru*] is all you can do, but it is difficult to do so gracefully [*kirei ni*] when there are still things you don't understand, can't accept, or continue to feel unsettled [*warikirenai*] about." The party was a way of encouraging each other, sympathizing with each other's feelings, and trying to reach not so much an intellectual understanding as an affective consensus.

The Party

This party was held at a Chinese restaurant used by Unikon workers for special occasions. A large, Japanese-style room was reserved, people came dressed up, and the food was elaborate. We were all seated on floor cushions around large round tables, but people still managed to stand and move about, mingling freely and exhibiting the comfort of familiarity and the enjoyment of each other's company. Several of the women brought homemade pickles which they distributed to grateful friends around each table. Each person had her own special reputation where the making of pickles was concerned, and few occasions went by without them.

As always there were formal greetings. This time they were uncharacteristically subdued. The young woman who had organized the party thanked everyone for their help and introduced the secretary general of the union, the only official present or invited. He spoke tensely and vaguely, thanking people for their lengthy participation. He did not talk about the future of the company or speak in a celebratory fashion about the Unikon victory. He briefly mentioned people going off to different companies and wished them good fortune. The tone of these greetings and the few which followed reinforced the mixed feelings that were the culmination of the weeks just passed. Workers had expected to be celebrating, drinking what they usually referred to as "truly delicious sake" (*hontō ni oishii osake*), but instead they were "just drinking" (*tada nonderu*). When people gathered for happy occasions or when they felt "singleness of feeling," they described the sake they drank together as "truly delicious." In contrast, when they were drinking over problems they described it as "untasty" (*umaku nai*) or sometimes as "not too bad" (*mā mā oishii*) or "ordinary" (*futsū*). Like the sake they use to symbolize their moods and feelings, the parties they threw also were transformed by the conditions surrounding them. The party was less an opportunity to escape and enjoy frivolity than an attempt to transform feelings and reach a satisfactory state of mind with which to face, in this case, the end of their many years of working together in both production and union activities and to allow a new phase to begin.

This party had the usual elements. Following the greetings there was eating, conversation, solo singing to recorded music, and dancing, then finally adjournment to a series of smaller parties at smaller pubs and drinking establishments. It was characterized by more serious talk than usual, and somewhat forced gaiety. One older woman came in smiling in all directions at once and bubbling in an uncharacteristic way to everyone, prompting the person next to me to lean over and suggest, "She is laughing on the outside and crying on the inside. That's why we are having this party, because we are all terribly sad, and that is why everyone will sing and laugh and dance."

The party was also the only occasion over these weeks when there was an open challenge to a leader. Where people had felt free in the past to speak in the presence of their leaders on the shop floor as well as in meetings, they now managed no more than sarcastic chiding. Workers would attempt to embarrass leaders at work, for example, by saying loudly enough to be overheard, "Here comes the guy who's making us all quit." But at this party the popular secretary general was confronted, and I was involved as audience.

One of the older women took me by the hand and told me to come over and see "the man responsible for firing us all." She walked over to

his table and accused him directly, saying "Here is the one responsible for our heads rolling. Explain to Christena why you did that!"
He was terribly embarrassed. He stuttered out something about
the federation, to which Unikon belonged and to which it owed allegiance, having made the decision and essentially summed it up with
"The order came from above and there wasn't anything I could do
about it." He was uncomfortable all evening and was the brunt of
extensive chiding, softened by occasional mention by others that he
personally was not completely responsible and that they should probably lighten up a bit.

There was some determined joking and a rather bitter humor intermingled with conversations. At my table, for instance, one of the young
men was teased that since he thought that what had happened was
reprehensible, and since he was a foreman and thus had experience
running things, he should start a company of his own and employ all
those who quit. "We'll all give you ten thousand yen and you can start
your own company. How about it?" And young women joked about
dropping off their kids at public day-care centers and making rounds of
each others' homes to stave off loneliness and boredom for a while, none
of them being optimistic about finding new work.

People were still trying to interpret what they had been through and
understand their own responses and feelings. What was most troubling
to them seemed to be their own resignation and inaction. Aoki-san, the
woman who had encouraged me to stay on through the transition,
started talking about the importance of resigning oneself to a difficult
situation (*akirameru*) and why everyone was having such a hard time
doing it and feeling right about it. She started talking to me and said she
thought maybe comparing American and Japanese workers would make
it clearer. The difference, she continued, is like the difference between
baseball and sumo wrestling.

In baseball, no matter how badly you do or what happens to you, there is
always another inning, where you can start fresh again and maybe even win.
Over and over again in the course of a game you get another chance. In sumo
you put everything into one try and no matter how you feel about the loss,
if you lose the only thing to do is to resign yourself to it and give up, because
it is over. It is over in a single try [*ippatsu shōbu*].

That is what everyone here is trying to do—to resign themselves and to
give up, so that they can go on. But it isn't easy, because there are so many
things that are hard to understand about what happened and hard to accept.
It is very difficult to resign yourself to having spent ten or twelve years with

a union and nearly three years working for something and then have it taken away. But that is what everyone is trying to do in their own way.

I had been told many times over the past few weeks that "the really serious mental distress [*nayami*] you must handle by yourself. You can't really get help from anyone. Each person must deal with their feelings in their own way." This distress is coped with individually, but it is communicated and, hopefully, sympathized with socially. Parties like this one as well as the bowling and walking and other social events were opportunities for this kind of communication, a discourse at once interpretive and affective. That night, through eating together, drinking together, and joking or being sarcastic, with nods of mutual understanding, people were sharing what they could of their feelings. The most effective communication of personal feelings at parties is thought to be singing, which people say is "not music but the individual heart [*uta wa ongaku ja nakute, hito sore zore no kokoro da*]." "There won't be much crying," I had been assured a few days earlier, "because there will be recorded music for people to sing to." "Singing," people say, "is a way of expressing your personal feelings." Not only lyrics, which often but not always match the feelings of the singer, but the music and the voice communicate effectively a person's mood and state of mind. At this party the songs were old Unikon favorites. They were sung, as are most songs at Japanese parties, over a microphone, solo, to the accompaniment of recorded tapes. One called "Youth," a song with nostalgic meaning for Unikon workers, was sung but with much less enthusiasm than usual. This song has a very lively tempo and is usually joined in by the whole group. There were also ballads and folk songs centering around themes of lost love, personal sacrifice, hard work, and disappointments of life. Themes of giving up gracefully and of carrying on in the face of difficulty were among those expressed in these songs. There were tears in the eyes of several of the women as they sang, and in none of these performances would anyone think of joining in.

This was a party with no sense of conclusion. Most Unikon parties begin with greetings and proceed through somewhat predictable stages, ending with a sharp rhythmic clapping (*sanbon jime*) signifying both the end of the party and the united spirit of those present. This party dwindled out and reconvened in a nearby pub. The dwindling and moving was inspired by the waitresses hovering about as though to encourage dispersion. Things at the pub lasted until very late, beyond the last trains for some. Usually people are not so reluctant to leave and the second and third parties are gradually smaller until just a devoted core of four or five is left. This night we had trouble finding a pub big enough for us, since no one left until after the second party, and even then it was an indecisive parting. People wanted to go on to a third place but there were not any more of sufficient size. Finally, standing on the sidewalk with passersby trying to get around all of us, we decided to just break up and go home. People promised to see each other "if" they decided to show up at the formal public reception in honor of Unikon's victory, to be held a month later. "We might as well all go. After all, it is free, and besides we can at least get to see each other again."

The party ended as it had begun, and as the last few weeks had continued, with people wondering why things had turned out as they had, trying to explain to themselves and to me why they had not been able to do anything besides talk and hold a party, and trying to communicate and work out a better way of feeling as they moved on to other things.

Partial Understandings and Irresolute Actions

The question I have most often been asked by colleagues and students when discussing this incident is "What really happened?" Interestingly enough this is also the question Unikon workers asked each other and me for months after all was said and done, and it is a continuing issue for many from supporting labor unions who look to Unikon as "the jewel of every worker still struggling in bankruptcy disputes" and an inspiration for other movements.[1] My most recent communication with the former Unikon president included his suggestion that we get together again to continue discussing the events and decisions around the time of settlement.

Unikon leaders faced choices, made decisions, and planned the form of the new company. Rank-and-file workers faced and coped with a transition in their organizational lives, their perceptions of the goals of their struggle, and their consciousness. When Unikon won its dispute they were awarded the resources to reopen their company under their own choice of management. At that point the organizational processes which had carried them to victory in this and other disputes and which

1. From Unikon union documents.

had become taken-for-granted structures in their organizational life changed. The change was the result of a decision made by leadership that there were too many opposing opinions to hope for resolution through open argument, debate, and compromise. Their choice was to close down argument, make decisions themselves about what was best, and thus ensure a smooth and efficient transition into a new company organization.

This choice to alter internal democratic processes was linked to their decision to restructure the new company as an "ordinary company," a decision they were convinced would be unpopular with the rank and file. Unikon leaders were certain, however, that to become a viable company in a competitive capitalist market economy, the productivity and efficiency of a capitalist enterprise was necessary. Leaders of supporting unions have been sympathetic to these concerns of viability, which echo their own dilemmas. In the months following Unikon's reopening, Universal leaders spoke of their own frustrations in trying to combine the more egalitarian and responsive characteristics of the union with the harsh and competitive characteristics of capitalist enterprise. The dilemma is central to union management and not easily resolved. Universal is still dealing with these issues, as will be apparent in chapter 8.

If there was widespread sympathy with the issue of creating a viable workplace with union management, there was less consensus about the particular solution chosen and even less about the process through which that solution was reached. An official of the Eastern Tokyo Regional Federation who worked with Unikon throughout its struggle was concerned that Unikon members trusted their leaders too much. He recalled that at meetings only members who had experienced former disputes would speak to difficult issues, that many would remain silent. "Sometimes," he said, "Unikon members knew nothing. I, as an outsider, knew more. I wondered what was going on." Others would say frankly that at the end Unikon leaders forgot to act like union leaders and acted instead like managers. The president of an affiliated union saw in their solution a potential disillusionment for many workers in other struggles. "If the goal of the struggle is to fight loss of jobs without due consultation, the solution cannot be the loss of jobs for half the workers without democratic process!" On the other hand, Unikon had shown to all other small unions that it was possible to wage a brilliantly organized struggle and win against "big capital." Conversations with supporters of the Unikon union in the months and years following this resolution inevitably come to this kind of irresolute conclusion, swaying back and forth between praise for the union's strength against capital and frustration or criticism for the union's forsaking of ideals and established practices of democratic process within the organization.

On this point there is a strong similarity between rank and file and external leaders and officials. What accounts for the "all's well that ends well" approach of many rank and file and for the attendance of nearly everyone at the final July celebration for their victory (described in chapter 1), was this sense of pride in their accomplishment as workers. As members of the Unikon union and as participants in its dispute, they had been part of a respected and praised struggle with acknowledged significance for Japanese workers trying to negotiate a more secure role in a changing economic environment. As bankruptcies in the small and medium-sized firms increased and economic growth slowed, workers as individuals and the labor movement as a whole were challenged. Unikon was one of a few unions which took political action, made some impact on the labor movement, and set some limits on actions companies might take in rationalizing their operations or carrying out bankruptcy proceedings.

Appreciation of these accomplishments did not diminish but rather enhanced the frustration and confusion over the elimination of jobs and of democratic process in their achievement. On this point Unikon rank and file and outside supporters seemed equally distressed. Unikon leaders were not of one mind either, but their differences were aired among themselves and a collective decision made, although with significant unresolved feelings on the part of several. One of the many ironies of the situation was that one of the leaders who had most opposed these decisions, the secretary general, continued to be invited and to come to rank-and-file parties, and he became the object of betrayed looks, snide comments, and the confrontation at the final party. Even the president, who had been the moving force behind this approach, had his own frustrations about the "necessity" of taking these actions against his preferred "ideals." He suggested years later that they would have preferred a situation where all workers could continue to work at Unikon, but it just wasn't feasible. What's more, most leaders had known this for some time but had not divulged the information to rank and file because they "knew" it would be opposed and would cause significant disruption. If the timing of the internal conflict were not managed skillfully, it could have threatened their negotiating strength during the dispute. Unity was an important part of their strength in winning the dispute.

While the situation for leaders was often frustrating, because of their lack of information the situation for rank and file was confusing. Among the most notable characteristics of their consciousness over this period were the sense of partial understanding and the inability to conceptualize or take confident action. Most workers threatened to quit, but only two did, and one of them came back. Challenges turned into bitter jokes and frustrated threats to their leaders spoken only to one another. Past understandings were thrown open for reappraisal, past actions for reassessment. What to do in the present and future was debated to no satisfying end. When the decisions were finally made to have the final party, to stay through the moving, not to speak up at the final meetings, and to go along, albeit complaining and grumbling all the way, there was still no sense of resolution and people were self-critical about these choices.

Their conversations and actions suggest the importance of metaphor, memory, and habitual practice over explicit ideology and reasoned argument. In the process of responding to the plans for settlement and company reconstruction, rank-and-file workers mixed explicit arguments about democracy, equality, and fairness with assumptions about the naturalness of exploitation of the "ordinary folks" by anyone with power. Principles did battle with historical memory. Habitual practice was perhaps the most confusing, taking both sides at once. Their union had made them excellent protesters and motivated participants in the managing of their own factory. Through study groups, through their experience representing their union to other unions, through demonstrations and other collective actions, and through the daily experience of worker-controlled production and union activities, they had learned, through practice, how to be members of a relatively democratic organization and how to fight with confidence and success for their rights as workers. Practice had also taught women to be cautious about their subordinate position, so much so that they had actually foreseen and gotten reassurances about the possibility of their own jobs being cut should the union win its victory. Practice had also taught rank and file how difficult political action is to organize and how important timing is to victory. So in these six weeks of struggling for consciousness they would swing back and forth between knowing that they must do something, must fight against the undemocratic and arbitrary actions in their own organization, and seeing that their chances of successfully accomplishing a different outcome were very meager.

CHOICES

Some of the ways in which human agency operates in its relevant cultural fields and institutional and social contexts are evident in this series of experiences, choices, and understandings. It is particularly interesting to see the fluid way in which what Anthony Giddens (1979) refers to as "structuring" and "structuration" interrelate in choice, thought, and action. The Unikon workers were constrained by their institutional "structures," practices, and processes and at the same time were making choices that either reinforced them or created different ones. They did this, inching along, thinking with one another, drawing on metaphors for organizational life or for class structure and behavior, recalling memories from school accounts, stories, or popular culture assessing their own history, and drawing on the knowledge gained from their own social lives. These messages conflicted as often as they reinforced one another. They were in different and differentially powerful forms. They had relatively more or less of "what makes reality real" (as Taussig would say), so they were in the end more or less convincing. But everything was brought into the conversations, and all was sifted socially, with coworkers, family, and friends, to achieve understandings that motivated and were themselves motivated by particular choices about how to act.

Some of the most important values of their organizational life at Unikon were challenged, and their choices were made in the context of these values. Unity, one of the most important elements in the image people held of themselves as members of Unikon's union, was shattered and their identity threatened. Many actions which they had habitually taken, including all forms of collective action as well as daily work routines, were viewed and experienced in the context of doing them "together, as one." In addition, this particular bankruptcy struggle had created such a public image for them, and their solidarity and its presentation as such had been so important an element in demonstrating strength and winning their dispute, that unity took on the additional dimension of strategy.

It is in this state of challenge to their notion of unity that it broke down, not into an entire lack of cohesion, but into its component parts.

As unity splintered in response to the breakdown of important institutional processes, leadership and rank and file became more distant, language of "above" and "below" and of more and less powerful surfaced, and stories of manipulation and even exploitation at the hands of their own leaders were told. Solidarity suffered in this process more than community. Solidarity revealed itself to be constituted both by a sense of organizational purpose and by unity with a distinctly ideological dimension, whereas community remained relatively strong but excluded leadership. The years of education and experience, learning to protest, learning about democratic and egalitarian principles and about interpretations of social and organizational life, prepared people for a sense of betrayal at the hands not only of their leaders but of their teachers as well. The solidarity of the union had been built in part on these efforts. Their consciousness of unity, their sense of the justice and significance, their feelings about their struggle had all been formed through these experiences. Their feeling that Unikon was a pleasant place "to live" and the importance to their lives of having come through so much "together as one" had built a sense of community based less on ideology and more on habitual ties of affection, mutual respect, and deeply felt shared experiences. Consequently the actions of leaders and the changes in democratic process in their organization had much less effect on this dimension of their idea and feeling of unity.

The consequence for their choices about action were very important. The things which rank and file chose to do, like throwing a party, convincing the young woman who quit to come back, and working through the move date, were choices made to "stay together through the end." The encouragement of the young woman to return was made quite explicitly in these terms. Those who encouraged her, successfully, to return did so with the argument that after ten years in the union together and two and a half working through all the hardships of the bankruptcy, she shouldn't quit before the rest did; they should see this thing through to the end and quit together. During these six weeks, and in making the choices that were made then, the language of workers' rights, of struggling for democracy or the labor movement, or even of fighting in opposition to their owners was gone. In fact, at this point workers' rights, democracy, equality—all the labor movement ideology was brought up as problematic, as a source of disillusionment and confusion. The conflict between their internal politics and the "struggle for democracy" which their union had waged in Japanese society at large was too great for them to resolve.

The choice to stay became one more choice to stay through something difficult. The continuity experienced in this choice came from all their other decisions to stay through hardships—ideology blurred, the differences in and rationale for the various hardships submerged. There was a relatively easy movement from identifying themselves with the hardships and suffering of workers, which motivated collective action in their dispute, and identifying with the hardships and suffering of workers and other "commoners" and "ordinary people" now and in the Japanese past. As their union leaders became managers in the new company, the rank and file shifted from feeling like workers unified with their leaders in struggle against capitalists to feeling like workers and common folk being taken advantage of and even exploited by those in power. The fact that those in power were their union leaders made their disillusionment strong. The fact that familiar processes in their organization were changing made rank and file feel unsettled and uncertain about the thing to which they were and had been committed. The strongest force for continuity was their community of coworkers, and its strongest single element was the sharing over many years of daily life and of a series of hardships. This suffering linked them to one another and to an image of the past and motivated a meaning which resonated for them with social reality as they saw it.

WOMEN WORKERS, PART-TIME WORKERS, AND UNITY

A potentially divisive force at the time of settlement was the transparent invitation for the women, particularly part-timers, to quit. This could have divided rank-and-file men from women, or part-time from regular employees. It did not. When union leadership announced plans to move to a distance known to be inconvenient for part-time workers, to eliminate child-care services making work inconvenient for regular workers with children, and to pay part-timers less than they were making under self-management, there were two well-understood messages. The first was that efficiency and productivity were important to the new firm, and the second was that women, especially those with children, and part-timers were the least efficient and least productive workers. The latter message could have aroused argument or debate within the rank and file, but it did not. Men and women rejected the interpretation as inaccurate and exploitative, referring to how bad things are for Japanese workers in general, and how much worse they are for women.

In his account of leadership's reasoning at Unikon, Inoue cites their problems coping with the imbalance between "strong egalitarianism and democracy," which extended to all workers, and a "highly variable sense of responsibility among workers" (1991: 250). The variation he writes about is gendered. Women workers, he says, were in the habit of taking their paid holidays and speaking up about their needs and rights but not working as much overtime or otherwise exhibiting a full sense of responsibility for their workplace. Inoue takes the explanation for the final exclusion of mothers and part-timers from reconstruction further than union leaders attempted to do. He concludes that to have included women in the final reconstruction would have been impossible because "female existence and behavior, which are focused on reproduction and nurturance, are remote from the principle of efficiency demanded by capitalist economics and company management," and he goes on to say that "female principles of existence" are contradictory to the "unlimited responsibilities of self-management" as well (252).

Rank-and-file men and women alike had a different perspective, but one that acknowledged and opposed the kind of interpretation Inoue writes about. One of the male supervisors in the assembly section discussed the issue of productivity with me shortly after the settlement plans were announced. Part-time women workers, he explained, could be viewed as less productive if you didn't take into account their shorter hours. "But," he continued, "that is why they are 'part-time' in the first place. They aren't supposed to work full-time and they aren't given any of the additional benefits to do so. That doesn't mean they aren't full union members or that they are less important to production." The rank-and-file perspective centered around the privileging of membership in the union and contribution to the workplace over a calculation of hours or output to evaluate a person's worth.

Interestingly enough, prior to settlement and in public statements even after the settlement, leaders and federation officials praised Unikon women as "the strength of Unikon" and claimed openly that the struggle would not have been possible without them. The part-timers' union was blended with the main union, and at the beginning of the dispute they asked for and were given assurance that a final settlement would include them. Their request for such an assurance stemmed from knowledge of the lesser respect given to part-time workers in Japanese industry, of the commonsense assumption that they are the expendable workers who make stability of employment possible for regular workers, and that as women they worked in a vulnerable political space.

The final solution restored patterns of employment practice dominant within Japanese firms and reintroduced assumptions about women's fundamental role being internal to the home and marginal to the workplace.[2] The day-care center was abandoned as economically impractical and work hours were to be more strictly enforced, eliminating the flexibility which had allowed women with small children to integrate their responsibilities as workers and as mothers. The transition from worker-controlled firm to capitalist firm was marked by a return to patterns of time-discipline and separation of personal and work lives which had most benefited women, both young full-time women and middle-aged part-time women. Not only did Unikon leaders decide to recreate an "ordinary company" as a capitalist firm with labor-management relations, they also recreated "ordinary" employee relationships with women workers. Their trimming of the work force followed the same patterns that are followed in all Japanese firms, letting part-timers go first and assuming that younger women with children will not be fully responsible workers. The difference between Unikon union decisions and those of "ordinary companies" was that Unikon leaders had to move against explicit and highly visible ideological arguments and practices embodying gender equality, the social responsibility of companies to the needs of workers as people, and the fair treatment of part-timers. The very "ordinary" and commonsensical practices with which they replaced those of their self-management phase were no longer unexamined, inevitable, or commonsensical to the rank and file. Unikon leaders felt uneasy and the rank-and-file workers were outraged.

As with other calculations of futility, living lives as women workers and as part-time workers had taught women how vulnerable their positions were. As is clear from accounts in this chapter their husbands and coworkers often expressed aggravation about their treatment more aggressively than they did. Gendered discrimination against women and part-timers was so much a part of their social world, however, that aggravated acquiescence to Unikon leaders' decisions seemed more realistic than open opposition. When I listened to women's voices, however, the more painful part was the fall from idealism. They had grown convinced over the two-and-a-half-year struggle that day-care centers were organized in response to their needs, that flexible time

2. See Kondo 1990 for an extensive discussion of the complex relationship between gendered identities as workers and as women in families.

schedules were created to allow them to be both responsible mothers and responsible workers, and that even as part-timers they were to be treated as full members of a union and full participants in a protest to improve lives and secure employment for ordinary workers. The final solution returned them to a very familiar world, but with an uneasy feeling that it could have been otherwise.

IRRESOLUTE ACTS

In the concerns with unity and its disruption were frustrations over changes in organizational practices of a democratic and egalitarian nature. The ultimate choice made by nearly everyone was to take no open action to challenge the suspension of argument, debate, and collective decision making, and similarly to take no action opposed to the suspension of working conditions designed to increase equality. Here again, however, these choices were not comfortable ones. The power of both their years of learning and their years of experiencing such practices had made them ever more disappointed, frustrated, and wholly conscious of the unfairness of this change. They even cynically suggested to one another that their advanced consciousness was one of the reasons they were silenced, that they had learned too well how to speak up and demand fairness, and that that was now inconvenient.

The power of familiar patterns of action surfaced quickly as rank and file tried to evoke initiative from their leaders. They had no experience taking initiative themselves. Their democratic process had always been initiated, structured, and managed by their leaders. Consequently, in trying to regain their voices, people would joke or make loud and cynical comments as leaders walked by or were within earshot. This time, however, these actions were ignored, and there were no other actions familiar or comfortable for them to take. They debated various acts of open protest and disruption, which they had taken with their leaders' guidance against others, but which they had never taken within their organization. In conversations workers threatened such actions and blustered about the fear of their leaders that such would occur. There was never any planning for such actions, however, and along with such suggestions came "realistic" voices pointing out that the timing was all wrong, that no outcome could be achieved now, and that all that could happen was a messy, publicly embarrassing show of disunity. The very tools of embarrassment by show of internal friction and unfairness, which they had used against their owners so successfully, inhibited their taking action against their leaders.

Their unsuccessful attempts to evoke initiative over this six-week period began to motivate conversations reassessing their past. Many began to wonder if they had had the democratic processes they had assumed they had. Had they really been consulted, listened to, taken seriously? Or had their meetings and discussions been attempts on the part of leaders to keep them happy, go through the motions, and make it look like they were involved? As leaders showed their unresponsiveness during this time such fears were expressed ever more frequently, accompanied by new recollections from their past. "We felt comfortable leaving things to them [leaders]. We had meetings and we discussed things, but come to think of it, the conclusions always seemed to be the ones they went into the discussion wanting." One young man recalled over a lunchtime conversation his own attempts at expressing a conflicting opinion at a meeting in the past. "I spoke up, and everyone listened patiently. But then everything I had said was just massaged into sounding like what they wanted us to accept [*marumekomarechatta*]. I still speak up, but I am realizing that being allowed to speak up doesn't necessarily mean being listened to."

One observer of the Unikon struggle had a conversation with President Sasaki in which he described how leaders found it more effective to present rank and file with ways to fight rather than to open discussion about whether or not to fight. Many who followed this dispute concluded that the strong centralization in the Unikon union from the beginning was part of their strength and ultimately a potential source of dissension. Totsuka has said in interpreting the Unikon struggle that the rank-and-file workers developed a consciousness of class and of democratic process which demanded continuation of their work there and a degree of participation in management greater than that desired by their leaders. The leaders didn't count on workers coming to that degree of commitment or to that degree of radical ideology.[3] The irony is that in the end they had to oppose what they had nurtured all along, because their most radical strategies were just that, strategies seen to be unrealistic as goals or final outcomes.[4]

Through conversations like those recounted in this chapter, Unikon workers began to differentiate between the form and the process of

3. These comments were made in private conversation with Totsuka Hideo, also the author of numerous studies of this and other struggles. See the bibliography and citations elsewhere in this book.
4. The issue of control and participation as goals of worker-control struggle is also discussed in chapter 8.

democracy in their organization and to find both wanting. The "truth" of their past experiences of democracy is not possible to ascertain at this point. It is interesting, however, to see how the past was held up to reassessment, memories recalled and reframed, in an effort both to understand their present dilemma and to figure out what if anything could be done about it. Their answer was, of course, that things could not be changed. Memories of history and images of contemporary social structure and the importance of a power structure against which it is hopeless to struggle without significant organization and resources resulted in a sense of futility. There were many different versions of this futility.

Interestingly enough, historical memory most often entered discussion as a reason to see a difficult situation as inevitable and unchanging. Memory of how bad things were in the past for workers permitted difficulties in the present to be tolerated with a sense of perspective. Labor radicalism and activism of the early twentieth century or of the early postwar period never, in my experience, arose to provoke faith in the strength of labor or hope for victory. Hope and strength were modeled more often after foreign labor movements or examples of worker struggles, or declared "new" and "democratic" and "without precedent." As workers, recent memory seemed the more dominant force, and the conservative power of governments not only in Japan but also in the United States and England were frequently mentioned as evidence that the situation for workers was bad at the end of the twentieth century.

For some the power structure was simply impossible to fight. For most, though, their experience in the labor movement had taught them that it was possible, but that it required organization, resources, and leadership. At this juncture rank-and-file workers could not mount such an action. There wasn't time and there were no resources, and the best leaders, those good enough to lead them to this particular victory, were the very ones they would have to oppose. All that could result from any open action was disruption. They could inconvenience and possibly stall or frustrate leadership attempts to structure and set up the new company. But they couldn't see a way to participate in that process and bring it to a different outcome. Their choice was to acquiesce unhappily.

WARIKIRENAI: WHAT STILL DIDN'T MAKE SENSE

The language of "choice" which I am using was, significantly, not the language of the workers. I use it to indicate the agency

I saw working in the conversations and ultimate actions taken or not taken. Many choices, however, evolved more than they were made. That is to say, there was also a way in which the conversations about what to do and about how confusing and frustrating the situation was lent themselves to carrying people forward through time without making clear decisions. In fact there were no contexts or procedures where rank and file were called upon to make decisions collectively. Individually people had to decide to stay or to quit and when. The overwhelming inertia of daily life played an important role in their staying. To quit before things were set up at the new company would have required a clear decision to do something different. Staying required only that people continue doing what they had been doing for the past ten to twelve years, coming to work and working together, dealing with hardships and the ups and downs of a strenuous set of circumstances. Some of the dissonance experienced by workers at this time had to do with their own struggles for sensibility as the weight of continuing their daily routine pulled them down a pathway which didn't lead in a direction or to a goal with which their own ideas and ideals could be comfortable.

At the time, and months and even years after this event, the word which "in the end" characterized the event for many was *warikirenai,* an interesting term meaning literally to be unable to cut, separate, or categorize. It is most like the English phrases "things don't add up" or "things don't make sense." Workers, including those who quit and those who did not, continued to gather for end-of-the-year parties and cherry-blossom viewing and other events for the next several years. At such times the events at the close of this dispute inevitably surfaced, and just as inevitably *warikirenai* would end the conversation, accompanied by shaking of heads and some resigned smiles of inevitability.

What never quite added up, the lines which could never be clearly drawn in the understanding of events, clustered in two areas. The first was a broken trust and the second was the gap between what people thought they should have done and what they did and did not do. While the actions of the leaders and the cessation of democratic process all ended up being understood in terms of history, power structures, capitalism, and common practice, the breach of trust which was experienced between the leaders and the rank and file never "added up."

In their acquiescence during these six weeks workers tried to do something very difficult: they tried to resign themselves to the situation. Resignation was not passive, easy, or equivalent to "doing nothing." It was quite a difficult task, as people pointed out around the time of and during the party. That most were unable to achieve that resignation was a continuing source of concern. It may be indicative of the slow progress of social change that actions which allowed solidarity to be broken and which allowed a relationship of power to be preserved could not be experienced as comfortable even with efforts to understand them as inevitable. The living of what Fantasia (1988) calls a "culture of solidarity" had made enough of an impact on people's consciousness to complicate their lives as lived within the world of "ordinary company" organization. Nothing seems more evident to me than the complexity of their consciousness and of the process of its forming, responding, and changing. As Geertz has suggested, the "social changing of the mind," is characterized by a "twisting, spasmodic, unmethodical movement which turns as often toward repossessing the emotions of the past as disowning them" (1973: 319).

All those who quit went into other, similar jobs in small companies, mostly without unions. All but eight of those who didn't quit at the time did so within the next three years. These workers lived their lives in the context of Japanese society as a whole, with friends and relatives involved in a variety of work and living in a variety of different situations. In other words, Unikon was indeed a "lifetime experience," a powerful time and a powerful memory for them as they moved on. The lack of resolution and neatness in their understanding of it seems to resonate uncomfortably with the lived experience of their lives. The complexity of their consciousness, the "contradictions" with which they live, think, and act, are lived within the equally complex relationships and processes of social life, and may even make the living and understanding of such lives possible.

PART TWO

Universal Shoes

CHAPTER 5

Routinizing an Ideal

Democracy and Participation
in Union Meetings

Early in June 1980, as Unikon was experiencing both the
disorder of moving to their new company and the dissonance of their
internal postvictory struggles, one of the Unikon leaders took me on my
first visit to Universal Shoes, where I would begin working in July. We
met at the train station nearest the company and walked from there. That
walk, the area we passed through, and the physical structures and spaces
of the Universal factory confirmed at every turn descriptions I had heard
about them from Unikon workers. The images were very striking. Having come to Universal from Unikon my mind was sensitive to the
differences. Whereas Unikon was located in three- and four-story, ware-
houselike factory buildings spread across a city block adjacent to the train
tracks, the Universal buildings consisted of one one-story and one two-
story wooden structures with pounded earth floors on about an acre of
land. Surrounding Unikon was a cement wall. Around Universal was a
wooden fence, just tall enough to prevent seeing inside. Bright red flags
with the union name were placed at about eight-inch intervals atop the
fence, giving the whole factory a somewhat festive appearance. The
buildings themselves were open to the weather, with doors and windows
open to breezes, whereas Unikon's had been closed up, many work areas
without windows, and all with climate-control systems of some kind.
People were not in uniforms at Universal as they had been at Unikon,
they were in comfortable work clothes and aprons. Between Universal's
two long rectangular buildings was a yard where the vans could pull in
and load or unload shoes and where people could gather. Behind one
of the buildings was an open field, part of which was being used by

workers to grow vegetables in their spare time, the rest of which was vacant and used for exercises and spontaneous ball games at lunchtime or for factory festival events. The walk from the train station to Unikon was short and crossed streets with a few shops and some apartments. The walk to Universal was long, about twenty minutes, and wound through tiny streets crammed with small houses, factories, and a few shops. The area was too far from train stations to be attractive to developers, so it was growing slowly and erratically into an area with both rebuilt homes and factories and older ones, all still on tiny plots of land with very modest resources. Unikon workers had referred to Universal as a "real *shitamachi* factory," referring to the old-fashioned neighborhood environment of the place.

What I found at this first meeting in June was a fascinating juxtaposition of images of tradition and traditional social values, on the one hand, discussed with pride by leaders and rank and file at Universal, with on the other, a commitment to ideals identified with socialism and democracy and a determination to protest, fight, and make personal sacrifices for an indefinite period of time to achieve union goals. This chapter is both an introduction to Universal and an account of one of its highest ideals, democracy, and the troublesome way in which, despite good intentions and significant efforts, that ideal evaded realization as routine organizational practice.

Introductions, Ideals, and Democracy

Nakahara-san, one of the Unikon leaders, and I met the president of the Universal union, Kishi-san, in the reception room of the factory. We spent only a few moments on the introduction of my project, about twenty minutes touring the small factory and meeting several workers, and then the three of us settled down for some tea and spent the next hour and a half chatting about a wide range of labor movement and union topics.

Kishi-san told me how hard he and other Japanese labor union leaders were struggling to realize democracy in their unions. He said that the most important aspect of socialism was workers being able to have "control over their own lives." He smiled and referred to Universal as a "tiny socialism" (*chiisa na shakaishugi*). It is very hard, he continued, to succeed in a capitalist economy as a "tiny socialism," but this was, for him, the real inspiration for Universal's struggle. They were determined, he said, to win their dispute and reopen as a worker-owned and worker-managed firm. With this, the conversation roamed in the direction of Unikon's recent victory and its plans for the future. Nakahara-san looked somewhat uncomfortable as Kishi-san expressed the ideals and goals of the Universal movement, and when he started to talk about Unikon he shook his head and sighed and expressed his growing acceptance of the difficulties of achieving labor union goals in a capitalist country.

Kishi-san's age (forty-two), his status as union president, and his long experience in the labor movement gave him the status he needed to offer extensive advice to Nakahara-san about how hard Unikon should work to be a model for other struggling unions. They should, he said, strive for a smooth transition from the workers' control of production during their struggle to a successful new company. The conversation turned to the differences between Universal and Unikon, reiterating most of the characteristics which Unikon workers had been telling me about. Kishi-san turned to me and said that one thing I would find at Universal which would make it very different from Unikon was that people here had trouble speaking up. Unikon is filled with younger workers, he said, and they are bold and understand better how to be democratic. "Here at Universal, however, there is a major problem of not speaking up [*ha-tsugen mondai*] and that is probably the central problem which we have to solve in order to realize democracy or socialism." The sense of importance given to issues of organizational procedure at Universal was of keen interest to me, having just emerged from the internal struggles over these issues at Unikon.

While I had never heard the phrase *hatsugen mondai* at Unikon, recent events there made his characterization of their union as untroubled by the problems of realizing democracy seem ironic to me. The difference apparent to me from this initial meeting was the degree to which democracy and new and different ideals for organizing a workplace were placed explicitly as ideals and as goals by their president in his vision of the meaning of their struggle.

Meetings

The most routine aspect of union membership is attending meetings. Even before their dispute Universal workers had been accustomed to convening several times a year for general meetings and more often for shop floor meetings. When I met them, Universal workers had been involved in their worker-control struggle for just over three years. It was the first major dispute in their twenty-five year history, and so far it had involved workers doing leafleting and attending arbitration sessions. The first demonstration in the history of their union was scheduled after I began working there, in an effort to speed up the resolution of their dispute.[1] Their leaders participated in extensive union networks and had managed to gain widespread support, including the support of the labor union of the parent company, Custom, but the rank-and-file workers had had very limited contact with those wider networks of workers.

One of the most important differences between Unikon and Universal lay in the relative independence of Unikon and the relative dependence of Universal. Universal had been operating wholly as a subcontractor to Custom, so they had no sales department and no experience designing, marketing, or independently procuring materials. Their union members were relatively inexperienced in company operations because they had not been as independent as they had to become after their bankruptcy. Once the backing of Custom was pulled out, they had to create their own networks for supplies, sales, and design. Most of this they did themselves by relying on union networks for advice, financial support, and additional management and labor power in the form of visiting officials working at the factory on a daily basis. They bought vans and utilized national networks of federations to market their shoes throughout Japan on a strictly informal, union-to-union basis.[2]

The Universal struggle was itself characterized most regularly by work routines and tenacious persistence. They put on factory festivals for neighborhood solidarity and threw occasional parties for their supporters. For the rank and file, the most frequently experienced form of explicit union action was the meetings. At the meeting described in this chapter, Universal leaders outline proposed changes in that strategy, changes meant to involve rank and file more directly in protest activities and more actively in the management of the company.

1. That demonstration is described in chapter 6.
2. Years later, when I was doing another project and dropped in on a union leader at a Toshiba factory near Tokyo, he asked me what other work I had done in Japan. When I mentioned Universal he beamed at me, pointed to the shoes he was wearing, and said, "They make great shoes! I bought these years ago and they are still in good shape!" He went on to praise their determination and success, particularly impressive considering how small they were.

Meetings held during their dispute were not altogether different from those held before, but they were substantially transformed, serving as a reminder of their struggle as an occasion for contact with supporting unions and federation people. For Universal workers, their struggle was evident in their daily lives as well, in that they had ongoing interactions both with workers sent from affiliated unions to help in production or management and with workers from their neighborhoods or their networks who bought their shoes. Representatives from these unions and from the Socialist Party came to all of their general meetings and to all of the special events.

Meetings had an additionally important purpose for Universal, in that their union ideology took an explicit stand in favor of workers controlling their own factory and making decisions in an egalitarian manner not only now, as part of their strategy, but as a long-term goal of company reconstruction as well. Democracy was an explicit ideal, as was the creation of a "tiny socialism." The first thing that Universal leaders asked me to do when I showed up for work my first day in July was to go to a meeting. It was clear that for them this was in many ways the heart of their union. I attended a Joint Struggle Committee meeting, the meeting of officials from regional and industrial federations gathered in support of the Universal dispute. Only Universal's officials were part of this committee; all other members were outsiders sent to direct and assist the struggle. Unikon also had such a committee, but I was never invited to its meeting. Universal leaders wanted me to attend these sessions, and I was more than happy to oblige.

I discovered the complexity of their small organization quickly, however, when on this first day I emerged from the meeting and went to the work station I had been assigned. I was working in the cutting and sewing section with six workers, all with long experience in shoemaking and at Universal. They broke the ice by telling me that I already knew more about their union strategy than they did, because they never got to find out what went on at those meetings. Only the *erai hito* or "big shots" got to attend those. I had only heard language like that used toward outsiders at Unikon. Here it was inclusive of their own officials and others on this committee as well. I was alerted already to the difficulties around decision making and democratic process within the union. The internal struggles which surfaced at the close of Unikon's settlement came to mind, as did the frustrations expressed by President Kishi about *hatsugen mondai,* the problem of people not speaking up, at Universal.

As the Universal union entered its struggle, the Custom union joined in supporting them. They were fighting their own struggle against further rationalization and loss of jobs at Custom, and they believed that the Universal bankruptcy was intended to frighten Custom workers into voluntary retirements to assist in the employee reduction management was attempting. The two unions had grown increasingly close over the past three and a half years, and Custom union officials were friendly, well-known faces around Universal. They often sent workers to help with production when deadlines were tight, and they always contributed financially when there was a need. While the Custom union was trying not to create an alternative form of workplace but rather to guarantee the jobs and benefits of their own rank and file in a successful company, they were also struggling with some of the same internal issues. Their union president raised the issue of democracy after one of the first general meetings I attended. "Unions," he said "are really the grass roots of Japan's democracy." It is the responsibility of union leaders, he said, to make it work in their own organizations, not just for the sake of the labor movement, but for the democratization of Japanese society as well.

At both Universal and Unikon, union leaders shared some of these feelings and accordingly made serious efforts to "educate" their workers, to "encourage" self-expression and participation in meetings, and to get rank and file involved politically at this most basic level. "Democracy is new to Japan," one leader told me, "and people have not had to fight for it. They don't really know what it is about. Our job is to educate our members." At Unikon workers had learned to speak up and say what they liked for much of their history. In the face of a major conflict they had not been able to find a voice or take oppositional actions, but in less polarized situations they had learned to engage in discussion. What that participation meant was, of course, seriously questioned and debated during their final weeks. At Universal things were quite different in this regard. Rank-and-file workers were inhibited in their expression not only of potentially discordant ideas but even in discussion of less problematic issues as well. Rank and file, however, did not feel it was so much an issue of education in democracy as one of leadership failing to lead "democratically." A Universal worker had this analysis: "Democracy doesn't work because our leaders act like samurai. As soon as they get any power, they start acting superior and stubborn. They don't even want to hear differing ideas, and they are scared that their own power might be weakened if differing opinions come out in the open. Consequently they try to suppress any debate. You can't have democracy with that kind of attitude!"

At both Universal and Unikon, and among both leadership and rank and file, democracy was highly valued as an ideal. At Unikon democratic process was abandoned by leaders when circumstances seemed to them to make it impossible to pursue, but that in itself became a serious internal problem, thus attesting to the significance this ideal had attained and to the movement, albeit imperfect, toward making its practice routine. The word and related terms were used informally in conversation by workers and by leaders in both unions to express positive aspects not only of their unions but of modern Japanese society.

I attended meetings regularly at Universal and watched the fascinating counterpoint between discussion during these events and discussion before and after. The following is an account of one of the most important meetings, an annual meeting where a major shift in union policy was announced and left open for discussion. The thoughts, actions, and feelings which constitute the experience and consciousness of democracy emerge both through this event and in actions and conversations on related topics from daily life.

The Twenty-Fifth Annual Meeting

"There is a general meeting this coming Saturday," my coworkers reminded me on a Tuesday. "Are you going to come?" I said I'd love to, that I was looking forward to it, and that I found these events very interesting. This must have been the response they were waiting for, because it set into motion the by-now familiar round of smiling, laughing, and good-natured teasing of the American anthropologist which had come to characterize their treatment of my research activities. It was early November and I had been working with them since July, so we had come to know, enjoy, and relax with one another. "You're always finding the most boring things interesting. That is what is interesting!" More laughter followed as others in my work group joined in talking about the boring and repetitive nature of these events.

I asked how late the meeting was likely to go, and several spoke almost at once, "Seven-thirty." This took me back, because they didn't say "about seven-thirty" or "between seven-thirty and eight" or anything similarly flexible. I followed up on this asking how they could be so sure of the exact time. "Because," they said, "we've been told to stay until seven-thirty, so for us it will end at seven-thirty sharp."

Suddenly I recalled the last large meeting I had attended, where I had been amazed to see virtually all the rank and file disappear simultaneously. At five minutes to eight they had all been there and at five after eight they were gone. I asked now if that was why they had all disappeared at the stroke of eight last time. They laughed and said, "Of course, didn't you know?" "For you," my group leader explained, "it may be different— something new and something to learn from. But for us it's just the same thing over and over and over again. We'd much rather be home."

If people didn't expect a fascinating experience or even an interesting one, they did, nonetheless, admit the importance of these events. When more than a couple of months elapsed between general meetings, people would complain that they were not being kept informed, that they didn't know what was going on. That they might have preferred a different format will be apparent later in this chapter as they discuss their feelings about democratic process in their union, but in the absence of anything better, they did expect these meetings to fulfill an important informative function.

They also expected a lot of work. In the Universal factory there was a large meeting room on the second floor, but it did not have any permanently set tables or chairs. Work tables had to be brought up the stairs for desks, chairs from work stations for seats, and various things like a podium, flags, and flowers had to be arranged. In addition, these meetings were always followed by one and sometimes two parties, for which food and drinks were served. All the work for these preparations was done by the rank and file, some during working hours but others after work. Cleanup, too, was done by them. Since outside guests were invited, these preparations were undertaken with additional care and thus effort. People anticipated the time and effort beforehand and talked about it afterward.

PREPARATIONS

On Saturday we quit early, about four o'clock, and started preparing the room upstairs for the meeting. All day long the women in charge of refreshments had been in and out of their work stations, working a while and then off shopping, cooking, cleaning. They were looking overworked and talked about being exhausted already. After we quit work, the men began moving benches upstairs and setting up the room. Two of the people I worked with told me to grab a seat cushion and follow them. I did so, and they took me upstairs. "We want to get good seats, so the best thing is to come up and put your cushion down, then even if you get here a little late, you have your seat." The "good" seats? The back row near the door. I teased them about acting like school kids trying to get as far away from the teacher as possible. They said that last year they were "stuck sitting in front" and "it was awful because in front you can be seen so easily." In contrast, the back of the room is relaxed (*raku*).

Conversation was not too different from that on other days at work. People did not talk much about the meeting and took the whole event in stride. When I did not bring it up, no one else did either. Meetings were, after all, the most routine events of their union and company lives. When I asked what to expect of today's meeting, I was told, not much; there would be speeches and greetings by leaders and visitors, and the Universal rank and file would just listen. "Wait and see, there won't be a peep from any of us. We'll just keep quiet. It's always like that."

The meeting room was very nicely decorated. The room itself was in a building which had survived World War II, in itself very unusual for Tokyo. The structure was wooden, with windows on two sides, and quite simple. Flowers were placed on a podium arranged as a stage near one end. There were red union flags, proclaiming the name of the Universal union and the "Unity" slogan. The sun was still coming through the windows, but it was cold. Since it was still November, heaters were not in use yet, and the inside temperature was in the high forties at four o'clock. It got colder later, and throughout the meeting this was a topic for mumbling to one another. Even in wool clothes, several layers of them, sitting still for a long time made us very cold.

To the right of the stage was a desk where the secretaries sat recording and keeping track of various papers. On each side of the room were chairs set up facing the rank and file. The chairs were to be occupied by outsiders, members of affiliated unions, Diet members, supporting union organizers, and other guests. Some of the Universal leadership also sat with these people. The rank and file were to be seated on benches and chairs, arranged facing the stage area with long tables in front so they could use them as desks, both to lean on and to write notes on.

THE MEETING

Once the room was set up, we all waited until one of the leaders came and said everything was ready, and as we filed through the door we were each handed a long forty-six page agenda booklet which included an overview of the past year, a short financial profile of the union, and a plan of action and discussion of union strategy for the coming year.

Welcoming Address. The meeting was opened by the chairman of the Kyōtōkaigi, the Joint Struggle Committee, the committee in charge of making policy suggestions and managing strategy. Made up of the most important members of Universal's executive committee and affiliated unions and federations, it was widely acknowledged that their word was usually taken and their suggestions inevitably followed.

The first speech was by the Universal union president, who began the meeting reminding people of the twenty-five-year history of the union. He continued to say that this year's meeting took on its own special character because of the fact that the union was in the midst of a labor dispute. Thus, this year's meeting would be different than "usual." In explaining this he linked the idea of a successful conclusion to the dispute to a successful protection of workers' livelihood, to a basic, grassroots style of democratic process. "We have to worry ourselves about how we can live. In this the most important thing is to get together and say what we think. If everyone says what he's thinking, we can use that as a starting point and make a good plan for our union and find a swift and desirable solution to the dispute." President Kishi emphasized the twin goals of building a democratic organization and settling the dispute—which would allow their union-designed, socialist-inspired organization to continue as a legitimate company. The purpose of this meeting, the president explained, was to talk about the goals and aims of the union members in their struggle, and that, he said, should not be left up to leadership and federation officials to decide. "So, today, let's make this a real meeting, let's exchange opinions [*iken o dashiatte*] and find the best way possible to protect our way of life." He ended his welcoming address by raising his voice in encouragement, "Speak your minds at today's meeting!"

Reports. The general secretary gave the first report. It was a long one, and he asked people to refer to specific pages of the booklet we had been given as he went along. He summarized activities and accomplishments of the past year and made generalizations about their struggle and the meaning of worker control.

In his specific reports on the year he mentioned dates for court appearances both past and immediately future, spoke about sales records over the year, and then singled out the absence of accidents and injuries on the job and the fact that no worker quit during the year as particular accomplishments. He linked the low accident rate to the introduction of daily calisthenics (*rajio taisō*) during afternoon breaks. "Moving the body keeps us alert and increases our safety record."

He also tried to put the strategy for the coming year in the context of the past, reminding everyone of what, after three and a half years, they might have forgotten: that the purpose of engaging in a struggle is to find a solution as swiftly as possible. "After a while the fact that we are still fighting becomes second nature to us and we forget that we have to put great effort into a solution. We can't afford to settle into complacency or we will never get back to a normal state." Universal leaders had begun to worry that tenacity and negotiation might not be enough. Perhaps, they thought, they would have to put more pressure on their parent company or on the financial institutions which backed them. He suggested that a new tactic might be called for now and that such a shift in strategy could be a breakthrough. The Universal workers had been just waiting for it to end "somehow," but they must now try to bring it to an end more quickly, in particular because of the numerous elderly workers and part-timers. A large ratio of these workers was always felt to be a sign of weakness, and it was often said that those they fought against would not take them seriously because of it. These workers are seen to lack the commitment and tenacity to last very long in a difficult labor dispute.

The general secretary also emphasized the larger social significance of the Universal struggle, saying that the Joint Struggle Committee, with its members coming from so many different areas of the labor movement, is in itself representative of the broader political and economic battle which they were fighting. The point of departure for their dispute was "anger," but the meaning of the struggle over three and a half years had become much more than that. It had become "everyone's problem, all workers' problem." He also mentioned Unikon's successful conclusion and the situation in other companies struggling to solve their own labor disputes, trying to link these and to generalize the significance of Universal's efforts to national labor movement politics and the betterment of conditions for workers in Japan as a whole.

When he finished, he asked for opinions and comments. There were none. He called for applause to verify that there were no further comments, questions, or additions to his report.

The assistant general secretary reported on their financial situation, and one of the shop floor stewards reported on production and productivity for the year. There were two straightforward questions asking for clarification of points made in these reports. They were both very short. Following them the new officers of the union were introduced, and each said a few words asking for understanding and cooperation and promising to do their best. Several reiterated the importance of everyone speaking up and expressing their opinions. One made the same link the president had made earlier between serving the union, making good shoes, and the livelihoods and way of life of the workers at Universal. "First and most importantly I will work to put food on our tables [*mazu meshi o kutte iku tame*] and to make good shoes. I am only one man, but as one individual I will do all I can to serve in this position." Others emphasized the importance of working together. "Alone we can do nothing, we must continue to work together as we have for three and a half years."

The Break. By now we had been sitting for nearly two hours and people were getting very tired. The leaders and various outside guests all headed downstairs and outside for the ten-minute break while the rest of us stayed inside. The benches were wooden and without backs, and the room was getting colder as the evening came, so the break was filled with activity and chatter, focused on warming up by moving about and releasing some tension by stretching and talking to each other. Several people paired off and gave each other shoulder massages, comparing techniques and talking about who did it best. Many commented with smiles about what "good talkers" these guys all were. There was no conversation whatsoever about the content of the meeting so far. Most of us were getting hungry and restless by now, and there was some longing expressed for the refreshments we had spent the day preparing and which were waiting downstairs. Some wondered how much more we had to listen to before we could get something to eat. Things did not settle down until the first of the leaders came back into the room, then we all took our seats again and the meeting reconvened.

Guest Speeches. The first speaker after the break was the Sōhyō organizer who had come to Universal for the duration of their struggle, to help them and to act as an adviser as well as a link to the wider resources of the national federation. He had been wounded in World War II and was missing one arm. Both his daily presence working at

Universal and his attitude toward his handicap seem to have impressed people. He was probably the best liked and most respected of the outside organizers. His handicap gave him a certain credibility when he talked about struggle and overcoming odds. Through their union networks many groups of handicapped workers appeal to them for help and support, and the most sincere expressions of support that I witnessed were toward these groups of people, whose efforts to overcome adversity were favorite stories.

His remarks were very serious and focused on the wider significance of the Universal struggle both for Japanese workers in general and for the individual Universal worker's own life. In developing this theme, he delved into the meaning of life (*ikigai*). "You have to think," he said, "of your own death. In thinking of your own death you will begin to ask yourself what you hope to accomplish in this life. That, after all, is all we really have, what we accomplish in this life. A struggle like the one Universal is involved in has that kind of greater importance." He turned next to a discussion of love (*aijō*) and its role in holding people together for all this time. He mentioned a piece I had written in the November Universal newsletter. He said I had penetrated to the heart of Universal's strength when I said that love of family and friends combined with pride in craftsmanship were in many ways more important in maintaining people's spirits over the three and a half years than ideological commitment. "This," he said, "is the real heart of the struggle. The dispute may have started with anger, but it is the love and affection of parents for their children and children for their parents and between workers all over Japan which is the root of our strength. Without this, struggles like Universal's cannot persist or succeed." He concluded by asking people again to always think about the "real purpose of life."

The next two speeches, very short ones lasting only a couple of minutes, were by Socialist Party Diet members. These men were both noticeably better dressed than anyone else present, including the business representatives from the federations and other visiting guests. Their three-piece suits were expensive, fashionable, and looked all the more striking in this old wooden structure, surrounded by people dressed casually and inexpensively and sitting mostly on long wooden benches. Each was introduced as a Universal adviser (*komon*) and with the explanation that he had a very busy schedule and regretted that he could not stay for the rest of the meeting. Their themes were the unfortunate success of the Conservative Party in the recent elections, the dangers of Conservative rule for the working class, and the backward (*okureteru*) policies of Japan toward its workers. The Universal struggle "is of particular importance to Japanese workers," said one of them, "because it is an example of people standing up to these backward policies." As an example of the backward policies he mentioned excessive working hours. Each of the Diet members was sent off with applause—none of the other speakers had received this courtesy.

The President's Address. The President's presentation was lengthy, lasting about thirty minutes. He discussed the direction of the struggle, strategy for the upcoming year, and the meaning of what they were doing. He outlined a twofold goal: to bring the dispute to a close and to reopen under their own union management. To this end, they were going to begin a more aggressive strategy, the first concrete manifestation of which was to be participation in the Sōkōdō demonstrations that month. "Sōkōdō," he explained, "is an organization of unions amid disputes, affiliated for the purpose of mutual support. Through participation in this, member unions can amass hundreds of demonstrators rather than just the few in their own unions."

He then enumerated seven themes which he said Universal members needed to discuss and debate. He encouraged people to do so starting right then, at the meeting, and to continue through the year. Throughout his discussion of these he wove some of his favorite themes, namely, equality, democratic participation by all members, and the importance of raising their consciousness of themselves as workers in a capitalist society. His seven main themes were: (1) workers' consciousness, (2) everyday life and livelihood, (3) workplace issues, (4) education, (5) economic concerns, (6) sales issues, and (7) self-management.

He emphasized considering the wider meaning of their action, not getting too bound by the particularities of their situation and their own problems. "We must clarify our thinking, not get too wrapped up in just making shoes. We have to develop a consciousness of ourselves as workers. Together we must think about the meaning of our struggle and of self-management." He concluded this topic by encouraging people to think about what kind of consciousness is necessary for workers to control their own enterprise.

He focused here on daily life (*seikatsu*) and its links to the necessity of earning a living. "We are wage workers," he said, "but that is not all. We also have a responsibility, to make ours a truly cooperative society. To this end we have to realize equality in our daily lives, starting in our union and our workplace." He emphasized that at Universal, equality of wages was important, and that each employee, whether part-timer, elderly, female, or temporary, should be paid without inequality.

President Kishi saw the most critical workplace issue to be participation and sharing in decision-making. All should be concerned with the organization of the work place and with working conditions. As an example, the president suggested people think about how to pay new employees when they want to hire additional workers. Should they be paid any less? What about seniority and job titles? "We have been working here through such difficult times and over such a long period. We have shared many things. How are we going to deal with new employees when the time comes?"

It is through the theme of education that so much of the orientation of Universal to society and issues of meaning are brought up. The president reiterated a familiar exhortation to try and get beyond the day-to-day routine and the particularistic way of envisioning the struggle. He spoke of the dangers of falling into a "capitalistic way of thinking. We have come all this way absorbed in what we are doing, not thinking clearly and precisely about our actions and their meaning. What we want is a socialist way of thinking, not a capitalist one, and we need to educate ourselves to achieve this." He emphasized the wide variety of issues related to this, saying that everything from the "meaning of our own actions" to "marketing" needs to be discussed and examined, to make sure they can achieve a "really socialist way of thinking."

As he moved on to talk about "economic issues" he continued to emphasize education and discussion, tying their importance to the "particular circumstances of each worker's life. Each of you has a particular standpoint [*hitori hitori sono tachiba ni tatteru*], so keeping quiet, thinking 'Oh well, nothing can be done anyway,' just won't get us anywhere. That kind of consciousness must be changed. We need to hear from everyone, every individual, about each particular situation and set of circumstances." He went on to say that especially on issues that affect people's livelihood, "we [leaders] are only human, so we cannot have all the responsibility," and he concluded this topic with an exhortation to help make their workplace an "environment in which it is comfortable for everyone to express their feelings and thoughts."

He emphasized as well the importance of sales to their success. Once the labor dispute is over, how would Universal choose to sell their products? Up to now this has been done through union networks. The president asked people to look forward and, in light of their desire to have a socialist way of thinking and doing business, consider how they might build their own "consciousness and work to sell to other workers as much as possible."

He concluded very briefly about the broad meaning of the term "self-management" (*jishukanri*). Everyone should be thinking about the political, economic, and social meaning of the term. Returning to the notion of everyday life and livelihood, he reminded them that managing their own workplace has great implications for their own lives as well and that they must take responsibility, each and every individual, for this. To this end, everyone's thoughts and ideas are important and must be expressed and discussed.

Final Greetings by Guests. There were a series of greetings offered by other outsiders of rank. They were short, encouraging Universal workers to continue to struggle without losing hope, even though their dispute had dragged on already for three and a half years.

One of these was longer and more elaborate, offered by an official with the textile workers' union who had been so involved from the very beginning with Universal that workers tended to refer to him as *sensei* (teacher), a term of deep respect implying their debt to his advice all along. He chose this time to tell a story about a young woman in one of his unions who had committed suicide not long ago out of depression. Her problems were personal and she had nowhere to turn. "If," he said, "our unions had been doing their jobs, if we had been as good as we should be, she would still be alive. She would have had some place to turn, someone to talk to and understand her. Our unions have to be places where we care about and understand each other. That is the most important meaning of what we are about." He continued to talk about human relations in unions, concerned now with worker control of production.

We tend to forget that the mistakes of one are the mistakes of everyone. We tend to accept that what we make belongs to everyone and that our accomplishments are shared. But when it comes to a mistake or an error, suddenly it's the other guy's fault. If self-management is to work, we have to share but we also have to realize that each individual is the main character, the star of the production. We are each individually responsible.

He ended by cautioning everyone that economic life in Japan is a "harsh reality" and that they must not look on it too naively.

The final "greetings" and statements of encouragement came from telegrams read by the general secretary from other federations and unions who had been unable to send representatives in person. This brought the formal session to a close.

PARTY SETUP

Once the leaders and outside guests left the room to wait, all the rest of us broke into activity. Men began moving the furniture from rows facing forward to sets of tables with benches encircling them for eating and drinking. Women hurried to and from the kitchen putting finishing touches on the refreshments. Men started carrying cases of beer and soda in, and we all helped arrange things on tables. By now we were all freezing cold, so the activity was exaggerated somewhat in our efforts to warm up by moving around. It was already about eight o'clock, so the meeting had gone on for three and a half hours, lasting far longer than had been predicted.

Once we got set up, we all took seats around the three tables in the back of the room, leaving the three across the front to the "big shots." No one had had dinner, so we were all starving and consequently frustrated by the length of time it took to get the others back in after we finished setting up. We started laughing about ourselves sitting there shivering and starving, looking at all that food right in front of us and unable to eat it. It was miserable but suddenly appeared funny to us, and the whole room filled up with the comedy, joking, and laughter.

Finally, we heard them coming up the wooden stairs, people made a point of stifling their fun, and we all quieted down, but we continued throwing knowing glances at one another. The guests and leaders all filed in and sat at the front tables, where the general secretary stood, ready now to convene the party, formally called a *kōryūkai,* or literally a "social interchange meeting."

THE PARTY

The party began with a toast and then everyone began eating and drinking. Food was similar to that served on other such occasions: deep fried cheese, some grilled chicken, sushi, potato chips, dried squid, lettuce and tomato salad, some fruit, rice crackers and small wieners. There was a generous quantity of beer, sake, and soda.

The general secretary, acting now as master of ceremonies, requested short addresses from several of us. This time I had to say a few words about my impressions of Universal thus far, then a young man who had come from Unikon at the same time I did spoke for a few minutes. He said he was grateful for the chance to work here while fighting his own court battle. He had been laid off and was in the process of suing. He and I both emphasized the way in which the Universal people had made us feel welcome, their warm and casual way of interacting at work, and the enjoyment of being with them.

Between these greetings there was more space than in the formal meeting. These were just short addresses done while people continued to eat and drink. The tables in back were subdued and relatively quiet now. At the ones in front, leaders and guests were clearly enjoying themselves, the mood lively and talkative. This was clearly more their hour. Food disappeared quickly at our tables in back, and conversation continued to be subdued.

There was the familiar pouring of sake or beer for guests and leaders by rank and file. It is a gesture of gratitude and/or deference to pour for someone, and most of the women and many of the men made a point of doing this. In a gesture of reciprocation, the union president and one or two of the organizers came back and poured for a few of the rank and file.

There were continuing addresses by other guests, which continued to emphasize wider contextualization of Universal in the labor movement and in the international arena. Twice during this time Reagan's election and his politics were mentioned as a serious sign of worldwide danger, both as a military threat and a sign of the conservative trend in world politics.

About nine o'clock the majority of the rank and file left; they had already stayed beyond the time they had expected to and were tired and ready to go home. I waited until nine-thirty and walked back to the station with three men with whom I wanted to chat. One was a Universal leader, one from an affiliated union, and another was an official of the Custom union.

We stopped, as is customary after these meetings and parties, in a coffee shop for something to drink and a chance to relax and chat. By now we were even more miserable from the cold and wanted to warm up. Our conversation wandered from topic to topic, and they talked with me about my fieldwork, complimented my efforts to actually understand what people thought, and once again remarked that anthropology deserved great respect for the time taken to get involved in people's lives. "Most scholars don't bother." They complimented me further for the essay I had written for the union paper and said they wanted to help me in any way they could, because they felt I was without preconceptions

(*yokubō ga nai*) and so might actually be able to understand. We also discussed the long hours they put in as leaders. They work full shifts and then take care of their union responsibilities. It is largely, for both leaders and rank and file, their own very demanding and often exhausting schedules that give them a respect for the efforts of a field-worker which they do not have for those who try to get as much information as quickly as possible in interviews. Effort and hard work are such dominant values in these contexts that I even found them complimenting me when I would occasionally miss a day just out of sheer exhaustion. "She works so hard," they would brag to outsiders, "that she forgets about herself and even gets ill sometimes."

We talked about their own work, how tired they get, their sense of achievement, the difficulties they face, and about the purposes and meanings of meetings like this one. This topic ended up focusing mostly on democracy in the Japanese labor movement. These men had between them experience in a variety of union contexts, and they lamented both the absence of "real participation" and "real self-expression" and the difficulty of getting rank and file to broaden their perspectives and identify with workers all over Japan or in the international arena. The Custom union official worried that it was his job as a leader to "give life to that democracy" which was more or less handed to the Japanese after the war. "Unions," he said, "are its foundation," and "it is not working in our unions. It should be, but it isn't. It's our job, as leaders, maybe our most important one, to make it work. If democracy cannot succeed in our labor unions, it can't succeed anywhere in Japanese society." Not only democracy, the others joined in, but even being workers (*rōdōsha*) is new in Japan. "Our own parents were in most cases not workers. Those with two generations as workers are quite rare, and those with three generations even rarer. There are only a few." Our conversation ended on this historical note, a very common one in people's conversations. The sense of historical achievement, conceptualized inevitably in terms of personal, generational succession, seems to be an answer of sorts to some of the more frustrating or intractable problems faced within their unions and companies.

DISCUSSION AND OPINION

This four-hour meeting had transpired with only two questions from rank and file, both of which were straightforward requests for clarification of information about company sales and finances. The plethora of exhortations to speak up and have discussion was in stark contrast to the silence of the members. The silence was context-bound, however, as the following days and weeks illustrated.

This meeting had seen discussion of several new strategies. The more aggressive efforts, centering around demonstrations, the filming of a movie to publicize and gain support for Universal's struggle, and the consequent need for putting in more hours to finance these and to actually participate in the demonstrations. The informal discussion of these at work and at after-work walks to the station or get-togethers in restaurants or coffee shops, indicated not only deep interest but considerably divergent opinions as well.[3] When, however, these conversations were going on at work and a leader walked into the room, the discussion stopped and people waited until he left to resume. The president continued his efforts to hear what people thought, and would drop in on us from time to time during work just to ask, but no one would say anything. I asked people afterward why they would not say some of the things they were thinking to their leaders, who seemed very sincere in their desire to hear opinions and discuss issues. Rank and file would respond by lamenting the absence of discussion, even tying it to the length of time their struggle had been taking to reach resolution. One man explained, "The leaders here just aren't very capable. They can't seem to take decisive and unified action, and that's because no one knows what the bottom [*soko*] of Universal is like."

I asked what he meant by "the bottom."

"The people on the very bottom, the lower level of the union. No one knows them or what they're thinking . . . and the bottom won't talk."

The tension between leadership and the union organizers and affiliated officers on the one hand and the Universal rank and file on the other was a stubborn problem, and the silence of the rank and file remained unbroken in spite of widespread agreement on both sides about the importance of bridging that gap and of communicating with one another.

The Ideal

Rank and file shared with leadership a sense of the importance and value of democracy and of democratic process in their unions. Unikon had built strength from efforts to create such organizational practices and had faced severe internal problems when these were

---

3. The content of these discussions is part of the following chapter.

suspended. At Universal leaders spoke of *hatsugen mondai* and wondered how to get rank and file to speak up, while rank-and-file workers were frustrated by the unwillingness of their leaders to listen to them. A sense of achievement historically mixed with a sense of inadequacies remaining in contemporary practice. While there was considerable disagreement about the source of the problems in its realization, there was widespread agreement about the nature of the ideal. The ideal itself had a number of references, and I came to realize that it was through its ability to represent so many other valued ideas and concepts as well that democracy had taken on so much importance. At Universal, efforts to work toward socialism meant most centrally a commitment to worker autonomy, equality, and control. Democracy embodied that. Their consciousness of themselves as "poor people" and as "commoners" allowed them to relate democracy to increased benefits in daily life for "ordinary folks." The following are some of the most frequently discussed clusters of meanings within which the notion of democracy was constituted in daily conversation and in meetings and other collective union events.

DEMOCRACY AS THE ABSENCE OF TYRANNY

The word *minshushugi* (democracy) was used frequently with reference to history or historical change, primarily in memories of older workers as recounted to younger coworkers or to their own families. For the younger Japanese worker there are no memories of Japan as anything other than a constitutional democracy. For those in their fifties and above, however, the memories of prewar and wartime society not only color their own ideas about contemporary society, but also emerge forcefully and frequently in discussion at home and at work.

In addition to exposure to personal memories of older relatives and coworkers, younger people also have their own education, the popular press, and the entertainment media to elaborate on their image of Japan's past. As a result, for the common person, contemporary democracy is defined largely in contrast to the tyranny experienced by the common person in the past. Furthermore, since in the most recent past the ruling power was the military, it is also conceptualized in direct contrast to militarism. Consequently, workers frequently juxtaposed tyranny, the daily coercion experienced by workers, and militarism and placed them together in opposition to "democracy" and "freedom."

A seventy-five-year-old former textile worker responded to her daughter-in-law's complaints about the lack of democracy at Unikon, for instance, by saying how much worse things used to be.

Things used to be much worse. Thanks to having lost the war [*maketa okage de*], things began to change. If it weren't for that, we'd still be living the same way.

I went to work when I was thirteen. My parents were paid a lump sum by the textile factory and for the first year I wasn't even allowed outside. There were huge fences all around the mill so we couldn't get out or escape. Girls died from the harsh conditions and were never allowed to see their families. We worked twelve-hour shifts, and it took me three years and three months to work off my debt so that I could leave.

The trouble is, once you left, you usually ended up doing the same kind of work in the same kind of place, because that's all there was.

And young men were being drafted into the army, and beaten to keep them in line. I have a friend who lost his teeth from so many beatings. And they would threaten your family.

After the war, democracy and freedom suddenly came into Japan, and had it not been for that, things would still be the same as before.

Democracy, when spoken of in this way, is described more by implication than by specific reference to institutions or democratic processes, whereas the tyranny it replaced is recounted in elaborate and personal detail. The resulting vagueness of the concept allows it to be used as a powerful symbol of what is to be hoped for in postwar Japanese society. Almost everything which people associate with increased freedom is apt to be labeled at one time or another "democratic." The Universal union president, for instance, associated it even with the basic freedoms of daily life. "We poor people have been greatly helped by the democratization and the Americanization of Japan. Now we can wear jeans and look casual [he pointed to his own apparel], and go anywhere. Before, we needed a new suit, a bath, and hair cream just to go to Ginza! All that cost money, so if you couldn't afford it, it showed. Sometimes you just had to stay home."

What constitutes this notion of democracy, which was not infrequently associated, as here, with Americanization, seems to be a basic idea of increased freedom and decreased susceptibility to arbitrary power for the average citizen. Democracy in this sense was often associated with other ideals like equality and freedom, but not with any particular system or institution. In this usage, it represents more the expectations and hopes that workers hold than concrete goals. It is illustrated more by what it replaced than by what it ushered in, and contemporary problems are quickly attributed to a residual undemocratic tradition, even while institutions and procedures that constitute the structure of Japanese democracy are looked upon with some cynicism.

THE LABOR MOVEMENT AS A "STRUGGLE FOR DEMOCRACY"

In both the Universal and Unikon unions, their disputes were referred to as "struggles for democracy" (*minshushugi no tatakai*), and in the frequent attempts to link their particular struggles to broader labor movement goals the ideals of democracy, equality, and freedom and the protection of constitutional and legal rights of workers were explicitly emphasized. The general secretary's speech in Universal's annual meeting spoke to this theme, asserting that the original anger over their situation was specific, but that now their struggle meant more than that, it was now "everyone's problem, all workers' problem." Similarly, President Kishi made a point of asking everyone to think about the meaning of their struggle to develop a habit of thinking of themselves as *rōdōsha*, workers.

After one of Universal's general meetings, in which the phrase "struggle for democracy" had been used, I told the people I worked with that I found that an inspiring thought. They laughed and gave me friendly reassurance that after a few more meetings I would "learn how meaningless all the words are." I pursued this, suggesting that in some sense they must feel that their lengthy dispute was serving the purpose of enhancing democracy and the welfare of workers in Japan. The five people there all tried to explain what to them was obvious, and with much shaking of heads and wavering, one spoke up, saying, "Not really . . . it's hard to explain, but things just aren't like that, not on the inside. They may look like that from the outside, but that's just show. No one really takes any of that kind of talk seriously."

This is not to say, however, that rank and file lacked appreciation for or sense of the importance of the laws and institutions of their society, the political apparatus and the operation of politics both in general and within their unions and union federations. These were more than adequately understood, and knowledge of contemporary political issues was extensive. The idea, however, that the maximization of democratic goals was to be achieved through these structures or the political process at this level did not inspire much faith.

Rank-and-file cynicism toward the political process and its institutions nevertheless was combined with their involvement in political action as union members. Even prior to the bankruptcy disputes which I observed, and during these disputes as well, they participated in actions aimed at furthering the interests of workers as a whole. Shunto (Spring Labor Offensive) demonstrations and May Day parades were only two examples. Not only in their meetings, but also in their celebrations and demonstrations, speeches and slogans emphasized the role of the labor movement in furthering democracy in Japanese society.

The threat of antilabor policies of the Conservative government and big business was also portrayed in such contexts as something against which workers must, through their unions, wage a stubborn struggle. For these Universal and Unikon workers, engaged in major labor disputes, their own specific problems and their efforts to fight against losing their jobs were represented as part of the greater labor movement, and of relevance to Japanese workers as a whole and, sometimes, to workers internationally.

Rank-and-file members did recognize the necessity of affiliation with union politics and national politics at this level. The collective weakness of the opposition parties was seen as related to the weak position of workers in Japanese society, and their relative strength or weakness at any given time was even thought to have some impact on the speed with which particular union disputes were settled. Affiliation with political parties and federations and the presence of Diet members at union functions received only equivocal support, however. Because participation was so indirect at this level, through representatives, it was hard for people to feel they had a clear sense of just how things were handled, and consequently they relied on evaluating the political process by its achieved benefits—of which they characteristically felt they did not get an adequate share. Because of their unions' small size and relative lack of resources and significance, they were skeptical about what they could gain from efforts of the labor movement at this level. Primarily such benefits went, it was felt, to workers in large firms whose unions were stronger and more financially sound and were taken more seriously by government and big business as industry leaders.

While leadership continued a concerted effort to arouse interest in and commitment toward the labor movement as a force for furthering the interests of workers and thus Japanese democracy, the rank and file persisted in a sort of well-informed apathy tinged with cynicism. This attitude contrasted sharply with the deeply felt commitment to the ideal

of "democracy" in general and to the goal of individual participation in
decision making within their own unions.

DEMOCRACY AS PARTICIPATION
IN DECISION MAKING

Democracy most often inspired conversation at Universal,
as at Unikon, when linked to participation in decision making and
involvement in discussion. Other forms of participation in union politics,
like voting and attending or sending representatives to meetings, while
taken advantage of, did not evoke high expectations for maximization
of democracy in their unions. Attention was focused instead on discussion, debate, and consultation. And this made the inadequacy of procedures at meetings a topic of considerable complaint and comment.
While the meeting discussed here is one of Universal's regular large ones,
the level of discussion in smaller meetings was not considered by rank
and file or leaders to be high enough either.

Smaller meetings were more informal, occurring as people sat in their
work areas. In these people tended to ask more questions and make
occasional comments indicating some frustration or disapproval, but
there was still no discussion aimed at exploring ideas, opinions, and
feelings that contradicted the suggested policies or strategies of leadership. Meetings at this level were convened, as were larger ones, at the
initiative of leadership, with particular topics for discussion in mind.
They were predominantly informative in nature, and as such their value
as well as their inadequacies were recognized by rank-and-file workers.

Why then, in these forums, where ostensibly democratic process was
possible, where leaders even encouraged and asked people to speak up,
was there so much silence? This question plagued the Universal leaders
as well as the membership. Leaders guessed that inexperience in democracy, political apathy, or passivity on the part of workers might be
the cause. After all, one federation official joked, "The average Japanese
worker doesn't have any consciousness." Consciousness in this context
meant class-consciousness and union-consciousness. It was to the end of
"raising" such consciousness that leaders at all levels of the movement
worked.

The rank and file presented a different picture. Their interpretations
of the problem centered around (1) powerlessness, (2) personal insecurity, (3) inequality, and (4) formal procedures. These four aspects of
their situation combined, they felt, to create an "atmosphere" in which

people felt it to be unwise to speak up and sensible to remain silent. This was not an atmosphere of harmony and consensus, nor one of authoritarian subordination. It was rather a well-calculated acquiescence, a response which cultural orientations and political realities made sensible to these workers.

Powerlessness. Perception of themselves as politically weak, both as individuals and as an interest group, was one of the most pervasive elements within the social consciousness of the Universal workers, and one with a particularly strong impact on their understanding of their own potential to be active participants in a democratic political process. It was a widely used notion, providing explanations for why workers must organize on their own behalf and why they could not possibly do so, for why they must stand up for and defend their own interests and why it was most often futile to bother trying.

This sense of powerlessness or weakness was a relative one, conceptualized within the context of certain relationships, within each of which rank-and-file workers saw themselves as the weaker partner. The four most frequently mentioned were (1) rank and file to leadership, (2) union to management, (3) small union to federations and Sōhyō, and (4) workers to government and big business (or capitalists). In each of these the possibility of participation of the weaker side in a democratic process of decision making, policy making, or collective bargaining was seen as ideally possible and desirable but in practice difficult to the point of being unlikely. The initiative and responsibility to create the specific mechanisms or procedures for such democratic process were seen most often to lie with the stronger side. Any perceived failures, therefore, in achieving democracy at these levels were usually considered to be the fault of the stronger partner. The weaker side, with which they inevitably identified, was not only free of blame or responsibility, it was also thought to have very limited possible responses. At an afternoon meeting at Universal following the annual meeting discussed here, rank-and-file workers had been silent in response to further planning for the new policies, which I had heard them criticizing ever since the annual meeting where they had been announced. I returned to my section to find people pantomiming and joking. An elderly man was bowing elaborately in the feudal style, uttering the humble sound "Haaaa" to the delight of his coworkers, who in turn joined in the mimicry.

He turned to me as I came in and said, "I bet you can't figure out what's going on around here, can you? But don't feel bad, most of us can't figure it out either. You know, before the war, this was all we were allowed to do, just bow and say 'yes sir' this and 'no sir' that, and keep our mouths shut. If it weren't for the defeat, we would probably still be saluting."

I asked why, if things were so different now, people didn't speak up.

"What can we do? It's always the same around here—a one-way street [*ippō tsūkō*], with everything coming from top down."

I persisted, "If you spoke up, then by definition, things would no longer be a one-way street, would they?" People then started joking that that might work in America, but in Japan leaders are not skillful enough to know how to handle that, to behave democratically.

"We aren't given a chance to say anything. They just say what they want to say and all we can do is keep quiet and go along with it."

The idea that there is "no opportunity" to speak has to do with several things. In part it is the problem of seeing "democracy" as the absence of tyranny. The authoritarian structures of the past are seen in relatively clear ways. What is dreaded and recalled has specific and daily life form, what is aimed for does not. Power can and often is experienced to be exercised through procedures of a nominally democratic form, and thus these procedures—like voting and being represented by leaders at strategy sessions or more broadly represented at the national level by Diet members—are not convincing.

The idea that they have "no opportunity" to speak has also to do with two widely held commonsense assumptions: that their own behavior is a response to the action of leaders and therefore dependent on it, and that it is leadership that is responsible for consulting and encouraging discussion. Thus, when the Universal workers pantomimed their own behavior, the object of their sarcasm, while appearing paradoxically to be themselves, was in fact their leaders. Their own silence was, in their view, the inevitable response to the undemocratic behavior of the leadership. However, the notions that they could in any way alter the situation themselves or that their own acquiescence might itself be partly to blame were in no sense part of their interpretation. This will perhaps recall the efforts to evoke initiative at Unikon, when workers felt frustrated by leadership's failure to initiate democratic process, and the inability of workers either to imagine an effective course of action or to be satisfied without one.

What many Universal workers openly objected to was a set of circumstances over which their leaders had control and which represented to them both leadership's power and their insincerity concerning real rank-and-file participation. They controlled information, the timing of its release to membership, and the meeting agendas. Because rank-and-file members had no say in any of these areas, they claimed that they never had the necessary information prior to a final decision and that they were always in a position of reacting to decisions which had in fact already been made. In short, they felt like subjects rather than participants. At Unikon it was only in the end that people started wondering if, in fact, the way meetings were orchestrated had harmonized their opinion even without their realizing it. At Universal workers were worrying about this even in the absence of specific crises, and it was of concern for both rank-and-file workers and for their leaders.

Rank-and-file thoughts on these experiences and on their own actions were filled with paradoxes: people recognized the need for the leaders to lead, to have first and greater access to information, to represent them to the outside world, and to make many decisions without daily consultation with the entire membership. Most workers wanted to delegate as much as possible to their leadership and content themselves with their daily work and home life. In the decisions that most directly affected their daily lives, however, most felt they should have, but rarely did have, a voice. Most felt a frustration about not being consulted on these matters, but they did not feel obligated or even able to insist upon it, and felt it more sensible to blame their leaders for being old-fashioned, undemocratic, and acting only in their own personal interests. These rank-and-file feelings of frustration, anger, or betrayal were, in turn, generally dealt with informally and without any consequent action.

Powerlessness was also raised in the context of the broader social structure, workers tending to divide people into two basic groups, "the strong" and "the weak." The specific identities of these changed depending on the context, but again they always identified themselves with "the weak." They also called themselves "the bottom" (*teihen*), "the poor" (*binbōnin*), or "commoners" (*shomin*) and identified with various historical tendencies referred to as "Japanese tradition." After seeing plays and movies about the Dickensian conditions of peasants or Meiji-era female silk workers, for instance, people commented on how "our company is just like that."

However impossible it is to believe that conditions can be as bad now as they were in feudal or prewar times, it is an important aspect of the historical consciousness of workers that they saw enough continuity of weakness and victimization at the hands of "the strong" to refer to the past of the Japanese commoners, workers, or peasants when explaining their own inability to act or their own position of weakness or difficulty.

This perception of themselves as contemporary bearers of a tradition of powerless commoners, peasants, and workers, coupled with a concrete sense of their weakness within their unions, helped them explain their own political passivity. The consequence of these self-images was a feeling of political sovereignty in the abstract sense of belief in the ideals of democracy, but with a very low level of political efficacy in their daily encounters with the political processes within their own unions.

Personal Insecurity. The importance of their own families to Japanese workers is probably impossible to overestimate. In addition to natural ties of affection, the responsibility to provide them a bright and cheerful life (*akarui seikatsu*), an omnipresent slogan at demonstrations and parades, is a basic motivation for much of their action. At both Universal and Unikon, workers talked about work itself and their participation in their unions and in the labor disputes as being "for the sake of my family." Yet when people discussed their participation in union politics, they also cited their families as the central reason for their silence or hesitation.

At an informal Universal shop floor meeting soon after the annual meeting, for instance, "the problem of people not speaking up" at general meetings was introduced by the foreman for discussion. "They [leaders] say they want to know why we aren't expressing our opinions and participating in discussions. I'm not sure what we can say about this, but it is a serious problem and I think we should really tell them what we are thinking." There were several brief comments followed by unanimous agreement, to the effect that "everyone has a family, so what can you do . . . ?" The other common response to the question was "raising children is a big responsibility." The link, which to everyone seemed self-evident, between keeping quiet and having a family was insecurity, a repeated theme throughout conversations about participation in their unions. "You don't want to end up in an insecure position—you don't want to be argued with," concluded one man.

Ultimately, the source of this feeling is the fear of losing their jobs. I asked one of the men I worked with one day why he thought people were so quiet even though they had so many opinions of their own and were willing to express them informally. "People just don't want to stick their necks out [*medatsu*], especially the older men. They can't afford to." While it seemed unlikely that speaking out would actually lead to losing your job, it was a very real and well-considered concern to these workers, one which they repeated in recalling examples of friends or coworkers who had faced such situations in the past. There was a story at Universal about a well-liked man who tried some years ago, before the bankruptcy dispute, to make his views known. He spoke out and expressed himself well at meetings even when he disagreed. The result, it was said, was that he was bullied and given such a hard time that eventually he was forced to quit. What people experienced as insecurity, of course, was in part due to their union being an enterprise union. For all their twenty to twenty-five years at the company, employment there had equaled union membership, so being out of favor with their own union also meant that there was at least the possibility of losing their jobs.

Yet another source of insecurity for these workers was the relatively limited social services in Japanese society. Workers often talked about having to rely solely on themselves and their own resources. Housing is expensive, old-age pensions are small, health insurance programs do not cover everything, and their children's education can be expensive. All of this adds up, they would say, to a heavy sense of responsibility. As one Unikon worker put it, "For those in large companies, their companies provide everything for them. For us, as soon as we leave at five o'clock, we are on our own. You are all by yourself and no one is there to help you." With all this responsibility, and a sense that there was nowhere to turn for help, workers felt they could not afford to risk losing their jobs.

To understand their feelings of insecurity, it is also necessary to understand their feeling that it is almost impossible for expressions of opinion to lead to discussion, compromise, and decision making in a peaceful democratic process. What people envisioned when they talked about speaking out was, essentially, a fight. In their responses to either an abuse of power or simply a policy or decision with which rank and file did not agree, a polarization of alternatives occurred. Workers felt that they must choose between either inactivity, accompanied by suppression of their own ideas and feelings, or extreme opposition. Extreme opposition, when conceived of as an individual effort or an unorganized effort of a small group, promised great risks in personal security for those involved. When such an opposition was thought of as an organized effort it was dismissed as too complex a task to undertake and, in a small union, just too impractical, in part because the only members skilled in political organization were already operating as leaders.

The consequence of this polarization of alternatives was severe constraint on any democratic participation that would include expression of divergent or opposing views. Universal workers pointed to the so-called "minority" unions or breakaway unions in large companies as the only form which internal differences of opinion could feasibly take. Unikon workers, seeing things in this light, felt constrained by the chaos they imagined if they spoke up about their disapproval of leaders' action. Thus the alternative available and seen as most sensible was a quiet, calculated acquiescence, albeit accompanied by persistent informal complaining and discussing.

Acquiescence was consistent both with their sense of being too weak to succeed anyway and with their sense of responsibility to their families and the necessity of avoiding insecure positions. But this had one, albeit weak, political effect as well. While it was not a strong statement of opposition, their silence was in fact accompanied by a withdrawal of sincere commitment and was recognized as such by leadership. This in itself provided some of the impetus behind the efforts by Universal's leaders to break the silence of their rank and file. Behind it, they knew, were divisions and uncertainties which were compromising their solidarity and their strength. The exhortations of President Kishi at the annual meeting were efforts to achieve a breakthrough, to learn what was at the heart of the rank-and-file feelings, and to forge a unity around common experiences and common goals.

The Distance between "Top" and "Bottom." The distance between "those on top" and "those on the bottom" was considered to be at once the source and the consequence of vast differences in goals, ways of thinking, and strategies between leadership and membership. In addition to what was considered a "natural" distance necessitated by their different roles within the organization, pursuit of personal power and status, available only through the union hierarchy, was also seen to give leadership a very different set of goals. "Without the labor movement there isn't any way for them [leaders] to become or to associate with big shots [*erai hito*]. They don't want to do things simply, they want to show off their positions and act powerful to outsiders." At Universal "they" were seen by many to be "just going their own way," "taking detours," and "not really caring what we think." This us-and-them terminology (*oretachi/watashitachi* and *mukō*) was by far the most common way for Universal rank and file to refer to themselves and their leaders in conversation. Included in "them" as in "big shots" and the "top" were members of the executive committees and all higher officers as well as the affiliated federation and Sōhyō officers.

Basic to the perceived distance were the differences in "ways of thinking" and the "unwillingness" of their leaders to "really listen" to their ideas. Leaders announced things, requested cooperation, explained policies and strategies, and tried to convince rank and file that they were right. "Even when you do speak up, the discussion is still a one-way street going wherever the leaders have already decided it's to go."

Many union leaders at various local and national levels expressed to me their feelings that "the average Japanese worker" was egotistical, selfishly individualistic, and lacking in consciousness, concerned only with the most personally relevant social issues and with their own personal benefits. "All they care about," one Sōhyō leader complained, "is what the union can offer them. They have no concern with the labor movement itself or with strengthening their own unions. American individualism is tempered with a sense of civic responsibility. That allows for a spirit of compromise and in turn democracy. Japanese individualism is untempered. The average worker has no sense of social responsibility whatsoever. He is interested exclusively in his own personal well-being, his own personal material benefits." Unikon and Universal leaders often expressed similar sentiments, although tempered with a sense of inevitability, given the low incomes and disadvantaged situations of their workers, but also with a sense of progress. The gap between themselves and the rank and file was both created and expressed in such perceptions. Because leaders widely believed this to be true, they felt that they must "manage discussion" and lead it in a "productive" direction. And because of their positions operating in the larger theater of regional and national labor movements, they were involved on a daily basis in issues of wider concern than were their rank-and-file members.

Union leaders were as concerned as members with this gap, and they tried in a variety of ways to overcome it, or at least lessen inhibitions about communicating across it. Paradoxically, their efforts often served instead to reaffirm the vertical distance even while denying it. A speech by an official at this annual meeting, for instance, urged "equality": "In our union we are all the same. We are all equal union members and equal as workers—all of us—from the president all the way down to the part-time women [*shita no pātosantachi made*]." Their efforts were further impeded by the polite and deferential attitude and language which common sense dictated in interactions between persons of unequal status. Workers said that they should not speak too much or disagree too openly with their "superiors" and that they must use "correct language." While appropriate discussion and even disagreement was a possibility, it was a linguistically and socially sophisticated one which most did not feel the confidence to attempt. Lacking that confidence, workers tended to avoid situations where it was necessary and, failing that, coped by speaking as sparingly as possible.

From both sides of the gap came the notion of great distance between them in terms of goals and strategies. From both came a feeling of near futility in closing that gap. Leaders made frequent efforts to achieve real participation, but in their very efforts they often demonstrated their own stubborn unwillingness to listen. Furthermore, the practices of Universal, unlike Unikon's, had segregated rank and file from leaders throughout their struggle. Leaders were operating outside and in the networks, and except for leafleting at their own parent company and attending—as spectators—their own arbitration, rank and file were always inside their own organization. Their primary contact with the larger networks of the labor movement came in entertaining them at meetings, special events, and visits to the Universal factory.

Formal Procedures. Like the inherent restrictions presented by their language, Universal workers talked about the inhibitions inherent in the formal procedures of their meetings. For them the meetings seemed to be performances demonstrating at once the hierarchy and unity of their organization and very inappropriate contexts for discussion, much less mention of anything oppositional. The formal procedures acted as an invitation to silence. People's common sense made it seem "natural" to be quiet. They experienced as contradictory the exhortations of President Kishi to speak up and discuss things in the context of a meeting structured around practices which highlighted hierarchy and made silence and consensus implicitly and even aesthetically appealing. His repeated requests at such events for discussion contributed to suspicions by rank and file that he was not sincere. Were he sincere, he and other leaders would ask for opinions in situations where it was possible to give them. For their part, the leaders at Universal talked about transforming their meetings into truly democratic meeting places, just as they wanted to transform their workplace into a "tiny socialism." The difficulties of doing so arose in the conflict between spoken ideologies and intentions and unspoken, implicit knowledge of appropriate practice.

It was to the carefully planned and absolutely predictable structure of their meetings that rank and file referred when they talked about it being "impossible" to speak out. The complete lack of any kind of spontaneity in these gatherings was itself a kind of mandate against membership participation. Even the time of their own departure—although not that of the leaders—was set, at once reinforcing the prearranged nature of the event and the differentiation of rank and file from leadership. The agenda, printed up and handed out as people entered the room, was followed and the meetings began and ended on a very orderly and predictable note. Since the officers and guests came with previous knowledge of the agenda, since they were the ones who made it up, and since they had prepared speeches, they were able to participate in a fashion congenial to its formal and orderly proceeding. Rank and file saw the agenda for the first time on entering the meeting room, and if they had something to say or ask they had to do so on the spot. They "haven't time," they complained, "to work out just what we want to say," and consequently they opted nearly always for remaining silent.

The order of speakers was a further inhibition. Greetings and addresses were given roughly in order of status. Proposals and opinions about them were offered first by officials of affiliated unions and their own executive committee members in the form of speeches to the membership. In addition, these proposals were printed up and handed out at the door in pamphlet form. It was only after thirty minutes to an hour of such addresses that rank and file were encouraged to express their opinions and ask questions. Following their almost inevitable silence, they were asked to approve policy proposals by voice vote or applause.

The fact that proposals were already approved by higher authorities according to accepted procedures, that they were offered already in print and supported by well-prepared speeches by high ranking officers, in lucid and correct language, all combined to create the "atmosphere" of which rank and file repeatedly spoke, in which it was "impossible to say anything." Later, in the party following the meeting, the status hierarchies were further rehearsed and dramatized by the pouring of sake by those of lower status for those they respect.

These meetings were, nonetheless, taken seriously by rank and file in one sense, as a necessary show of solidarity and unity in their struggle to win their dispute. They recall a performance more than a meeting, and it was here that harmony came most directly into conflict with democratic participation. Workers took a great pride in being able to bring off one of these affairs with success, and reflected on their own competence in depicting harmony, unity, and solidarity with good-natured humor. Their motivation in this effort was to display strength, and since conceptually harmony is linked directly to strength, a show of dissension in this environment would defeat what for rank and file appeared to be one of the primary purposes of the gathering. The repeated experience of participating in such demonstrations of unity and strength may well have been an important factor in the difficulty Unikon workers felt in speaking out at their own final meeting or in disrupting the occasions which were available to them. Addresses all emphasized these themes of unity, solidarity, and strength as well as universally relevant themes like improvement of livelihood and protection of jobs. The utter impossibility of breaking the image being created by standing up and disagreeing with some issue was understood by everyone as a kind of unquestioned common sense. Clearly, to do so would be something like an actor in a play suddenly discarding his role and asserting his own personality.

When I began asking rank and file what situation would not make it "impossible" for them to speak, several suggested a "seminar" (*zemi*). As they envisioned it, this would be an atmosphere devoid of formality where information would be made available and issues discussed prior to actual decision making. The proper timing for these sessions seemed critical, since one important complaint was that nothing was ever discussed until decisions had already been made. The agenda would also be flexible, with an opportunity for rank and file to introduce topics of concern. Results of these sessions should then be reported to union officers and their opinions integrated into policies at that level. This suggestion itself, while held very widely and with some enthusiasm, was never put formally to officials—because rank and file "have never been given a chance to do so."

Routinizing Democratic Ideals

Democratic ideals and values have had considerable success in penetrating the consciousness of rank-and-file workers. The ideals of democracy have been embraced so enthusiastically that the word itself sometimes has the awesome ability to represent almost anything that is good about postwar Japanese society. The democratic structures of the polity, however, have come to be taken for granted after nearly forty years. And while their constitutional and legal rights and institutions are considered basic to the operation of their political process, they are not by and large considered sufficient to the realization of democracy.

The operation of politics itself is given the most cynical of interpretations, stemming largely from a certain perspective not on formal institutions but on power within their social world. As workers see it, relationships of power determine the uses made of democratic institutions and procedures, not the other way around, and these structures of democracy are not widely considered capable of checking the misuses of power which rank and file observe around them. While formal procedures may guarantee informative and expressive opportunities, these cannot guarantee real participation and involvement because they are not capable of altering or even substantially moderating the critical structuring relationships, "power relationships," or "the system."

To the Universal workers it looked as though the further realization of democracy in contemporary Japan was being threatened by traditional Japanese power relationships surviving relatively unchanged within the formal structures of capitalism and democracy. To their leaders the picture was rather similar. Both were working to make things better but doing so in a hesitant way, with their own commonsense notions of appropriate behavior frequently conflicting with the goals they hoped those actions might achieve. When leaders tried to emphasize equality but ended up saying things like "from the top all the way down to the bottom," they reinforced the inequality they spoke against. When Universal called more meetings to have more discussion but structured those meetings around procedures which made open debate seem impossible, the conflict between commonsense practice and intentional effort was obvious.

The task is a complicated one, to make routine what is an ideal, to facilitate in practice what is explicitly believed to be sensible. The consciousness of these workers, like their experience, was changing, forming, being challenged, feeling comfortable in one context and dissonant in another. The ambitious goals and ideals of Universal in trying to win their dispute, achieve a "tiny socialism," and organize their workplace democratically set the rank and file and the leaders on a troublesome path. They had, at every turn, to struggle to feel their own acts to be sensible in a field of widely varying interpretations of appropriate and inappropriate actions and of valued and rejected ideals.

In the interpretation of Japanese social life, it is often at junctures like this one that "traditions" of harmony and consensus are called upon to explain how "tradition" is conflicting with "modernity." But it is not, I believe, that the "traditions" of harmony and consensus inhibited the voicing of opinion, thus stalling democracy, but that the important decisions were made behind the scenes without involvement or consultation by those in charge. Too often what was intended to be consultation was little more than an opportunity for expression designed to appear democratic, the substance being handled somewhere beyond their reach. At Unikon this was apparent in their final settlement and appears to have been used intentionally by leaders to control opposition. Rank-and-file workers made these generalizations about politics at all levels, from the national arena to their own shop floors. Within their unions, responsibility for initiating democratic participation, discussion, or debate, was seen to belong to leadership. On the national level, they relied on representation by federations and resigned themselves to their relatively disadvantaged and underrepresented position as small-firm workers within these organizations. Efforts to change this situation faced stubborn and unexamined habits on the one hand and well-examined fears of disorder or inefficiency on the other.

In my experience with workers at Unikon and Universal, the past, or "tradition," was as often recalled to help understand conflict, excessive use of power, or divisive acts as it was to imagine unity or harmonious relationships. Modern, and by implication "western," notions of democracy were no more evident than were modern and western notions of organizational procedures which, like agendas at meetings and hierarchically organized union leadership, make internal democracy difficult to achieve even within unions fighting for social democracy through the labor movement. This conflict is not new to other modern western societies, as the classic by Lipset, Trow, and Coleman, *Union Democracy,* attests. This struggle, like others engaged in by these workers, was about human agency in social change and the gradual evolution of consciousness over time and through experience.

The complexity of their situation as Japanese workers was noted, usually with some humor, by Unikon and Universal workers as they pondered the sometimes uncomfortable western origins of both the capitalism which they were challenging and the socialism with which they were challenging it, not to mention the democracy which they were routinely assuming to be appropriate to both. The world of these Japanese workers has no impermeable borders around either their geographical location or their temporal location in the flow of Japanese history. Their struggle to make sense of and to make a practice of democracy continued while I was working with them and continues still, in this international and intergenerational context.

The consciousness of these workers is characterized more by a series of competing motivations and attitudes than by consistencies. Some of these are habits of the present rooted in the past. Others are ideas for the future being rehearsed and tested in the present. Habits are created, and their creation is a process which, at the level of human agency, is about both the past and the future, both what is imagined and what is assumed to be real. The "traditional" is as often what people are consciously avoiding as what they are unintentionally re-creating. And the "modern" is as likely to take the form of a hidden assumption as it is to be an explicit ideal.

In trying to make democratic procedures routine in their daily lives, Universal and Unikon workers acted out of a calculated acquiescence as often as out of a committed consensus, believed more in the ideals of political sovereignty than in their own political efficacy, and found themselves striving for political participation without demanding political equality. Harmony within their unions was more a strategy for showing strength and achieving certain goals than it was an end in itself, and their commitment to their union itself stemmed in large part from a sense of individual vulnerability.

CHAPTER 6

Arousing Thoughts,
Persuasive Actions

*Identity, Experience, and Consciousness
in a Demonstration*

At the Twenty-Fifth Annual Meeting described in the last chapter there were two major shifts in strategy: a movie project, and the decision by the Joint Struggle Committee that Universal should join the Tōkyō Sōgi Kōdō demonstrations and thus take a more aggressive posture against both their parent company and the financial institution backing them. Rank and file had many reservations about these new projects, the movie project because it would cost too much and require a lot of extra hours of work to pay for it, and the demonstration because it would be uncomfortable to do.

Open conflict was not taken lightly by Universal workers, and while their labor dispute had already lasted three and a half years and their worker control of production was a public act of defiance and protest, this would be their first experience going into the streets in open and disruptive protest. It would take place outside their own neighborhoods and even outside their local area of Tokyo. As time drew closer to the event the contrast between rank-and-file and leadership attitudes toward participation grew more evident to me. While both were quite serious and determined, union leaders expressed genuine excitement in anticipation of this new form of collective action. They did what they could to alleviate reservations of the rank and file and to encourage enthusiasm from them. The leaders had explained their viewpoint that to win there was no choice but to get involved in demonstrations, and although rank and file had real apprehensions, they gradually became resigned. "This kind of thing," they would repeat to one another, "is probably inevitable." Because this was Universal's first demonstration, it was possible to watch the impact participation had on consciousness and on other daily life activities. It was also possible to follow workers through preparation for, participation in, and reflection on this event.

I had already been through the Tōkyō Sōgi Kōdō demonstrations with Unikon where, because of their particular history, the demonstration was already taken for granted by most workers. At Universal, in contrast, it had a distinctly transformative impact on the consciousness of most workers. The action itself drew people directly into a set of social relationships with other workers and unions which they were otherwise experiencing only through representatives or through words or supportive gestures. Participation also situated the Universal workers inside a collective protest, inspiring emotions and reflections about their own identity as workers, about the meaning of their struggle, and about the form it was taking. Explicitly stated ideas and the unspoken sensations of the actions themselves together constituted an experience which urged their consciousness to shift toward greater awareness of their identities as workers and toward increasing comfort with collective protest. This chapter is about this changing of minds and about Universal workers "getting used to" these actions. It is a story not of certain, swift transformation, but of hesitant and uncertain shifts, feeling better about past habits than about present actions, and thinking unsure thoughts about the meaning of their own struggle and its new protest strategy.

Universal's Demonstration

PREPARATION

There were twelve days between the announcement at the annual meeting and the day of the Sōkōdō demonstration. There was not much reference to it until three or four days immediately preceding it, and for the most part this consisted of sighs accompanied by resigned comments anticipating the approaching date. The day before the demonstration, however, was filled with conversation both on the job and during lunch and break time and focused on misgivings about participation.

I had already been at Universal for several months by then, and it was the first time that I had witnessed people discussing an upcoming union event. I had never heard a comparable anticipatory conversation about meetings or distributing leaflets, but on the day prior to the demonstration that was the only topic which kept people's attention for very long. Other topics, like the marriage that day of one of the most talked-about young singing and acting stars, Yamaguchi Momoe, simply came and quickly went. Even the radio, which was on most of the time during working hours, did not inspire the usual chitchat about news items and star gossip. The most startling thing to me was that the conversation was entirely negative in tone. Having been introduced to such events at Unikon, I was prepared for some reservations but surprised by the degree and extent of them.

At break time, we talked about nothing else, and some talked or nodded in agreement while others expressed their apprehension. Heavy sighs accompanied comments like, "How I hate the thought of tomorrow! [*Ashita wa iya!*]" or "Being seen at an event like that! [*Ā iu tokoro de mirarete . . . !*]." In this particular conversation, the majority of the talking was done by the three women present and the bulk of the agreeing by the three men. I told them that I was honestly surprised that they were not looking forward to it. This comment brought real amusement on all sides. "How could anyone look forward to something like this?" I asked if maybe they were at least pleased that it was a change of pace from their work. Everyone quickly agreed that they would far rather be working all day. They talked to me about the new emphasis by their union leaders on taking Universal's struggle out into the public eye and getting more attention from other parts of the labor movement and from the public at large. For this each and every Universal worker would have to participate in various demonstrations now and into the future. They seemed to agree that this might be unavoidable, but that no one was really anxious to get out and do that kind of thing. Into these conversations crept mention of the film and then memories of similar union events which cost money and consequently cost workers hours in extended work demands. Some thought the leadership was just too idealistic and trying to fight for too much when things might be speeded up by settling for less. Such activities were referred to sometimes as "detours," taking time and energy away from a simpler and swifter settlement.

Criticisms of this kind surfaced at times like this, as general concerns expressed in exasperation when workers were up against new or additional demands. While it was always clear to me that there were reservations about union goals and strategies in their lengthy dispute, it was not clear at the time whether or not these would become serious objections. Conversations with leaders were similarly fluid, with options and strategies juggled while decisions were being made about what to do and what to try next. I was catching Universal at a time when their struggle was still without hope for a rapid end and when workers were still debating the most effective ways to act, and for some even the sense of staying with the struggle into a very uncertain future. These debates took only informal forms for rank and file and both informal and formal forms for leaders. Reservations were expressed more frequently when facing changes or when tired, under pressure, or discouraged by lack of progress. The process of forming a strategy and getting most people, or ideally everyone, committed to it and enthusiastic enough about it to carry it out was a complex one. Leaders had to put constant effort into understanding what rank and file might think and feel and then into choosing a strategy that might succeed in demonstrating the strength and determination to bring the union into serious negotiation with Custom and the bank behind Custom. The demonstration was to be one element in a new strategy, an attempt to force financial backers of Custom to pressure the company to negotiate seriously and bring the struggle to an end. Having so decided, they had now to educate, encourage, and prepare their rank and file. For their part, rank and file were trying to work up some enthusiasm while harboring serious reservations about the potential usefulness of this strategy chosen by their leaders. Their position in the struggle and lack of experience with such action made it very hard for them to see or to appreciate the potential power of the demonstration.

The day before the demonstration, in addition to informal conversations, there were significant efforts by leadership to prepare for it and to create an enthusiastic atmosphere. Their efforts did not meet with easy success. Toward the end of the day a meeting after work was announced. People complained that it was not going to take place during working hours, but were reassured that it would only take a few minutes. The purpose was to prepare everyone for tomorrow's demonstration. After the union leader who had announced it left, people wondered out loud what could be left to discuss after the smaller shop floor meeting held earlier in the day. Kanto-san, the man in charge of the cutting and sewing sections, had called us all to his workbench area, given us the details for tomorrow's activities, and answered questions about time and place. It had been a brief and informative meeting. There was no discussion and no issues were brought up. People did not seem interested in discussing tomorrow's activities any more than was absolutely necessary. The excitement of the union leader who came in to tell us all about the meeting after work provided a very striking contrast. He was clearly caught up in the preparations, of which there were many, and spoke with animation, not seeming to notice how quiet his fellow workers were in response to his conversational comments about how much work they had done already and how much was left to complete. He spoke with the air of one who was enjoying being busy and not entirely looking forward to the lengthy and exhausting task coming to a conclusion. He presented an attitude in stark contrast to ones I had been working around all day.

We all went upstairs after work at 5:15 P.M. and began changing into street clothes. People hurried, trying to get assembled quickly so that the meeting could get started. There was some suppressed sighing upstairs and mumbled comments about being tired and not needing yet another meeting. The lockers where people dressed were at one end of a long, second-floor room used for meetings and other union work. Once people dressed they gathered there on benches set out for that purpose. Everyone clustered as near the door as possible. The room was strewn with half-finished banners and chest signs, paint and brushes, and other paraphernalia needed for demonstration preparation. There were half-a-dozen union leaders, all from Universal's own union, working there on these things, and four of them talked to us during the meeting. Tanabe-san, the general secretary of the union, began by saying that we had been called together to be given details about tomorrow, and that he would not keep us more than a few minutes.

The first thing we were told was to dress well, since it was necessary to make a good impression on passersby and on the press as well as on the bank personnel, not to mention on members of other unions. He explained that he did not mean we should be dressed up, but that we should come looking neat and respectable (*kichin to shita kakkō*). This was listened to quietly with no comment or question, but a couple of the other union officials started joking to the group as a whole about the sight of somebody coming looking sloppy and the funny things that might be said about Universal if that were to happen. The other leaders present, who were continuing to work on their projects, laughed and joined in. The rank and file just sat quietly making no response. Tanabe-san began again, starting to tell us about the schedule.

One group is to start at 8:30, actually they will meet at 7:30 for leafleting at the Asakusa factory of Custom. They will be leafleting workers on their way into work. Another group begins at 11:30 and will go straight to the Tōyō Bank to prepare for the demonstration there later in the afternoon on

Universal's behalf. This will include leafleting passersby and setting up signs and welcoming the Sōkōdō marchers when they arrive. Both of these groups are to continue through the evening, until 5:30 or later, but older people and less fit persons may quit whenever necessary.

The morning group was almost entirely men, mostly middle-aged and mostly within the leadership of the union. Older men and most women went in the afternoon and worked at the factory in the morning. These assignments followed the usual Universal pattern of grouping older men and women together, separate from the middle-aged men. Both gender and employment status overlapped largely but imperfectly with these categories. Most but not all women were part-time workers, and all older men were postretirement workers. Both part-time and postretirement workers received lower wages and fewer benefits. As at Unikon, the union included these categories of workers, whereas most Japanese company unions do not. Their shorter assignment at the demonstration was explicitly linked to a concern with their stamina (*sutamina*) and implicitly associated with their status. This protective attitude toward women and the elderly was sometimes perceived as patronizing and as unwelcome. One elderly man asserted his status as "an equal union member" and insisted on being sent out to distribute pamphlets, although he had been told that it was exhausting work and he need not go. For the most part, though, this protective demeanor was accepted as reasonable and welcome when it concerned the elderly, but was much less appreciated when it concerned women.

Toward the end of this announcement people began getting impatient, and someone even reminded Tanabe-san that we had already heard all this in the earlier afternoon meeting. He said that there were just one or two more things, and continued. By now it was already nearly 6:00 P.M.

He continued to sketch out for us the general plan and shape of events for the demonstration and march as a whole and began to detail the activities scheduled for the Tōyō Bank site.

The first thing to be done is the leafleting of passersby in front of Tōyō Bank. This should begin about thirty minutes before the main body of the marchers reaches the bank, so our afternoon contingent of Universal workers will go there ahead of time to prepare everything, put out the signs and flags, and so on. Then they will wait for the marchers. Some leafleting for the All-Japan Leatherworkers Federation will also be done.

While the demonstration is going on there will be a few Universal people trying to get into the bank to talk. This may or may not succeed. Sometimes

banks cave in and allow the spokesmen for the union in to talk, but sometimes they do not. Since banks are soft on women, we are asking Miura-san
to be one of those who tries to gain entrance [*Ginkō wa josei ni yowai kara,
Miura-san ni haitte moraimasu*]. The others will be Kishi-san [the union
president] and Nakahara-san [a federation officer working closely with the
Universal dispute].

This last remark about banks being soft on women brought chuckles
from a number of people and eased the mounting tension in the room
somewhat. But there remained the overall atmosphere of some thirty
people wanting to go home and half-a-dozen wanting less to quickly
inform than to speculate about and enjoy anticipation of the next day's
events. It was becoming a very uncomfortable situation. There was a lot
of looking at watches and even easing toward the door. Some made
rather a point of putting on their coats. Tanabe-san and the other officials
didn't seem to notice. They were very much caught up in the excitement
of the moment. It was 6:15 as Tanabe-san continued,

After the Tōyō demonstration, Universal is going to continue marching,
going to sites of other unions' demonstrations. We want to return the
support given to us at our own demonstration. We will be staying all through
to the end. Actually about ten of us will be there through evening, and we
are having the rest of you go home earlier. But, please don't look too obvious
about leaving. We don't want to give the impression that Universal is only
there for its own interests, is only staying for its own demonstration, accepting the support of other unions and not returning the favor.
  So anyway, don't make a spectacle of a whole bunch leaving en masse.
Leave a few at a time [laughter and a short pause]. Just sort of sneak behind
a tree, remove your headband and chest sign and walk away looking non-
chalant.

Everyone started laughing at this caricature of themselves trying to get
away with minimal participation. The laughter helped raise people to
their feet, and the meeting seemed to disperse spontaneously.
  Those of us who usually walked to the train station together assembled on our way out and waited around for Kanto-san until we realized
that he would have to stay around, as a union steward, with the union
officials to help out for a while. There was a great deal left to be done,
and those remaining talked feverishly about it and were proudly showing
their finished signs and banners to anyone they could get to stop long
enough. As we went out the gate people were saying "Poor Kanto-san,
he'll be there all night!"

On the way to the station about six of us talked about that day's meeting and the next day's events. The mood continued to be apprehensive and low-keyed. The meeting after work was said to have been too long and too repetitive. People complained that they should have been home by now and felt sorry for Kanto-san. I mentioned that it seemed that the movie people would be there shooting, and an older man from the section where soles are added to the shoes spoke up, saying, "I hate having pictures taken at things like that [*ā iu tokoro de shashin o torareru no wa iya da*]." A man not usually given to voicing his opinion too easily, he surprised us somewhat by elaborating, "They [leadership] are telling us it [the movie] will be something to help us look back on all this later, but . . . well . . . I don't know . . . if it were something good, I mean, if it were a good memory to look back on it would be different, but this! Who needs to look back on something like this?" He spoke in his characteristic quiet manner, but others joined in agreement, prompting me to ask if he meant that he would like to see this dispute just get over with as soon as possible and then forget about it. Immediately he and the others expressed total agreement with that assessment. Michiko-san, a forty-year-old woman from the sewing section, agreed that being photographed doing things like demonstrating was something she did not appreciate. She continued, "Doing what we've been doing up to now is one thing, but going out where everyone can see you . . . that is different. Who knows who might see us tomorrow!"

The embarrassment which constitutes much of the strength of the demonstration as a strategy is itself a double-edged sword. It can be embarrassing to the workers staging the demonstration as well, since the acts taken are designed to disrupt and in the disruption lies its embarrassment and its power. The bank, leaders explained, would be humiliated in front of their customers and surrounding banks by having thousands of demonstrators on the street in front of their main office. They would in turn pressure Custom to settle quickly to avoid further embarrassment. The disruption, however, must be created by the workers, who themselves may feel embarrassed to be involved in disruptive acts. Leadership efforts to "educate" were in part aimed at convincing workers that these acts were legal, reasonable, and appropriate. The interpretation which uncertain Universal workers were trying to embrace held that they were in the right by virtue of mistreatment and even illegal treatment as workers, and that it was not they who were disrupting the social order, but rather the bank and Custom Shoes who were disrupting legal and customary practices. While it was not hard for apprehensive workers to understand and agree with the logic of this, it was very challenging for them to feel comfortable with the actions they were about to take on behalf of this sensible argument.

THE DEMONSTRATION

Everyone going with the earliest contingent was gone the next morning when I came to work. Those of us scheduled to go with the 11:30 group were working as usual until then. It was a rather subdued mood around Universal on this morning. In the section where I worked there were only three of us left; the others all had been assigned to go early in the morning. At 11:00 we quit and went to the cafeteria, where a very special lunch was waiting for us. It had been called in from a local restaurant and included fish tempura and soup. The daily Universal lunches were not generally so elaborate nor did they usually contain so much protein. The concern with people's stamina had been a repeated theme, both in union leaders' addresses and in casual conversations, and lunch seemed to express again the concern with the health of the older workers and the women. It was delicious and everyone ate heartily, commenting to one another that it was going to be a long afternoon of walking and standing, so it was best to eat well.

Conversation at lunch was dominated by the man in charge of our contingent, Nakada-san. He was a steering committee member, a man of about forty-five. He had been very excited all the previous day and was still exuberant. When he realized that I was joining them he got caught up in the thought and talked without pause about how vulnerable banks are to foreign opinion and how surprised Tōyō Bank would be to see that there were foreigners who knew about what was going on with Universal.

After lunch we all changed clothes and assembled to walk to the subway station. Nakada-san was leading us, carrying the banners which we would set up after we arrived at the demonstration site in front of the downtown offices of the bank. To me, his mood was contagious, but others were unmoved. There was a great deal of affection toward Nakada-san and people joked with him even now, but no one got caught up in his enthusiasm. He led us on a rather unique route to the subway station, one he was apparently famous for and continued to insist was a shortcut, although everyone else went by a more direct path. I had never traveled this way before and others laughed and joked about whether or not we would ever really get to the station, much less to the demonstration site in downtown Tokyo, if we were to follow him on this crazy route. He kept assuring us that he knew just where he was going, and we kept following him and teasing him about taking the scenic route. Nakada-san himself did not initiate any conversation that was not related to the demonstration at hand, and about that he continued to talk in a loud voice full of anticipation. "That bank is going to get a big surprise today. They've probably forgotten all about Universal by now, but they're sure going to get a harsh reminder today! They have to deal with customers all the time, so they aren't going to like us showing up. Wait till all those people show up in front of their main office. How will that look to the public!"

Meanwhile, as we walked along listening to Nakada-san's enthusiasm, people were making softer comments to each other. "Tōyō Bank has most certainly forgotten all about us. We are so small." "They may not even notice us today, we're so small." "What could little Universal really mean to such a big bank?" Clearly the rank-and-file workers with no experience of these demonstrations did not imagine them to be as Nakada-san and other union leaders described them. When Nakada-san occasionally heard one of these comments he would respond that there were to be thousands of people there that day, not just the forty-five or so Universal workers, and then he would go on repeating his prediction that they were going to be pretty surprised when everyone showed up at their main Tokyo office.

The mood was very much like that which pervaded most of Universal's activities and even the everyday work situations. People looked out for each other, tried to find little ways of reaching out to one another, and just generally expressed in innumerable quiet ways a certain warmth of feeling in each other's company. For instance, Moriyama-san, a man of seventy with a certain shy charm of manner, brought some hard butterscotch candy with him which he passed out silently to the women near him by simply slipping a piece in their pocket or hand. He was affectionately teased for flirting by all.

As we walked to the station, in the lunch period before, and in the leafleting activities after we arrived in downtown Tokyo, this mood prevailed, making people seem very much united in a common positive and caring attitude toward each other and toward their tasks. As is usually the case this general mood encompassed Nakada-san, but his excitement did not reach back and encompass the others.

When we got to Ōtemachi Station we all disembarked and reassembled on the platform, where we waited while Nakada-san tried to remember which of the many exits we should use. This is a huge station,
and as often happened when I came to this area with the Unikon workers
or the Universal workers, people did not seem very sure of themselves.
The geographical gap between the station nearest Universal and this one
is only about a fifteen-minute subway ride on one line, but the cultural
gap is very wide, and people just do not come to this area with any
regularity. As we had walked from Universal to the train station that
morning, we had begun in the small, factory-filled area immediately
surrounding Universal, had gradually walked into a residential area
threaded with tiny winding streets and pathways, and then into the
station area crowded with small drinking establishments. People on the
streets in this area are housewives wearing casual clothes and aprons, men
and women in work clothes from nearby factories, and a smattering of
young people in school uniforms. When we emerged from the subway
at Ōtemachi, we were standing on a beautiful eight-lane boulevard, lined
with trees. This horizontal spaciousness was reinforced by a vertical
spaciousness created by the tall buildings on both sides of every street
in this area. Those buildings which are not chic new architectural tri-
umphs are old, stately brick or stone structures. All are imposing, all are
landscaped with beds of blooming seasonal flowers and hedges, and all
the sidewalks in the area are wide and uncrowded. People passing by in
this area are well-groomed, fashionable, and for the most part in business
attire.

We arrived at the Tōyō Bank intersection a few minutes before
leafleting was scheduled to begin, about 12:30 P.M. The marchers were
expected to arrive at 1:20. The Universal people were not wearing any
identifying paraphernalia, so when we stopped in front of the bank and
began unpacking all the chest signs, headbands, and banners we had
been carrying, passersby did their share of staring. People quickly put on
their headbands and chest signs in little groups of two or three, helping
each other tie them securely. Leaving a few to put up the banners and
signs around the outside of Tōyō Bank, they took up their respective
posts on each corner of the broad intersection. After a while someone
moved into the center of the street as well, standing on the wide center
divider and handing out leaflets to people in the crosswalk as they passed.
While people carried on with this, I was moving around taking pictures,
watching, blending into the crowd, and stopping frequently to talk to
those who were for a few moments not busy. I was struck by how this

scene was visually reinforcing the comments made all the way here by Universal's workers about how small they were and how the bank was not likely to even notice them and their little company's problems. They certainly did look small, and it was not easy to notice them until you came right up to them. We were altogether a group of about fifteen, and that had seemed like a lot of people until now, but here on these wide boulevards surrounded by towering buildings and busy sophisticated people bustling by, we were hardly noticeable.

As people walked up to the crosswalks and waited for lights to change or passed by the bank, the leaflets were held out to them. Typically the Universal person would bow slightly as they held it out and the passersby would try to look past them, noticing nothing until that became impossible at which point they would receive the leaflet. A smaller proportion of the people would reach out themselves for one and begin to read it while walking. The task of getting strangers, especially in this area, to pay attention was neither an easy nor a very pleasant one. I could understand why people had said that this kind of thing would make them tense and tired afterwards. I began to have some understanding of why they were so reluctant to be photographed doing this kind of work, why they had said that this was not the fond kind of memory they were eager to look back on.

Despite the reservations they had been expressing, the Universal workers had risen to the task at hand and everything was being done conscientiously. Their attitude was of people doing their best at something they would rather not have to do. They were competent, unexcited, a little tense, and happy to have a diversion, like talking to me or to each other during a lull. Moriyama-san slipped over to me when the street emptied for a moment and slipped another piece of hard candy in my pocket, slipped back over to his place on the corner, and then looked over and smiled broadly at me. Others commented to me and to each other how beautiful the autumn leaves were in this area just now. Time was going by rather slowly and the marchers were late. After an hour of standing and walking we were all getting a little tired.

About half an hour after leafleting began, at 1:00 P.M., the movie crew, other union officials, and some federation leaders arrived. They gathered around the front of Tōyō Bank and talked about arrangements for the demonstration soon to begin. The bank was beginning to take some notice, and the number of guards at the door had now increased from one when we arrived to four. Supporters from other unions began arriving a few at a time, scattering out around the area. The federation people and the Sōkōdō officials were clearly in charge and had a very professional attitude toward their work. The Universal union leaders were obviously following their lead at this point. The general mood of excitement among Universal leaders prevalent the previous day was being replaced by a serious concentration on carrying through the planned action against the bank, and by an emotionally charged but controlled demeanor. Emotional involvement was not evident among the Sōkōdō and federation leaders. They remained throughout cool, professional strategists. They spoke to me before and after the demonstration about the potential effect of this on Universal's negotiations to end their dispute, and about how far it was wise to push the bank today, never displaying anything but intelligent, experienced, and concerned strategic thinking. I was even invited up for a tea break between demonstrations by one official who said that his office was on one of the top floors of a nearby skyscraper. He said it might be a chance to rest for a moment before continuing with the afternoon's schedule.

About 2:00 we began to hear the chants of the marchers approaching. By now they were about twenty minutes late. We could hear them for some time before they appeared. Universal people quickly left their leafleting posts and gathered by the steps in front of the bank. They lined up single file on both sides of the sidewalk facing each other, making a sort of reception line for the arriving demonstrators. A sudden flurry of color brought the demonstrators right into their midst, filling the sidewalks all around the bank and flowing out into the streets. They continued to pour in by the hundreds, walking through the applauding Universal workers' lines, all marching behind their own union's flag, invariably bright red, and all wearing headbands and chest signs with their own union's particular dispute's slogans printed there. These too were mostly red on white, with a few in bright blue or orange. The overall effect was colorful and impressive.

The Universal contingent arrived with these marchers, about twenty strong, all having been marching and joining in other demonstrations since early morning. They looked different than I had expected. They were concentrating, involved, serious, and the excitement of this massive demonstration had found them. They barely said hello to me before starting to talk about how incredible this day had been, how many places they had been, and how many people they had been with. When the demonstration got called under way shortly afterward, Michiko-san and Yokota-san, with whom I had been talking, dropped their sentences midway and turned back to the crowd. These two women had been among the most reluctant of the Universal workers. By now the members of the contingent with whom I had come were also getting involved. Their voices were raised along with their fists in the chants joined in by the hundreds crowded around the bank.

The demonstration activities began as a panel truck equipped with loudspeakers pulled up to the curb, and Universal's union president, the Sōkōdō organizers, and other union leaders spoke and led the crowd in chants. Meanwhile, other leaders and Universal's union members were crowded immediately in front of the doors of the bank pushing and asking to be let in to negotiate with the bank leaders. Kishi-san, the Universal president, spoke for some time. His address was strong and aggressive and spoken with an oratorical flair. While he was speaking a Sōkōdō negotiator, also with a microphone, was at the bank door trying to get them to let him in to talk. The movie crew was up at the door filming. The bank personnel were surrounded by guards by now, looking somewhat taken aback. After a few minutes a bank representative came forward, looking extremely expressionless. For perhaps ten minutes neither he nor anyone else from the bank said anything at all. They just stood there looking quite blank. Kishi-san, from atop the truck, was accusing them of standing in the shadows and being afraid to come out and meet people. He warned them that workers were going to combine their strength and fight wrongdoing on the part of the powerful institutions like Tōyō Bank. "The aim of these workers is nothing more than protection of their livelihood and way of life." Interspersed through this speech were several "Protect our livelihood" chants (*Seikatsu o mamore*) shouted with raised fists. The struggle at the door was continuing throughout all this, and there was enough pushing that those at the door were being forced back inward.

Attention turned to the negotiation attempt at the door. The Sōkōdō organizer and the appointed Universal people were continuing to ask permission to enter. Chants of "We won't give up" (*Ganbarō*) set the rhythm of the crowd pushing on the bank doors and against the bank personnel. Finally the bank representative began saying, "Please restrain yourselves [*Enryo shite kudasai*]," and "Please restrain yourselves just for today." He never varied from these two sentences. The union people and the camera crew were holding out microphones to the bank representative, who began to look more and more unsure of himself as this went on. To his continued "Please restrain yourselves" and "Please restrain yourselves just for today," those at the door of the bank replied in restrained and polite, yet loud and insistent language, "Why? [*Naze?*]"

"Why should we? [*Dōshite sō shinakute wa ikemasen ka?*]" and "When can we come back, then? [*Ja, itsu mata kitara ii no desu ka?*]" The demonstrators, meanwhile, continued in high, tense, angry voices, voices I had certainly never heard these same people use before.

After ten minutes or so of this, a sit-in was staged on the steps of the bank. The Sōkōdō organizer continued talking to the bank representative, insisting either on talks that day or on a promise for a specific future date for negotiations. He continued to explain in a loud and determined voice that Universal's three-and-a-half-year struggle and the threat to the livelihood of the forty-five odd workers and their families was the responsibility of Universal's "parent company" and of Tōyō Bank. He spoke of their social responsibility to these workers and accused them of neglecting it. The sit-in served its purpose, and the bank representative finally gave in, in a voice so soft that none of us on the street could hear it. With this the Sōkōdō organizer announced that for today the demonstration was finished and that they would be coming back soon for talks.

As the crowd dispersed and people lined up again to march to the next site, Universal workers were still very wound up. As we walked on, people talked to one another, with traces of excitement continuing to be evident for some time. "Whew! I really got worked up." "Everybody got pretty involved." "That was really something else!" Nakada-san was walking near me, his steps coming much higher and faster than usual. He was smiling, shaking his head, and saying, "These capitalists just don't care if a man dies or not. They don't care about anything but their own profits. Just look at these buildings. What do they care about a few little human beings?" We were walking at that moment through a narrower street, with the appearance of a sort of valley of sky-scraping bank and financial buildings.

The Universal contingent, combining now both the afternoon and the morning groups, continued to the next demonstration site and on through to the final demonstration of thousands in front of the Tokyo Metropolitan Government offices at about 5:00. The anticipated problem of people leaving en masse never materialized. The event had caught people up in its momentum and the great majority of Universal's workers were there until the end.

THE NEXT DAY

The next morning I went into work wondering how people would be feeling about the previous day's activities. Unlike the usual absence of conversation following other union activities, the demonstration of the previous day came up over and over again, and a certain air of excitement remained for most of the day. Early on Kishi-san dropped in and greeted us with "Yesterday was something else, wasn't it?" His spirits were very high, and he was a good deal more outgoing than usual, smiling and walking with lighter steps. He spent a lot of time talking to us while we worked, not about the demonstration in particular, just making friendly conversation. This was not a common occurrence. I asked him when he came over by me if he thought that yesterday's demonstration had had the desired effect. He said that it certainly had, but that it was important not to drop the effort now. Universal would have to persist and keep up the pressure. Nakahara-san, the federation official working most closely with Universal, had told me very much the same thing yesterday between demonstrations. He said that Universal's contracting company, Custom, would get a call from the Tōyō executives. Their company president would be scolded for creating a situation in which the bank became the target of this kind of action, and he would be pressured to bring the dispute to a swift end. Nakahara-san too had said that it was of vital importance not to let up now that they had begun to put the pressure on.

During work that morning people smiled, shaking their heads, and talked about how worked up everybody had gotten, how involved they had all felt. They were surprised at themselves, at how caught up they had all been. Since I was working near Michiko-san, I talked with her quite a lot, reminding her how reluctant she had been the day before the demonstration. She said, "Yeah, it was a first time for me, so putting on that thing [she motioned toward where the chest sign fits] was something I was dreading. But, you're not alone doing that, and even when something is unpleasant when you do it alone, if you do it with everyone together it is all right. There were so many people there yesterday! It was amazing. I didn't realize." I asked her if she would feel reluctant next time Universal was called to a demonstration, and she said no, she did not think so, she felt differently about it now.

Later on, while we were working, she began talking about the previous day's events again. "You know, workers alone just can't get anywhere. They're too weak. Workers have to get together and act with each other's support. Everyone has to combine their strength."

I asked her about the leafleting prior to yesterday's demonstrations. I said that it looked like hard work, giving leaflets to strangers some of whom will not even accept them.

She replied, "That is exactly right. It is tough work and sometimes very unpleasant. But you have to think about the necessity of doing it, and just go ahead and get it done."

Toward the end of the day a flier was passed around announcing a mass meeting in support of another labor union with its own labor dispute. Michiko-san remarked when she saw it, "Workers are, after all, very weak."

Not only was conversation uncharacteristically focused on labor movement topics, particularly yesterday's demonstration, but the mood too had perceptibly changed. It was lighter. People were working at a slightly faster pace, movements were sharper and the conversation exceptionally good-natured, tones of voice carrying something of satisfaction in them. They talked now and again all day long about how many people—thousands—had attended, about how long they had walked, and how far—several kilometers. They teased me about losing them once in the crowd and not being able to figure out which march their contingent belonged to. They talked repeatedly of the final stop in front of the Tokyo Metropolitan Government offices, where all the marches converged and literally tens of thousands of workers assembled. People had been very apprehensive about the previous day's demonstration, but something had been, in fact, accomplished, and they spoke about it with satisfaction and an appreciation of having reached a new understanding.

Persuasive Actions

This demonstration was a colorful, antagonistic, and vivid dramatization of open conflict and as such was very unusual in the lives of the Universal workers. Before they were convinced of the wisdom or necessity of participation, they were certain of its inevitability, and their response was to try to "get used to it." The forms which the actions took were themselves troublesome to get used to, being everything that they hoped their everyday lives were not. The demonstration aimed to create disturbances, its language was imperative, its colors bold and bright, its props large and flamboyant, and it was noisy. To create such an event was, for the Universal workers and all other participants, to behave in disturbing, imperative, bold, flamboyant, and noisy ways. The thoughts which were aroused during this event were embedded in the experience of these actions. People were sensing relationships, identities, and struggles through the forms of their actions quite as much as they were analyzing them and thinking about how sensible they might be.

DRAMATIZED CONFLICT

In dramatizing open conflict and antagonism, demonstrations are usually represented as a last resort, appropriate only because negotiation, accommodation, and similar cooperative methods of problem solving have failed. Speakers and signs reminded onlookers and participants that Tōyō Bank and Custom Shoes, not Universal, were refusing to reach settlement through such channels. Unikon signs accused their owners of "running away" and "disappearing," placing blame for the chaos of the demonstration squarely on their shoulders—as a last resort. The style and form of the demonstration are determined by its goal—to force negotiation and ultimately concessions. The strategy is to draw attention to the union's unwavering determination, demonstrate the union's strength, and embarrass the opponent.

Embarrassment as a strategy for gaining concessions is omnipresent. It determines the very scope of the action as well as the specific form it takes. The Sōkōdō demonstrations last for miles, winding through the financial district, and come into contact with a potential audience of thousands. The handbills printed up by each union discussing their specific grievances, however, are distributed only in front of and immediately surrounding the institution in question, not all along the route. Furthermore, all dialogue shouted or chanted at the demonstration site is carried out with people and loudspeakers facing the bank buildings, making every effort to address the bank and none whatever to address directly the onlookers. The strategy is to demonstrate in the most literal sense, to dramatize in as vivid a way as possible, the conflict between the institution and the union. That dramatized conflict itself, when exposed to the passersby, the neighboring institutions, and the customers both inside and out, is considered a potentially devastating embarrassment.

A demonstration like this could aim at educating the general public, drawing attention to itself and its plight, but it typically does not. Instead it is a dramatization of the fight per se, and as such aims primarily to demonstrate that there *is* a conflict and that that conflict was brought on not by the union but by the institution in question. The ensuing embarrassment, it is hoped, will force their opponents into negotiation and ultimately to a settlement.

What this drama requires from the participants is that they display their antagonistic feelings, even exaggerate them, and it puts them in danger of falling prey to an unwieldy emotional state of mind which they ordinarily control and handle with some restraint. Their demonstration asked Universal workers to act out, to show their most negative feelings, to express their frustrations and anger, and to disturb the usual peace-fulness of daily routine. The means of expression were largely prede-termined, and the sequence of actions was carefully orchestrated. Even the on-the-scene behavior was carefully watched and managed by an outside union organizer who himself remained calm and unemotional. For the rank and file, the emotional involvement was deep and the turning-on and turning-off of feelings quite difficult.

Under other circumstances, they were able to discuss and be calm about their struggle and their situation, and there was a great appreci-ation for not letting emotions out, for not expressing frustration too directly, for holding their tempers and getting on with everyday neces-sities. These are sensibilities common in Japanese society and become increasingly important with age, as they are commonly associated with maturity. They are also associated with gender, being even more im-portant for women. One young man at Unikon talked of the initial reluctance of many of his coworkers to be involved in these actions, remarking on the importance of peacefulness, quiet, subtlety, and in-conspicuousness for most workers. "Workers generally want to live without opposing or protesting things [*sakarawazu ni*] because they know that they have to protect themselves. They want to sort of blend into the crowd and not to stand out in any way [*medatanai yō ni*]." Although the original conflict may have been caused by the bank, the owners, or the parent companies, it is the demonstrating workers who initiate the disturbance and participate in what most Universal workers felt to be embarrassing (*hazukashii*) and disreputable (*mittomonai*) be-havior.

FORM AND STYLE

Particular colors, sounds, and language characterize dem-onstrations and combine to suggest drama, conflict, strength, and de-termination. These, too, echo forms of activity more comfortable for younger workers and for men. The demonstration is bright red, blue, yellow, green. It is lively, even noisy, and it involves being lively and noisy in public. It is imperative in language. Red as a color for demonstration headbands, chest signs, banners, and other paraphernalia, including individual union flags, is associated with left-wing political ideology. Everyone is aware of this association, and no one whom I asked failed to get to this eventually, if pressed. In daily conversations workers talked about their flags and other symbols as bright (*akarui*), good-looking (*kakkō ii*), and beautiful (*kirei*). Most assumed that these were the colors of labor unions everywhere and were surprised to hear that red was not in such widespread use in American unions. When the flags and banners decorate the shop and factory property, thus remaining within the boundaries of the workplace, people of all ages use these adjectives and seem happy with the colorful touch. When, however, they are taken into demonstrations, onto the street, older workers lamented the way red "sticks out" (*medatsu*) and calls attention to them, and they talked of the embarrassment of marching in public wearing headbands and signs in bright red. As with feelings of hesitation in being dramatic about conflict in general, red is objectionable in this context largely because it "sticks out," and thus those wearing or carrying it "stick out" too. This is very uncomfortable for many.

Colors, especially for personal wear, are rather well-segregated by age among the Unikon and Universal workers, as they are in Japanese society as a whole. It is uncommon for middle-aged people to wear bright colors or even softer shades of red. Subtlety in the shades of color you wear is appreciated and associated with growing up and gaining poise. Colors worn at demonstrations are otherwise worn primarily by children and young people through perhaps their twenties. There are exceptions, but the exceptions are generally people who want to be noticed. There was one such woman at Universal, who occasionally dressed in brighter colors and was criticized for her flair and for "not dressing her age."

Red is also a color for festivals and celebrations of all kinds. It has a very positive connotation in that context; there, red and other bright colors are for everyone. Young Unikon workers often described their demonstrations to me as "festival-like" (*omatsuri mitai*) and told me they went "half for the fun of it" (*asobi hanbun*). Universal workers never used this kind of description and older Unikon workers just laughed when their "young people" made such comments.

The noisy and physically active forms of the demonstration similarly challenge older workers and women while being fun (*tanoshii*) for some of the young men. Marching, fist raising, chanting, singing, and sitting in as protest are all physical activities performed in public and as such are felt to be inappropriate and uncomfortable by many. Again, age and gender intersect with personality to determine the degree of discomfort and ease of adaptation. Vigorous physical exercise, including dancing, is widely considered "healthy" and "youthful." Noise, too, is the privilege of the young. As such, these kinds of activities are tolerated and even appreciated by older adults. When selecting coffee shops for after-work gatherings with Universal workers, for instance, those where "students" and "young people" gather are dismissed with a smile as noisy (*urusai*).

Festivals and drinking parties, however, provide contexts in which all of these things are appropriate for all ages. Workers' parties are both noisy and involve a lot of moving around and dancing. They are not, however, held in public, where the noise could be considered a nuisance or where strangers could observe. When held in relatively public places, even parties are more subdued than when held in private, on the workplace premises, for instance. Festivals do not seem, for older workers, to be like demonstrations. The nature of the noise and the more structured form of the dancing are sanctioned by tradition and as such are suitable for public behavior. It is an interesting comment on the generational differences in the meaning of festivals and of demonstrations as contexts for behavior that while older people found the two so different, the young readily associated them.

Finally, the style of the demonstration is also constituted by its language, which emphasizes polarization and antagonism. While in fact the leaders are usually inside negotiating or at least talking about the need to negotiate, the speeches outside are inflammatory and uncompromising, serving to dramatize the conflict as extreme. While rank and file may find it reasonable to fight with the intention of discussion and cooperation, they find it difficult to participate in the stark and harsh discourse of the demonstration. Again, older workers find this more difficult, corresponding to the assumption that maturity develops with increasingly subtle and sensitive abilities and uses of language. Allowances are made for young people not appreciating subtlety and indirect forms of communication. It is easier to make sense, therefore, of youth participating in the harshly worded discourse of the demonstration.

Participation in these demonstrations was a challenge not only to ideas about protest or labor movement struggles, but to the sense of appropriate behavior and individual strength of character and maturity. The young men at Unikon frankly admitted that they enjoyed finding an outlet for their frustrations, an alternative to the daily necessity of controlling it, and they claimed that afterwards there was a feeling of being refreshed (*sukkiri suru*). Some even called it interesting and exciting (*omoshiroi*) or a chance to vent anger (*ikari o hassan suru*). In the cultural field of Japan, forms of activity characterized by color, noise, public physical action, and imperative language are associated for young people with being healthy, strong, vital, or simply appropriately childish or immature. For adults, and particularly adult women, they are more likely to be considered inappropriately lacking in poise (*ochitsuki ga nai*), even disgraceful (*mittomonai*).

Middle-aged and older workers at Universal prided themselves on being restrained and calm (*ochitsuite iru*). Before and after the event, they spoke of hesitating to "put on that chest sign" and "march around in public," and immediately following their demonstration they spoke of getting all worked up (*kōfun shichatta*) with a sense of embarrassment. Workers got used to demonstrations at different paces, depending on their age, gender, and personality. Middle-aged women at Unikon spoke of "getting used to it" by "following our young men." Overall, union leaders and rank and file assumed that it was easier for younger workers and for male workers to do so for precisely these reasons. It was, consequently, no surprise to leaders or to rank-and-file workers that Universal, with its configuration of older men and middle-aged women, had a lot to "get used to."

Being Workers

The intensity of emotions aroused during the demonstration motivated Universal workers to reflect on and attempt to interpret their own role in this event and in the labor movement. Amid the discomfort, excitement, even confusion of their own participation in the action, workers were faced with the explicit arguments made in speeches, signs, and chants and with implicit messages about themselves and their relationships to other workers as participants in the same event. The emotions of the event inspired more intense reflection than usual in daily life, but at the same time threatened to be exceptional unless repeated.

One of the most moving and inspiring experiences of the demonstration for Universal workers was of the social relations between themselves as workers at Universal and other workers from all over Tokyo. In previous union actions Universal workers had come into contact with small groups of workers from supporting unions, with federation officials coming to support them, or with the workers of Custom Shoes. This was the first time, however, they had encountered thousands of workers engaged in disputes as they were and committed not only to fighting similar struggles but also to helping Universal with theirs. Reports read in the news media or heard at union meetings were for the first time felt as personal experiences, and the impact was quite powerful.

Universal workers entered this demonstration, with all their apprehensions and lack of experience, knowing quite explicitly that they were workers. They used a variety of expressions to refer to this part of their identities, words like *rōdōsha,* with the connotation of worker versus capital, and *hataraku hito,* with a less political nuance of "working people." What this demonstration inspired was reassessment of their place in a broader set of relationships, experienced personally in these dimensions for the first time. Being in the Tōkyō Sōgi Kōdō organization, being there with unions of varying power or prestige, with greater or lesser numbers of women and older workers, and being from factories on the outskirts of Tokyo, all placed them in a particular location in a network of workers with whom they could share this protest action and with whom they could to some degree identify.

The word *rōdōsha* itself was understood and used in union events and pamphlets, but had not been a common one in everyday conversation at Universal. Following the demonstration, however, people spoke of themselves and of their union and of the labor movement using *rōdōsha* with renewed meaning and a new frequency. This experience had a dramatic effect on their perception of themselves as workers and of their union's struggle. The inhibited and apprehensive spirit in which people walked to the train the morning of the demonstration, worrying about being laughed at because of their small numbers and weak position, recalled their dispute's history. Universal's rank and file had felt they had been fighting essentially alone, even after four years of continued struggle. The cooperation and support of affiliated unions had been known and representatives had visited Universal, but it had not been experienced in such a direct way before this demonstration. The following day, and even more noticeably in the evening after the demonstration, people were in high spirits, encouraged, and talking at length about how much they had learned, about how surprised they were at the numbers of people joining in the demonstration. The leaflets which came by on the day after were given a new perusal quite different from the more matter-of-fact glance I had become accustomed to in previous months. They even encouraged some generalization and comment about the common weakness of workers and the importance of sticking together. One Universal participant remarked with a sense of newly gained understanding, "Workers have to get together and act with each other's support. . . . Workers alone just can't get anywhere, we are too weak."

While on the one hand reinforcing their identification of themselves as workers, or *rōdōsha*,[1] the demonstration also reminded workers of their particular place in the broad spectrum of workers, workplaces, and circumstances. They came away with a renewed sense of the specific relationships tying their particular union to other particular unions and with additional appreciation of the differences and inequalities between theirs and the others.

For all the sharing of a common language in organizing the demonstration around brightly colored and directly worded statements and for all the similarities in attire and form, there are extensive and explicit differentiations just as obvious to the participants. Each union, of course, marches with its own flag and with its own banners. This, rather than, for example, marching with common slogans and common banners, sets unions apart from each other and effectively demarcates them. Attire is also differentiated by union. Some unions come wearing their company uniforms or a company product, as is the case for one jacket producer, for example. The effect of this union-by-union differentiation is to make it very easy to spot other unions, judge their size, their overall spirit, their age and gender composition, and read their particular grievances. The next step, comparing theirs with one's own, is hard to resist. Small unions like Universal and Unikon come away with even stronger feelings of weakness and inferiority after comparing their union to others. So it was that Universal people commented on the size, youth, and male composition, and Unikon people on the size and male composition, of so many of the other unions. There are very few smaller than Universal and not many smaller than Unikon. But those too were spotted and talked about later. The even tinier ones made people feel that "it could be worse" (*Yunibāsaru wa mada ii hō*), and the bigger ones and younger ones made them feel that just maybe they were wasting their time. "See, Universal *is* tiny! Did you see the number of people from that union? And they were so much younger. There's just no comparison. [*Yappari,*

---

1. For a discussion of the ways in which demonstrations reinforce universalistic notions of worker identity, see chapter 2.

Yunibāsaru wa chiisai! Ano kumiai no ninzū o mita ka? Wakai shi . . . mō kanawan.]"

BEING PART OF TŌKYŌ SŌGI KŌDŌ

The Tōkyō Sōgi Kōdō organization, while a statement about shared conditions, is at the same time about the particularity of workers' consciousness. It is not an organization which brings workers from any and all sympathetic unions out to demonstrate on behalf of other troubled unions. It is an organization of unions involved in disputes, and they gradually fade out of the organization after their dispute is settled and they have "paid their debt" by participating after their own settlement as a gesture of gratitude. Of course, they never get involved in the first place unless their union is having a fairly serious problem in negotiating, and consequently it sets workers in disputes off from those in what they call normal companies (*futsū no kaisha*) and develops in them a kind of reluctance to be around workers from these "ordinary unions." May Day demonstrations are an example of this kind of reluctance.

Universal workers expressed mixed emotions about the upcoming May Day, which has evolved now into a demonstration in the nature of a celebration, with marches but no political actions of any kind. Unikon people expressed relief that, at the first May Day after their settlement, they could go with a light-hearted feeling (*akarui kimochi de*) because their chest signs would not proclaim them to be from a bankrupt company. A Universal worker expressed his reluctance this way:

I like the May Day demonstrations. They are even fun, with everyone getting together and marching under bright flags through those nice areas of the city, and starting from the beautiful Yoyogi Park. But it just isn't the same when you have to put on that dreadful chest sign so everyone can read it and tell that you are from a bankrupted company, from a union fighting a long and drawn out struggle. You don't want to advertise that fact, and it spoils the fun of going.

There you are with thousands of people from ordinary companies, and . . . I don't know, I just don't feel like going again this year.

While providing an important avenue for unity and strength, the Tōkyō Sōgi Kōdō demonstrations also give solid expression to the differentiation between workers who are involved in the trials and tribulations of labor disputes and workers who are free of them. It adds fuel to the fire of embarrassment and isolation felt by participants from unions which are fighting difficult and sometimes losing battles.

The Tōkyō Sōgi Kōdō organization ties unions to one another by bonds of indebtedness. Each union is indebted to (*osewa ni natteru* or *on o uketeru*) Tōkyō Sōgi Kōdō as a whole, but they are also indebted to several other unions in particular. These particular debts are less emphasized than the general debt at the demonstrations, but they play a part even there. The general debt to Tōkyō Sōgi Kōdō was responsible for Unikon's presence at the demonstration described in chapter 2, after their own settlement was all but concluded. They spoke and even joked about being indebted to Tōkyō Sōgi Kōdō, bowing and laughing and in general caricaturing various Japanese ways of expressing humble gratitude. And to the Universal demonstration described above, Unikon sent four members, because these two unions had very close ties and Unikon was indebted to Universal for inspiring its own struggle and for lending support of various kinds.

There is in this act the expression of the *on*, or reciprocal indebtedness, felt to be a defining characteristic of the relationships between unions, both for Unikon and for Universal. This indebtedness, the exchange of services, financial help, advice, and sentiment that characterizes the relationship, creates a debt which cannot, for instance, be repaid by simply joining in a demonstration for yet another union, or even by participation in the Sōkōdō demonstrations as a whole. It is the nature of these relationships to be independent in this sense. So Unikon must show its gratitude and give its support to Universal in particular. This kind of orientation is of course responsible for creating a certain specific constellation of participants at every demonstration stop on the route of the Sōkōdō marches, and it works against the participating workers feeling an unambiguous universalistic identity as workers, and encourages instead a sense of oneself as both a worker (*rōdōsha*) and at the same time as a worker of a certain company and of a union with specific characteristics, problems, and friends or allies.

BEING POWERFUL OR WEAK AS A UNION

The demonstration highlights the struggle between capital and labor.[2] It reminds workers of language otherwise uncommon in

2. See chapter 2 for a discussion of ways in which capital and labor were conceptualized in the demonstration and by Unikon workers. The categories and their usage in conversation were the same for Universal workers.

daily speech. Universal workers spoke of "capitalists" during this event and commented, with discouraged emotions, about the relative weakness of their union compared with the strength of Tōyō Bank. For instance, "What we're up against is capitalists! [*Aite wa shihonka da yo!*]" The tone of voice used by Nakada-san when he said this was, "Can't you see how difficult this is going to be?" After the Universal demonstration, as we walked away from Tōyō Bank and toward the next site, Michiko-san commented, "They don't need us. What can it possibly matter to them if Universal ceases to exist? Custom doesn't need our production capacity, and Tōyō Bank would be happy to be rid of us." The stark way in which demonstrations place labor against capital highlights the necessity of strength for the weaker side, the workers and their unions.

This does, on the one hand, emphasize the need for unity and solidarity, but it also impresses people with the differences between unions as well. Some unions have more political clout than others, they end their disputes more quickly and seem to have better leadership, better connections to powerful union federations, and better political strategies. The successful examples are repeatedly called to everyone's attention in demonstration speeches. Unikon was one such example. Unikon's struggle ended in a comparatively quick two and a half years, and it ended successfully. At several stops in the Sōkōdō demonstration which I attended with them right after their victory and again in one about six months later, Unikon was mentioned as an example to be studied and from which lessons could be drawn and which might serve as an inspiration. They were well respected by other unions, and the membership of Universal often spoke of them admiringly.

Because these two unions knew one another both through membership in their regional federation and in dispute-related organizations, and because they had been watching one another for lessons on strategies that might work, they had a special relationship to one another. There was nearly always a two-dimensional discussion when Unikon's name came up at Universal. On the one hand, workers felt a sense of encouragement in their victory in a situation very much like their own. On the other, the inevitable comparison of the two unions made Universal people wary. "Unikon has so much better leadership than we do." "They are so much younger and stronger." "They don't have so many old people." "Their federation is strong." "They didn't have the same kind of enemy as we do—they weren't a subcontracting company, so they only had to fight their previous owners, who had already gone bankrupt. We have to fight the strong Custom Shoe Company!"

Both the strengths and the weaknesses of other unions and of one's own become more obvious and more open to comparison in the context of the demonstration. More than other actions, this event dramatized the necessity and the purpose of strength. It did so by dramatizing the relationship between the unions and the financial institutions which back their companies. Were the unions and these institutions equals, the workers would be negotiating instead of demonstrating. And indeed it is negotiation which is the first aim of the demonstration. The Sōkōdō demonstrations, once negotiations are underway, are tamer by far than the initial Universal demonstration was. People commented afterwards that it was an exceptionally aggressive one and that Tōyō Bank had been particularly stubborn. The speculation was that they just did not expect such a "weak" union to be able to make such a fuss, and as a matter of fact, neither did the Universal workers prior to their experience. Their perception of the political strength of the institutions was heightened. Their perception of their own individual union's political weakness was recalled, but at the same time transformed by a new experience of unity and strength deriving from a much larger collective action.

BEING MORE FEMALE AND OLDER

The ratio of women and older men to young and middle-aged men in a union is considered to be a measure of both political strength and determination. At Universal, it was an often-repeated refrain that they were not taken seriously because they were too heavily female and elderly. At the younger but over half female Unikon, comments took the form of, "You aren't going to believe this, but our women are really something else! Even the middle-aged women [part-timers] are really energetic and committed [isshōkenmei]."

Universal and Unikon looked at themselves very differently, but used essentially the same criteria for evaluating their own strength and prestige. Unikon was at an advantage because their only drawback was the number of women, and "even" the older women were complimented for being committed. Age was clearly considered a liability when entering a struggle. Where Unikon built its pride around achieving success in spite of the high proportion of women, or because older women (in their forties and early fifties) were "really young," Universal saw itself as somewhat "unpresentable" because of the predominance of the elderly and of women. The "unpresentable" feeling was overcome to a large degree in the course of participation, lessened by the overwhelming reception and support given their union by thousands of fellow workers from a variety of other unions. People came away feeling visibly better about themselves. Nevertheless, for both Unikon and Universal the presence of a lot of women, part-timers, and/or elderly people was a liability to be overcome.

The dependent status of older people and of women is assumed as common sense, and the agenda of a labor dispute is aggressive fighting, requiring sacrifice, determination, and assertive acts. Women and older men are not considered suited for such action, so some kind of special care must be taken to form a collective action with such a work force. The proportion of women and older men at Universal was cited by some leaders as one of the reasons that demonstrations had been postponed for the first three and a half years of their struggle. Some had feared that their rank and file were not suited to such actions and might not be able to carry them out with the necessary commitment and strength.

These concerns reflect employment categories for women and older men as well. The logic motivating fears about adequate union commitment and action is quite similar to the logic motivating the employment categories for these people. The shorter assignments of participation in the demonstration reinforced both the separation of rank and file into these categories and the assumption that women and older men had less strength physically, less commitment, and a less significant role. This assumption of both physical weakness and lower levels of responsibility, dedication, and status on the part of women and older men was a sensitive issue within the union and at the same time contributed to its difficulties in creating an image of strength, solidarity, and determination externally in fighting its dispute.

BEING PROUD OF THE UNION

Related to images of economic or political strength are feelings of pride, but pride—or its absence—was often expressed in other contexts as well. Workers talked about everything from the kinds of services rendered or products manufactured to the attractiveness and creativity of the demonstrations prepared.

Unikon workers, for instance, were very proud of the fact that they produced cameras. They sometimes used signs at demonstrations in the shape of cameras. They once put a huge cardboard camera on top of the Unikon car which accompanied them to demonstrations and marches. A closely affiliated union whose workers manufactured jackets similarly claimed a certain prestige because of the good-looking jackets they produced, and they made a point of wearing them—all in the same color—to demonstrations, replacing chest signs with arm bands. For both cameras and jackets, status was derived in part from the product being modern and youth-oriented. In the case of cameras, additional pride was taken in the fact that they required a very high level of technology to produce. Universal, in contrast, never used shoes in this way. Shoemaking is an old industry and requires little technology. It is ironic that, in suggesting I go to Universal, Unikon workers had emphasized the greater skills and craftsmanship of the Universal workers. Where it takes only a few weeks to master most of the jobs at the camera factory, it is said to take eight to ten years to become a skilled shoemaker. The contemporary cultural field of Japan, however, inclines in the direction of "high-tech," youthful images. Their product is further removed from this ideal by being conservative leather shoes marketed primarily toward middle-aged men.

Pride also comes through in a good-natured competition concerning the attractiveness and originality of the paraphernalia and other signs of the effort of the membership in putting together a good demonstration contingent. Universal was recording their demonstration for their own movie. Unikon was very proud of their sometimes unconventional demonstration tactics and props, had them recorded on film, and had a lot of fun showing them off, recalling special signs, slogans, and actions which drew attention and were even copied by other unions. Before one of their demonstrations, one young man claimed proudly, "Unikon might be small, but we aren't going to be outdone by the bigger unions!" My participation in a demonstration with them was heralded with self-conscious enthusiasm: "Wait until they see our contingent this time! They're going to say, 'Unikon has done it again, a foreigner! You never know what they are going to come up with next.'"

Similar thoughts were expressed, but much less enthusiastically, at Universal, where the experience was dampened by the uncertainty of demonstrating for the first time. The concern with being dressed well, with "looking involved" even if you were not feeling enthusiastic, and with not making an obvious exit when leaving to go home all showed a concern with making a good impression. As one of the leaders put it at the evening meeting before the event, "Look at all these signs we're painting. And we have headbands and chest signs coming all printed up. It may take us the rest of the night finishing all the preparations, but we aren't going to be outdone [*makenai zo*]! We're going to put on a good show."

Attractiveness and originality are related intimately to evaluation of effort. And it is really the effort (*doryoku*) which is being evaluated implicitly as well as in the more explicit calls for at least the semblance of enthusiasm on the part of participants.

BEING FROM ACROSS THE RIVER

The demonstration brings people face to face with the unequal prestige of the different sections of Tokyo. Workers are so predominantly living and working "across the river" in the eastern sections of Tokyo that on demonstration days, both for Tōkyō Sōgi Kōdō and for May Day, the trains coming in from the east to downtown Tokyo are actually packed in the rush-hour fashion, crowded with workers and the equipment needed for the demonstrations. These districts are relatively low in overall prestige, and the ward governments of Eastern Tokyo are forever trying to improve the images of their areas to attract residents of, as they put it, "better quality," like "white-collar workers" and "people of better educational background." And these people worry about their areas having too many tiny companies, not enough modern fast-food restaurants, and generally being "backward."

There is a *shitamachi* or "old Tokyo" image which counterbalances this "backward" image and gives it fair competition in the evaluation of the areas in which the Universal and Unikon people lived and worked. For some the *shitamachi* image meant warmth, fellowship, tradition, closely knit neighborhoods, and a colorful though modest life-style. But even so, that image could not be very well maintained by the majority of workers, especially younger workers at Unikon, because they were living in low-cost government housing projects which give them few of the positive aspects of the old-Tokyo-style neighborhoods. Even for those older workers who were born and raised in this area, there was a kind of complex about the "backward" nature of their life-styles and the often rundown look of the neighborhoods. So while perhaps even preferring to live in this area, they also recognized their life-style and their area as being of lower status. One Unikon worker raised her eyebrows and lowered her voice a bit to tell me that her sister lived in a certain more prestigious western suburb of Tokyo. This was followed by a discussion of how conceited people were "over there" and how much more fun it was to live in the older neighborhoods of eastern Tokyo. There was no doubt, however, that enjoying life here did not increase its status vis-à-vis the western suburbs.

The areas where demonstrations and marches take place are without exception high-status areas, and demonstrations thus occasion a great deal of sighing and some wishful thinking. Some older women hoped for their children to be able to get jobs in the banks "around here," and people talked about cousins or friends' children who had jobs in a "building just like this one somewhere near here."

Opposition, Responsibility, and Human Life

The ideological and emotional power of the event prejudiced the conversations for the participants by placing them in an assertive role, arguing through their actions for a particular perspective and feeling through their participation a particular set of relationships between themselves and other workers on the one hand and between themselves and capitalist institutions on the other. Universal rank and file found themselves in an oppositional place of stark contrasts between capital and labor. Capital was represented in this action by imposing buildings, labor by thousands of supportive workers. Images of "small" and "large" stood out visually and verbally and began to take on power through their ability to stand for a variety of inequalities and implied injustices. The metaphor of size encompassed economic inequalities, as in such statements as, "Capitalists are so big, and workers are just little [*Shihonka wa dekkai shi, rōdōsha wa chiisai*]" or "Capitalists are so big, what do they care about little human beings [*Anna dekkai shihonka ni wa, oretachi mitai ni chippoke na ningen wa dōdemo iin da*]." Comparisons were made between big companies and small companies and between big labor unions and small ones, and words like "small" (*chiisai*) and "tiny" (*reisai*) were used to express both despair about one's own status and feelings of powerlessness. The actual size of a person, union, or company was, of course, not the point. Rather, the status, social position, or perhaps reputation was at stake. The demonstration not only provided a very direct experience of this distinction but reinforced it in signs like "Big Capital! Stop destroying small and medium-sized companies! [*Ōte Shihon! Chūshō tsubushi o yamero!*]" The setting for the demonstrations, putting people, however numerous, in front of enormous towering buildings of concrete, steel, and glass, gave rise to a great deal of big versus small commentary, all serving to reinforce the image.

If size was a primary way of conceptualizing inequalities, "responsibility" (*sekinin*) was central to the representation of related incidents of injustice that motivated the demonstrations and struggles. "Responsibility" was dramatized and recalled in the most emotionally arousing actions of the demonstration. The word's power stemmed at least in part from its ability to cross the boundaries of a number of different contexts, integrating valued forms of relating people to one another, ways of relating in "human" ways. People felt very deeply about taking, fulfilling, and shirking responsibility.

It was used on the one hand to mean a legal or contractual responsibility, a specific promise or obligation. Banks were told, for instance, to take responsibility for Universal's bankruptcy (*Yunibāsaru no tōsan no sekinin o tore!*) and speeches elaborated on this, saying that the banks deliberately put these workers out of jobs for their own financial gain. Similarly, they and Custom were accused of planning bankruptcies to break the union, and speakers cited the Labor Standards laws giving workers a right to organize. In this way, workers used responsibility to demand compensation, assign blame for quasi-illegal acts, and insist on the "social responsibility" of financial institutions to uphold specific laws and practices and the spirit of the workers' "right to livelihood."

"Responsibility" also resonates across many contexts to symbolize the appropriate care for one's own work or task and for those with whom one works, as well as for one's own role in furthering the fortunes of the organization as a whole. Thus it evokes images of individual commitment, egalitarian, horizontal working relationships, and integration of individuals into a workplace community. It also recalls the appropriate caring attitude of those on top of an organizational hierarchy toward those below, or of the strong toward the weak, the large toward the small. It draws, therefore, on traditional concepts like obligation (*giri*) and human feeling (*ninjō*), as well as on contemporary notions of cooperation, equality, and democracy. It is in this sense that at demonstrations banks were told to "take responsibility for Universal's workers!" These echoed as well the daily use of the term, giving it more in common with a diffuse notion of expected good will within a relationship than with specific duties. In daily usage it has the sense of caring for or looking after an individual or a group of people. Used in union activities it lends a sense of an almost paternalistic expectation considered appropriate and desirable to these workers.[3] The terminology of "parent company" further reinforces this sense in Universal's case.

---

3. For an historical interpretation of paternalism and labor movement ideology and practice, see Smith 1988.

While the more specific legal or contractual sense of the word explains its wide use in slogans, it is the more implicit and diffuse one which lends much of its affective power to inspire participants. It was while shouting "take responsibility" to the seemingly "inhuman" and insensitive bank representative and seeing his continued intransigence before their pleas for understanding (*oretachi no tachiba mo wakatte hoshii*), sincerity, and basic human treatment (*ningen to shite tōzen no yarikata*), that the protesters at the Universal demonstration got most keyed up. And it was following that, walking away, that their disgusted and by then edgy and tense voices complained to each other about the inability of capitalists to treat workers as human beings, about their insensitivity to the lives and needs of workers, and of the necessity for workers to fight together.

The power of this word to symbolize the problem with things as they are and at the same time a view of how things might otherwise be makes it a very important expression. It evokes both, on the one hand, the necessity of living up to negotiated promises, agreements, and laws that hold in check the tensions recognized as inherent in class relations, and on the other hand, the basic sense of appropriate norms of human relationships (including relationships of hierarchy), which people feel should be characterized by consideration, respect for individual circumstances, and compassion.

It manages to combine clear-cut obligations and general, affectively convincing notions of human feeling and caring. The most common use, in fact, is in expressions like, "Tōyō Bank! Take responsibility!" This usage encourages a unity, or at least a coexistence, of these two very different dimensions, effectively making the notion of legal responsibility and obligation more familiar and convincing through its link with the commonsensical and affectively convincing idea of considerate, paternalistic care expected or at least desired by workers from their owners and others above them in hierarchical relationships.

Changing Minds and Getting Used to Actions

Throughout the next several months there were no more demonstrations for the Universal workers. When one was finally announced, workers voiced, to my surprise, hesitations and apprehensions similar to those expressed prior to the first one. When I reminded the people I worked with that they had said they would not mind next time, that they had realized what an important and vital aspect of the labor movement and of their own struggle this was, they said, "Really, did I say that?" I laughed and offered to show them my notes. Then we discussed it, and they said that they had forgotten but, come to think of it, they were a little less reluctant this time. They still did not, however, like the idea of "parading around the financial district wearing those awful things [chest signs and headbands]."

After this second outing, the demonstrations continued at the rate of about one per month, and after half a year or so workers simply sighed about cold in winter and heat in summer and went. They were doing, they said by then, what was "necessary" and did not think much about it anymore. They were "used to it now."

In the course of the demonstration, participants learned to talk more explicitly about themselves as *rōdōsha,* or workers. They also began to learn to feel and to perceive themselves as part of the labor movement. Certain inequalities became increasingly visible, attention being drawn to them both explicitly and implicitly, and the inevitability of open conflict became more evident to them. At the same time, however, their conversation was filled with references to how distinct they were, how unique their plight, how peculiarly hopeless or difficult their struggle. They exchanged discouraged feelings about inequality and the futility of fighting. And they continued to get emotionally distressed about the lack of human feeling on the part of Custom, which was at the root of their commitment to their struggles. All these more-or-less new or reconsidered thoughts had their own patterns of use and neglect. Just as people forgot that they weren't going to mind demonstrating anymore, by the time of the second demonstration they had also forgotten some of the inspired ways of connecting themselves to other workers and to the labor movement. The power of these events is in the juxtaposition of participation, emotion, and reflection. The difficulty of making new insights and feelings lasting elements of consciousness lies in the exceptional nature of the action and the powerful inertia of the routines of daily life. As the demonstrations became more common the insights and feelings took hold more solidly, a process evidenced as well in the Unikon workers' experience in learning to protest.

Demonstrations were among the most intense events in which the Universal workers participated. They were moving, all-encompassing, clearly bounded events in which some of the most important aspects of their social lives and identities were involved. And they occasioned lengthy reflection on identity, inequality, injustice, and open conflict. That the resolution was not complete, their world views neat and wholly integrated or their understandings of good social relations entirely consistent, was both the strength and the weakness of these events. Workers felt that conflict was "inevitable" between themselves and "capitalists," but at the same time they admitted strong "anger" and "betrayal" when treated badly by them. While common identities with other workers were emphasized, Universal workers sometimes felt hopelessly bounded by their own small company, union, and concerns.

I never heard people try to reconcile the often divergent and sometimes conflicting understandings of themselves and their struggle. Notions of almost paternalistic consideration lived with assumptions of conflictual labor relations, the inevitability of mistreatment by owners and "capital" hovered just beside the expectation of consideration. Furthermore, their sense of the advisability of demonstrating and their feelings about participating were, for most, left similarly "unresolved." What helped people change their minds about participating did not necessarily succeed in changing their feelings about it.

It provided a context in which issues of enduring importance were argued. As such it moved people; it nudged them toward change. It provided a coincidence of action and idea, of shared thoughts and shared feelings; it tried to argue for a politically active, well-organized, and class-conscious union response to injustice in the workplace. Through the participants, wittingly and unwittingly, themes of enduring importance to the ethos and affective climate of labor relations and of the workplace were also present. Most workers felt, at least at first, reluctance to make a spectacle of themselves, to stir up even temporary disorder. They preferred to persist resolutely in adversity rather than to demand change and clung to desires to work together, cooperatively, under the skillful, considerate, and protective guidance of good ownership and management. Most workers in these demonstrations wanted, in short, a more subtle dialogue. It was a task of labor union leaders to encourage and strategically incorporate these reluctant and hesitant workers into actions which might change their orientation. Others, however, found the demonstrations exhilarating, exciting, and even fun. Youth and male gender eased the process of learning to protest, but the education and experience of union activities was effective in helping most workers "get used to it," if not become enthusiastic and wholly convinced.

The consciousness of the Universal workers was as complex as their various responses to their own collective actions. If they could not have the subtle dialogue most preferred, they did learn to engage in open conflict, of which the demonstration came to constitute the most dramatic and challenging form. They had ways of understanding and explaining adversity and antagonism, inequality and injustice, but these had not replaced completely their notions of how things might otherwise be. In the tenacity with which they held to such diverse and varying explanations and assumptions about their social world lay much of their ability to adapt to the rapidly changing circumstances of their workplaces.

Some thoughts, like the actions with which they were associated, were more "gotten used to" than realized in a successful argument or a sudden insight. People became workers through acting as workers; they became protesters through acting as protesters. Thoughts about their identity as workers, their relationships with other workers, the injustices inspiring their demonstration, and their own role in protesting grew on these Universal workers as they acted and reflected, the two processes being inseparably interwoven in their experience.

CHAPTER 7

Working as Protest

Dignity, Routine, and Daily Life

Over my desk hangs a poster made by Universal to paste
on telephone poles, fences, and neighborhood kiosks and to mail out to
affiliated unions all over Tokyo to advertise one of their "Factory Festivals" (Kōjōsai). Covering about three-fourths of it is a black-and-white
photograph of Kanda-san, the head of the cutting and sewing section
where I worked. Oblivious to the camera, he is concentrating over his
sewing machine, running leather under the needle as he did six days a
week all day long for most of the forty-plus years of his career. Over
Kanda-san's image is a bold diagonal banner of words reading "Our
sweat is glistening." A subtitle underneath announces the "Factory
Festival of Working Friends" (Hataraku Nakama no Kōjōsai). Under it
are cheerful, blue line drawings of four children, two men, a woman,
some goldfish, a balloon, two carrots, four potatoes, three daikon radishes, and four musical notes singing over them all.

What happens between meetings, demonstrations, trips, and pam-
phleting has mostly to do with concentration on work, with the production of shoes, with families, balloons, and radishes, and—on good
days—with music. This chapter is about daily life in its routine forms,
its meaning for Universal's protest, and its celebration of the commonsense world of being human. It is about repetitive and routine ways in
which objects, families, and dense networks of "working friends" were
created and represented. In an unexamined and taken-for-granted way,
the routines of daily life provided the counterpoint to the special events
and collective actions of their ten-year struggle. It was cultural practice
without the argument, the grounding for the occasional stirred-up emo-

tions, and an important source of assumptions about what was natural, desirable, inevitable, or real. Because it was what people did most of the time it had the pervasive power of common sense. Daily work routines were what people returned to following demonstrations. The shop floor was where disagreements and complaints were expressed and debated following meetings during which rank and file remained silent. In the sewing, cutting, gluing, polishing, and packaging of shoes, people practiced their crafts and felt their own skill. The repetition and continuity through time wove routines of familiarity, association, and consciousness which sustained this struggle through the union's fight with Custom and Tōyō Bank and through the internal dissonance which periodically plagued their own struggle for a coherent solidarity.

Sharing Time and Space

Daily work routines were at once goal, strategy, and substance of daily life throughout the Universal dispute. The objective of their worker-control struggle was to secure their continued daily practice of coming to work at the Universal factory. To achieve that goal, union leaders saw the persistence of daily work routines as critical to their strategy. At the factory festival mentioned above, one of the lawyers representing Universal praised the "perseverance" of rank-and-file workers in their day-to-day maintenance of factory operations as the most important factor pushing them toward victory. A powerful and tenacious image was thought to be crucial to forcing their parent company and the financial institutions backing them to take the small Universal union seriously enough to negotiate a settlement. In addition, keeping these routines going—literally sharing time and space on a daily basis—was seen by union leaders to be the minimum condition necessary to mobilize commitment for struggle.

To make ends meet immediately following bankruptcy, Universal leaders organized rank-and-file workers to make coin purses, train-pass holders, and leather covers for whiskey bottles (these covers looked like vests and hats, transforming the bottles into little cowboys). One purpose was to make a modest amount of income to tide them over until shoe production and sales could be organized by the union. The other purpose was to keep people together. Workers came to the factory and maintained the usual schedule in the usual place, but without making the usual objects. Leaders frankly claim that their struggle would never have gotten off the ground had they not convinced people to continue in this way. The story was the same at Unikon, where workers brought all their various types of piecework to the factory site at the same time and in their usual work places, to work on their disparate projects together. In their case they also pooled their accumulated money and divided it up according to original pay scales, maintaining the factory organization of labor time and approximate scales of wages. In discussion about decisions to stay and fight through their long struggle, rank-and-file workers consistently emphasized their feelings that they had been together all this time, so they couldn't quit while others stayed, or even that Universal was by now a "comfortable place to live."

The routine at Universal was a very usual one for small industry, with work beginning at 8:15 every morning and ending at 5:15 every evening. Overtime was not daily, but corresponded to special needs for money or production. In the morning everyone walked in through the open gates and punched in at a vintage time clock just outside the main office. The friendly morning greetings exchanged there turned into sex-segregated conversations as people split up to go change clothes at lockers upstairs behind the big meeting room. Unlike Unikon, Universal had no official uniforms, so everyone brought comfortable, older clothes and shoes to change into at work. In winter there were multiple layers of cotton underwear, nylon stockings, wool sweaters, and little hot-water bottles tied into scarves or sashes worn next to the body for warmth. Everyone wore much nicer, even slightly dressy clothes to commute to and from work, during which time they might stop at restaurants or shops. Not only was it nicer to be comfortable in clothes which could get soiled and were loose fitting for easy movement, but since buildings weren't heated or cooled, it was also important to adjust for weather. The buildings felt amazingly cold after working for a few hours sitting or standing still, and in winter people joked about how fat everyone looked all padded up to keep warm. This practice set a casual and relaxed tone to the workplace which clearly demarcated it from the outside world.

People tended to arrive at least fifteen or twenty minutes prior to their starting time. After changing clothes there were little gatherings around tea in each of the work areas where chatter about weather, families, and current events accompanied morning radio shows left on all through the day. By the time the bell rang at 8:15 everyone was ready to work. Work flowed smoothly and in patterns familiar to everyone. There were three breaks during the day. At 10:00 A.M. one of the women in each section would make tea and people would congregate around a small table for a few minutes before getting back to work. It was not a scheduled break with a bell but an informal one left up to workers on their own shop floors.

At noon a bell marked the lunch hour. As part of its effort to contribute to health and help family budgets, the Universal union had decided to serve a complementary hot lunch every day for all the workers. The whole factory was housed in very old buildings dating to prewar times. They were all wooden with old windows and hard earth floors. The cafeteria was a small room with windows on three sides and a tatami mat floor with several low tables to sit around. A big TV sat in the corner and was tuned to the public station's noon news broadcast. It began at noon and ended at exactly 12:15, which was, to my initial amazement, exactly the time everyone cleared out of the lunch room. I practiced with considerable effort and never managed to eat that fast. The lunch period lasted an hour, and the remaining forty-five minutes were filled with enjoyable things to do. Several men were growing a garden on land behind one of the buildings, and they would spend the rest of the time there, weeding, watering, and admiring the progress of their plants. At least two or three games of Japanese chess (*shōgi*) were always in progress, gathering onlookers when the contest came to a critical phase. Many workers sat and talked to one another, read newspapers or books, and relaxed indoors in winter and outdoors in hotter months. A large open space behind one of the buildings was adequate for modest games of catch, and some of the part-time women who lived close by bicycled home and back. Informal friendships complemented the structured sharing of work spaces and nurtured dense networks of association and community.

People shared the ups and downs in their energy and exhaustion over the course of the day. Afternoons usually saw more conversation, more commentary on radio programs, and some complaints about cold, heat, being tired, or things people needed to do after work. Complaints about being sleepy or about backaches or shoulder aches later in the day were common. Workers would massage each other during breaks and tease one another about getting old. The Universal workers had known each other for some ten to twenty years or more, so they had also watched each other age and overcome various physical problems. In the cutting and sewing section where I worked one of the women was suffering from hot flashes due to menopause. When she would begin to experience that discomfort others, including men, would ask her if she was all right, and someone would suggest she take a break and step outside if she needed to. One of the older men had high blood pressure, and in the winter when it was cold other workers would remind him to be careful and to come stand by the heater if he needed to warm up.

The third break of the day was for twenty minutes, beginning at 2:50 P.M. Everyone congregated in the largest open space where the head of the cutting section would place a portable radio-cassette player on the ground and put in a tape of calisthenics and music. Exercising was a great excuse for joking and playfulness, in that each person had their own style and level of enthusiasm, and fortunately no one seemed to mind getting teased about their imperfections of form as they tried to keep up with the voice on the tape. It was also the only time during the day that every worker, regardless of shop floor and section, did something together. In addition to the social aspect of this activity, people expressed appreciation for the physical relief from sitting or standing all day. Tea and sweets rewarded people back at their work areas following their exercise. This was the last break of the day, after which people worked through until 5:15. There were two bells at the end of the work day, one at 5:00 to signal the beginning of a fifteen-minute cleaning-up period and the last one at 5:15 at the end of quitting time. By the end of the day there were times when people would discover themselves all looking at the clock waiting for 5:00, and they would laugh and joke about their enthusiasm for working right up to the last possible moment. By the time the 5:15 bell rang, work areas were clean, and everyone was back into street clothes and—if their timing was just right—maybe even at the time clock ready to punch out. These little ups and downs formed the habits of working a very ordinary and accepted schedule.

This sharing of time and space doesn't take either much time or much space to write or read about. Its power lies in its repetition and in its association with ordinary, respectable human life. Nearly all Universal workers had worked this schedule for well over ten years, and had worked it together. It didn't change at the onset of their worker-control struggle. No one challenged it as the basis for efficient, productive work. Their protest actions interfered with it on occasion. Workers assigned to leaflet in mornings at Custom came to work a few minutes late. Demonstrations took from a half to a whole day away from work. Meetings and festivals required suspension of work routines for preparation. But for most days of most weeks of most months over several years the Universal workers had been sharing that factory space and the hours from 8:15 to 5:15 with one another. Routines like these were constitutive of fundamental ties of association, familiarity, and consciousness for them as workers and as workers in protest.

It is not easy to record the effect of daily life on consciousness. Workers didn't talk much about routines they were used to, although they were likely to complain when something interfered with them. These routines didn't receive any explicit attention until I started talking about them and about my experiences of them. That in itself elicited interesting commentary from people around me as they tried to explain things to me and to help me adjust. The process of settling in was for the most part comfortable and smooth. I felt constraints, however, around my own energy and time. The combination of evening note taking and daytime factory work left little time for other activities, including rest. I got sick from this schedule after a few weeks, and that brought unforeseen benefits in popularity and unsolicited advice. My reputation was permanently improved. Universal workers began to brag to outsiders, when they introduced me, that I worked so hard I got sick, but that "even then she didn't quit." Without any particular intention of doing so, I was beginning to build relationships with people by virtue of daily life habits and routines.

The advice I received sketched a picture of maturity, adulthood, and the value intrinsic to a work schedule. The first problem with me, Michiko-san explained with enormous sympathy, was that I was not yet a mature adult member of society (*shakaijin*) and consequently I was not used to the demands of the schedule. I still had too much looseness in my heart (*kokoro no yurumi*). When I got a real job and started receiving a paycheck that a family depended on, "things will change." The association of this work schedule with a full adult life in society is one of the most important assumptions motivating the antibankruptcy struggles. One observer of the Unikon and Universal struggles saw in the rank-and-file motivation the "human desire to labor." In my experience, these workers shared the simple notion that human beings must work, that perseverance and diligence is appropriate to that work, and that it is all tied to the support of a family. In this way the daily lives of their families are created by and given meaning by the schedule and the daily life of the workplace, and the work schedule is in turn given meaning through its creation of family life.

While it is inevitable that a description of daily workplace routine appear discrete, it is not lived outside of personal life. Days don't begin at 8:15 or end at 5:15. The recognition of the interlacing of home life and work life was apparent at all Universal parties, trips, and celebrations, through the direct involvement of family members. Meetings and collective actions recognized the links in speeches praising the patience, endurance, and support of families for the struggle and referring to the protection of family life as the underlying reason for workers to fight for their livelihood.

An important part of becoming a mature adult member of society was being "settled" into a schedule. That, people explained, came with getting used to the work and getting used to the people they were working with. Kanda-san reminded me often that it took at least ten years to learn this craft, and that nearly everyone at Universal had been making shoes for at least fifteen. Not being used to either the work or the people "uses more nerves" (*shinkei o tsukau*), and I would become less tired as I "got used to" the work, the place, and its people. The routines of work and of being together had a strong association with familiarity, relaxation, and comfort.

Making Things

The original reason Unikon leaders suggested I work at Universal for a while was their belief that the craftsmen at Universal would have significantly different consciousness than the Unikon workers. The differences I observed were more subtle than obvious, and the differences in the work people did were always contextualized by the similarities in the structuring of the day, the organization, the production process, and the union activities.

The most explicitly discussed difference had to do with wholeness. At Unikon workers sometimes referred to themselves as "just one part in a big machine" or talked about being "interchangeable." These were comments which arose, as did the feelings they expressed, in times of trouble and doubt, when workers felt their leaders were not taking them seriously enough or caring for their needs. The Unikon workers also joked at other times about how no one in the factory could put the whole camera together, because they only knew their own little part of it. Even the men who inspected the camera didn't know how to do each step of its assembly. The workers in the parts department were even more at sea in understanding where the tiny pieces they made would fit. Only the men who ground the lenses were considered to be "craftsmen," but even they could not see the whole camera. This aspect of their jobs was at once a subject for joking and for self-denigration. It also contributed to a hierarchy of prestige for the different sections of the company. The assembly workers were between the parts department "aunties," who were all part-time older women, and the lens department workers, who enjoyed the highest status.

At Universal I was assigned to the cutting and sewing section. Unlike Unikon where I could move about freely from one job to the next, learning in a couple of hours enough to do a respectable, though slow, job of assembly, at Universal there were very few places where I could work. The accepted wisdom was that it required ten years to become a shoemaker, and everyone at Universal, except for the six men who came from other unions to support the dispute, had worked at least that long, most at least twice that long. I was assigned to the sewing section because there I could glue leather together prior to its being sewn, a job which could be fixed should I make a mistake and which was extremely simple. Kanda-san, the head of this department, said that the definition of a craftsman was "someone who can make a whole thing." Kishi-san, the union president, went even farther, claiming that people who can make things start to finish have a very special feeling for objects. They care for things because they can see in them the efforts and skill of the workers who create them.

One difference in my own experiences at Unikon and Universal was in the things people wanted to teach me. At Unikon workers wanted to teach me their jobs, but very quickly they wanted to talk about other subjects. At Universal, throughout my participant observation work and later when I visited, I consistently had workers teaching me about shoes. There was a very strong pride and interest in the product they were making, and particularly in the process of making it. A very elderly worker bragged to me one day about his skill in inspecting the final shoes, showing me in great detail all the things he checked and explaining that since he knew how to make this shoe he knew how to make sure it was perfect. "I put myself in the place of the customer," he said, "and I wouldn't want a flaw in something I paid good money for." To demonstrate his particular care, he showed me as well how he wrapped the cleanly shined shoe in tissue so it wouldn't have a spot on it when the box was opened up. "This is the last time someone handles the shoes before they go to the customer," he teased, "so it's up to me to make everyone's work look good!" Kanda-san would talk to me for hours about how the leather should bend, how to sew along certain grains and not others, how to shape the cut and glued pieces just right while sewing.

One day he confessed that he couldn't tell me much about "consciousness" but he was confident that he could teach me anything I wanted to know about making shoes. Universal, on a daily and hourly basis, was permeated by this sense of skill, confidence, and pride in the quality of the products they were working on. The atmosphere at Unikon had, indeed, been different. People there worked quickly, and in evaluating their own skill they thought in terms more of quality and speed than of an expressed love for the process of making the cameras.

To convey what a day's routine was like is quite difficult. In describing the daily work schedule, the breaks, lunches, and starting and quitting times stand out because they are transition points and are thus relatively easy to describe. What constitutes most of the day's routine, however, is work, and work done standing and/or sitting in one spot. From 8:15 to 10:00 Universal workers were making shoes. From 10:10 to 12:00 they were making shoes. From 1:00 to 2:50 and from 3:10 to 5:00 they were making shoes. Making shoes is what they did most of the time every day. Most chapters in this book focus on particular incidents or special events and as such are much easier to write and, I would guess, to read as well. Events like demonstrations and meetings have clear structures of beginning, middle, end. The daily practice of work, on the other hand, has a structure which can be summed up in a few sentences, and a substance which would require pages of repetitive description.

Work doesn't happen for a couple of hours like a meeting, or once a month like a demonstration, or once every three months for two or three days like a trip. Work is the most continuous and repetitive practice in the daily lives of these workers. Minute after minute, hour after hour, day after day, week after week, month after month, year after year, the men and women doing these jobs follow their routines. And yet their working is never exactly the same. Kanda-san has been taking up bits of glued leather, molding them to form a three-dimensional shoe form, and running them under a sewing machine needle to stitch them together for nearly thirty years. At Unikon, the placement of the tiny black aperture part into the lens opening with long tweezers was unvarying for Suzuki-san, and had been for the twelve years she had worked on that assembly line. Their experiences of their work, however, were not the same on Saturday just before quitting time, facing a weekend off, as they were on Monday morning facing a full week of work ahead. Nor were they the same when there was a good conversation of gossip as when there was silence, or when there was an interesting game of chess waiting from the previous day's lunch as when there were no particular plans to

look forward to. It wasn't the same when the production targets had just
been raised as when one had just been met.

To convey what actions constitute daily routines of work at Unikon,
I might simply write something like this:

First she picks up the long tweezer, then with that she carefully takes a
¼" × ⅛" black aperture part from a small box filled with hundreds of these,
places it over a tiny silver peg and tips it at just the right angle so that it
overlaps the one before it just right. Then she picks up another ¼" × ⅛" black
aperture part from a small box filled with hundreds of these, places it over
a tiny silver peg and tips it at just the right angle so that it overlaps the one
before it just right. Then she picks up another ¼" × ⅛" black aperture part
from a small box filled with hundreds of these, places it over a tiny silver peg
and tips it at just the right angle so that it overlaps the one before it just right.
Then she picks up another ¼" × ⅛" black aperture part from a small box filled
with hundreds of these, places it over a tiny silver peg and tips it at just the
right angle so that it overlaps the one before it just right.

For each lens aperture, Suzuki-san put in fifty of these pieces. I have just
written about four of them. It would require about eight pages for me
to repeat that description fifty times. Suzuki-san does about five cameras
an hour, and that would take me forty pages to describe. An eight-hour
day would yield three hundred and twenty pages. A six-day week would
be nineteen hundred twenty pages. Suzuki-san has worked at this job for
about twelve years.

To convey in such a form what a Universal worker does is a little more
difficult because it is relatively less repetitive in the details. Kanda-san
always takes glued leather pieces, shapes them properly, and slides them
under the needle of a sewing machine to stitch them. But depending on
the particular leather and its cut and the "feel" of the form, he bends
it this way or that, fiddles with it, and adjusts the machine and his task
accordingly. He sews about seven pairs of shoes an hour, about fifty or
sixty a day, around three hundred a week. At Universal there were several
people doing each task. And each task led from one to another until the
whole shoe was finished. At any given moment parallel jobs were being
done, which created the flow of a single product throughout the factory
and from one person to another.

This daily flow of work, experienced together, was clearly facilitating
a sense of sharing skills, organization, fortunes, and lives. No shoes were
made without each section touching them, and in a company this small
that also meant that each worker knew the others who were working on
the same product very well. They knew the idiosyncrasies of their work,

their style, and their enthusiasm or lack thereof. The daily routine act of making shoes rehearsed the commonsense assumption that the Universal workers were sharing their lives and their livelihoods.

Managing and Being Managed

One of the frequently acknowledged problems with unions operating their own factories is the conflict between their egalitarian ideologies and organizational hierarchy. President Kishi spoke of the "soft" (*amai*) characteristic of union relationships and how they don't always mix with the "harsh" (*kibishii*) nature of factory management. Equality as union members conflicts both with the union's own internal hierarchy of officers and, in cases like Universal's, with the factory management hierarchy set up by the union as well.[1] Prior to bankruptcy and worker control of production, all union members were working together, sharing time and space and making the same product in the routine ways discussed above. Once the union began to manage production, however, union leaders all took on different jobs, jobs with different schedules, a different workplace, and none of them involving hands-on production of shoes.

On a daily basis, decisions about what to produce, in what quantity, and at what pace were all made in committees of union officials. Rank-and-file workers saw their union officers around the factory, but they were in the front office doing management work with one or two visiting federation officers. The work the leaders did was no longer the work of the shop floor, and there was a daily experience of separation and distance which enhanced whatever differences in opinion, strategy, or status workers might otherwise feel.

Decisions about what to produce, the quantity, the prices, and sales strategies were all made in committees which included Universal officers and outside labor federation officers. Rank-and-file members were told the results of these decisions, but for the most part they were working under the management and instructions of their leaders. Leaders were also doing the work of the union and as such were associating with outsiders, going around Tokyo meeting with federation officials, lawyers, and others involved with their struggle. Their worlds were bigger and clearly of higher status than the world of the factory. The union

1. For a discussion of this dilemma in similar companies, see Inoue 1981a.

leaders also joined different activities and followed different schedules. They did not eat lunch at a particular time and they rarely joined rank-and-file workers in the dining area. Their hours were longer and less clearly structured. The daily habits of work were themselves both expressive of and responsible for a gap in practice and a sense of inequality which contributed substantially to the problems of the union with internal democracy and equality.

The habits of management became, through daily practice, part of life for union leaders. In turn, their frustrations around trying to get rank and file to speak up, take part in discussion, and take responsibility for making decisions revealed rank-and-file habits of being managed.[2] The daily patterns of association between leaders and rank and file strained former relationships of equality and rehearsed in ongoing practice this confusion of status. The very leaders most sincerely concerned about egalitarian principles were trapped in habits of management within hierarchy that undermined the achievement of their goals for internal equality, democracy, and rapport between workers.

In December, when the end-of-the-year rush demanded higher output and longer hours, one of the workers in the cutting section missed work for a couple of days. Things were so busy that President Kishi decided to work in her place for a couple of days. Working the cutting machine had been his job prior to self-management and he would be a big help. When Kanda-san, the foreman, came back from a meeting to say that President Kishi would join us the next day there was silence. By now I knew that silence for Universal workers was itself a statement. Later, while we were walking to the station, I asked about that silence. They reminded me that President Kishi didn't treat me the same way he treated them, and that he was very "harsh" with them. Having him there would mean a very serious atmosphere. Furthermore, it would not be easy to talk because when you talk to "superiors" (*ue no hito*) you have to "be careful not to use the wrong words or something." Once again, as in reluctance to speak at meetings, the complexity of deferential Japanese language usage was cited as a reason for not bothering to speak.

The next day, President Kishi did come to the cutting section. It was indeed one of the quietest days I had ever witnessed. More interesting to me, however, was the way in which he worked, choosing not to follow the same schedule as everyone else. At the afternoon break when the

2. This is still a problem at Universal in its new cooperative company form. See chapter 8 for a discussion.

buzzer sounded, he did not stop working, and others were very slow to stop themselves. Gradually we all did, however, and walked out to the open space to exercise. He continued working. When we went back ten minutes later he was still working, and by now even I was feeling uncomfortable taking a break while someone else was working. It is quite usual at Universal, and at Unikon too, for people to break only when everyone else does and to leave only when their whole section is finished with a task. If anyone had to leave ahead of the rest, he or she went to each other coworker and apologized for leaving first. Once we had made tea, the woman pouring said under her breath to the others, "I suppose I should make one for Kishi-san too, shouldn't I?" They nodded that she probably should. It was becoming quite an awkward situation. Finally one of the workers called to him that tea was ready and he stopped work to come and join us. While one person was pouring tea another was finding him a good chair. As we began to eat our usual sweets, Kishi-san's secretary came in with sweets he had asked her to buy and bring to us. This generous gesture was also a little surprising, because it is the sort of thing which guests do when visiting, and once more reinforced a sense of distance. The difficulty many workers felt in speaking up at meetings or in feeling equal as union members or equally enthused about particular events seemed to be continuously strengthened by the simple practices of working in the factory. Attempts to argue for a new form for their organization, while convincing as an ideal, often seemed distant from the reality constituted by their ongoing experiences.

While continuing the daily routine of work was itself a powerful symbol of solidarity and strength critical to Universal strategy, once reestablished, union leaders considered that very routine to be problematic as well. They explicitly argued against settling into a complacent routine so ordinary that rank-and-file workers might lose the vigilance and determination necessary for their protest actions. The repetitive and familiar routines of daily life which occupied most hours of most days could fill up time, use up energy, and make days and weeks predictable in ways which provided calm patterns of activities. Workers were nurtured by them, and productivity was enhanced by such stability, but it often did become an escape from formative debates and unfamiliar actions necessary to their struggle.

Rank-and-file workers frequently expressed their desire to just do their work and let the lawyers and their leaders negotiate a settlement, and shortly after I began working there I started hearing people refer to their struggle as "calm" (*ochitsuiteru*). Clearly, the goal of the dispute—to continue their daily work lives at Universal—and the means to achieve it were to a great extent merged for many of the workers. Lawyers working for Universal claimed that this perseverance was Universal's most powerful weapon. On the other hand, the attendant habits of quiet daily life were obstacles to forging a strong, conflictual protest needed, for instance, in demonstrations. Leaders also worried that it might hamper their ability to represent themselves to the outside world as powerful enough to be taken seriously.

There were very few changes in daily work routines when the Universal union took over management of production. The daily work schedule didn't change, nor did the length of breaks and lunch hours. Information, on the other hand, was much more broadly dispersed once the union began managing the factory. Rank and file were more informed than ever before about day-to-day operations but experienced little difference in their own role in decision making. They didn't make decisions about production before and they didn't make them after their union began managing. Union leaders made a much bigger transition in their daily activities and associations. This dissonance was clear when leaders spoke about creating a "tiny socialism," about "equality" and worker control over their own livelihood. While most rank-and-file workers held these principles and ideals to be valuable goals, they were not experiencing them as directly as were their leaders. For them the picture was complicated by habits of management and of being managed which sustained hierarchies of organization and mediated against equality or the experience of direct control of their work. The political frustrations of incomplete forms of equal process were unwittingly aggravated by complacency about management of production. Rank-and-file workers were engaged in political struggle over the control of their livelihood more than over the right to manage their own workplace. Universal leaders were more idealistic, striving for control over both, but it was a control that they themselves were exercising and of which they had a daily understanding and experience.

When I asked people what had changed for them at work, there were two common kinds of responses. Some talked about the more casual atmosphere of work. Others talked about the insecurity of their livelihood due to the absence of professional management. Everyone said that things weren't that different on a day-to-day basis. The real differences were in the security and outlook for their futures. One worker put it this way: "Before the bankruptcy we didn't have to worry about where work was coming from, where it would be sold, and so on. Those were tasks for the managers. . . . The union had to take all that on and professional managers and sales people know more about what they are doing." For most workers this lack of security about their futures was more dominant than their experience of their present working conditions as "tiny socialism" or even as a significant break with organizational hierarchy. While the ideas expressed by their union about a future company owned, operated, and designed by their own hands was attractive, these ideas, even after several years of union management, were not yet experienced as real, and their feasibility was sometimes seriously doubted.

Seikatsu for "Working People"

For workers in antibankruptcy disputes, coming to work was in and of itself an act of defiance. The internal arguments about the form of the workplace shaped the conceptual meaning of their goals and strategies. The daily routines of making shoes or cameras, following a regular "ordinary" schedule, and making a modest but livable wage were familiar acts of fundamental significance in the context of their struggles. They embodied a fundamental association of human dignity with daily work lives on the one hand and daily home lives on the other. They defied the authority of capitalists to control whether or not a "working person" could work. These were not initially struggles over distribution of resources or increased participation in management of factory operation, although these issues became important internally during worker control of production. These were struggles over control, not over management. Workers were ambivalent throughout about how much they wanted to get involved in managing production and how well they thought their own leaders could even handle that job. No one was ambivalent about their fundamental right to work, and about the "inhumanity" and "irresponsibility" of capitalists who would deny them that without consultation or appropriate consideration.[3]

The motivation to fight over such long periods of time was sustained in union activities and arguments and nurtured in daily life associations of work, home, and human dignity. *Hataraku hito* (working people) was an expression which echoed through labor movement events, community

3. Dore 1986 presents an appendix with accounts of two cases of labor unions arguing for something beyond the contractual employment relationship. In both cases bankruptcy does eventually occur, but the unions insist upon "responsibility" and consultation in the process.

events, and daily life. It softly grounded the more ideologically motivated *rōdōsha* and labor-capital relations in the people and activities most real and most loved. The identities of Universal and Unikon workers as workers layered these terms, and solidarity played on their overlap as well as their distinctions. *Rōdōsha* was powerful and could be used in analyses, speeches, or shouted at banks. It could signify opposition and organization. The more richly grounded *hataraku hitobito* could be used in the same speeches, on banners, or chest signs to refer to the common plight of ordinary people working for a living. A bridge was frequently built between these two by using *nakama* (friend or colleague) to evoke strong horizontal ties of association, at once friendly and close but placed in daily routines of workplaces. These terms helped people imagine identities and solidarity extending from personal, daily work life through ties to co-workers with whom you share your organizational life and finally to all who share the relationship of labor to capital.

Seikatsu, like *sekinin*, or responsibility, was a versatile word and a powerful symbol in these struggles. Its meaning encompasses earning a material livelihood, daily life, and home life, and it served to unify all three in a deeply felt struggle for the dignity of work and "working people." It was the most frequent word to appear in slogans, and its "protection" was angrily fought over. The protests of the Unikon and Universal unions grounded their motivation and commitment in the protection of livelihood. Debate ensued about the degree to which livelihood was to be controlled by workers themselves in the long run, but there was no debate about the legitimacy of the demand. The language, however, was important in understanding felt commitments and determination strong enough to motivate these long struggles and their financial and personal sacrifices. *Seikatsu* did not have to be explicitly linked to family or to daily life because it was already, by definition and common, unexamined usage, fundamental to the imagining of what it is to be a human being in society. It includes within it the relationships to family, to work, and to daily association which constitute "ordinary life." It was an important touchstone, where ideological motivation to fight for the interests of Japanese labor was grounded in those immediate experiences of association that made workers feel that they "just couldn't quit" while their coworkers continued.

In the early twentieth century, Japanese unions struggled over "respect for the humanity of labor," a goal often translated by rank-and-file workers into the struggle for a "normal life" (Gordon 1991: 231). Gordon quotes one young worker describing her personal goals as just wanting "to do what human beings do" (1991: 228). At Universal's second factory festival, the schedule of events handed out to guests had a statement of purpose. "We have decided to begin our daily lives, our work, and our struggle again this year." The radishes, the children, and the glistening sweat were juxtaposed, just as were home lives, work lives, and protest. The festival itself was an impressive collage of activities attended by nearly two thousand people. Other unions under worker control of production were selling their own products at reduced prices. Universal set up a small "shoe bazaar" where they sold their Solidarity (*Soridarichi*) brand shoes. The Japan Philharmonic Orchestra, the musicians' union of which was just settling a lengthy dispute, gave two performances. The first was a "parent-child concert," and the second was an evening concert of baroque music emphasizing Mozart, where people were invited to "wear a nice jacket and some Solidarity-brand shoes and enjoy an evening of wonderful music." Food booths sold ice cream, barbecued chicken, kabobs of ground octopus, and drinks. Cotton candy was given away to children, and a large area of games and activities was set up especially for them, where they could fish for goldfish, pop balloons with darts, or buy masks of favorite cartoon heroes. A small railway ran around the perimeter of the empty lot where exercises were done during the workday. Tickets for kids and parents to ride on it were printed up as souvenirs. Over a red line drawing of an old-fashioned steam locomotive were the words "Solidarity Rail. Destination: Reconstruction of a Worker-Controlled Universal." Vegetables were brought in from local retailer cooperatives and laid out for sale. A singing contest awarded prizes for those with the most talent, and a portable shrine was borrowed from the neighborhood for children to carry around the factory yard to the accompaniment of auspicious drums and chants.

In presenting themselves, their factory, and their struggle, Universal workers created a collage of the most ordinary elements of an ordinary human life. The more mundane and familiar the object or event, the more powerful it was in creating their own images of themselves as ordinary working people and of their struggle as a strong one with unshakable determination to defy attempts to take their ordinary *seikatsu* away. The weaving together of families, craftsmanship, hard work, and an orderly routine gave people affectively convincing substance to the arguments and goals of their collective action. Their long struggle, and that of Unikon as well, endured in large part because they had the humor, simple pleasures, and affection of the *seikatsu* these "working people" were fighting to maintain.

CHAPTER 8

Endings

The Unikon and Universal unions waged struggles re-
markable for their length, for their success, and for their timing. In an
era of economic slowdown, decreasing labor activism, and political
conservatism, workers at Unikon and Universal, aligned with the Communist and Socialist parties, defied legal orders to disband, operated
companies under their own control, and won resources and the right to
reopen under their own ownership. Interpretations of the consciousness
of the rank-and-file workers in these struggles ranged from "the most
advanced class consciousness in Japan" to "they don't have any." Researchers looking at the movements' strategies and prospects tended to
overestimate the ideological consensus and class consciousness of the
union members. Union leaders engaged in mobilization of rank and file
joked in frustration about the utter absence of these same characteristics.
In this book I have explored the conceptual world of Japanese workers
engaged in protest and have tried to show the significance of practice in
the analysis and construction of consciousness. Direct experience and
discursive argument both played decisive roles in forming the ideas and
feelings which guided action. Decisive and successful social action can
be taken, and I would suggest inevitably is taken, while consciousness
is in the process of being formed. Unspoken assumptions and nonverbal
actions are as critical to such analysis as are direct discussion, debate,
reading, or intellectual pondering. Furthermore, all social experiences
matter, from daily life routines like those of a usual workday or casual
chatting over tea or sake, to periodic events like union meetings or

company outings, to exceptional occasions like demonstrations, formal parties, or internal union conflicts.

It is tempting to look for a single coherent belief system or for a particular content to consciousness, but what is clear from this account is that neither experience nor consciousness is truly at rest. As E. P. Thompson elegantly writes of class and class consciousness, "Like any relationship, it is a fluency which evades analysis if we attempt to stop it dead at any given moment and anatomize its structure" (1963: 9). Looking at social life as lived makes strategy and decision making central and the uncertainty of outcomes ubiquitous. To see how action engenders thought and how ideas and feelings inspire decisions is to see how people perform their cultural calculations and negotiate their actions during intervals when outcomes are unknown and strategies necessary. In short, it assumes their active role in creating their own lives and histories.

This kind of processual analysis is particularly important to the study of Japan, where stereotypes of tradition-bound, docile, and submissive workers continue to encumber our understanding. It becomes possible to see industrial workers as active participants in the ongoing evolution of their own labor relations, of their own social organizations, and of their own conceptual world. While their histories, their remembered pasts, and their embedded sense of what is natural or commonsensical shape their social and cultural worlds, they are themselves the agents of their constitution. Andrew Gordon calls industrial workers "assertive participants" in the evolution of prewar labor relations in Japan, arguing against the scholarship on Japan which relegates workers to positions of docility and dependence (1988). I would suggest that this is an even broader problem plaguing studies of Japan in that it is usually generalized to include all who are placed low in hierarchies of authority and power. In looking at the intellectual issues and cultural contestation in present-day labor protest, I have tried to bring the concerns of cultural conceptualization and assertive agency into an historicized present. I have also tried to show how life at the bottom of hierarchies is nonetheless life lived amid critical thought, careful consideration, and strategies for action within institutions. Industrial workers in Japan are engaged with their past, with the international community, with commonsense assumptions and ideological arguments from the political right and the political left, and their lives are shaped by their own efforts to change things for the better and to accommodate the inevitable.

Settlement and Reconstruction

Both Unikon and Universal continue as viable small companies. Unikon is still making cameras and Universal is still making shoes, but each has had to adapt to the competitive markets which conspired to drive their companies into bankruptcy in the past. They each continue to be active in the labor movement networks which supported their struggles. Although Unikon modeled its struggle on Universal's, and their settlements were similar in many ways, the decisions about how to reorganize and operate the new enterprises were dramatically different. Those initial decisions and the forms which their new companies took continue to lead these small companies down very different paths.

UNIKON CAMERA

Unikon's settlement was signed on June 27, 1980, and they began as a new company at the smaller Saitama prefecture site on July 21. About forty of the Unikon workers stayed to work there. The structure of the reopened Unikon was designed by the Unikon union leaders, and replicated the organization of "ordinary companies." From the point of view of most leaders, the primary purpose of their dispute had been the restoration of both the management and the labor-management relationships usual in capitalism. Management was separated from the union, which continues to exist and to be affiliated with the same federations. The Unikon union president became the new company president and the secretary of the union became the new union president.

There were explicit efforts on the part of union leadership to design a new company which would not be encumbered by its history of union management. Unikon leaders had worried, as had many at Universal and elsewhere, that when unions run companies the principles of equality and democracy which characterize the union interfere with the administrative hierarchy necessary to a successful capitalist enterprise.[1] In a conversation in 1989, the former union president explained to me that you cannot run a company without a "clear distinction between superiors and subordinates," and that on the other hand you can't run a union

1. For a discussion of this issue, see Inoue 1981b.

without equality. Their own history of commitment to the labor movement and to the communist and socialist ideals of the parties which
supported them were instead expressed in the nature of the products
which they would try to manufacture. The new management at Unikon
talked about forming a "socially significant corporation" by manufacturing cameras which were "user-friendly" and would take good pictures at a reasonable price (Inoue 1981a: 81).

The most pressing problem for the new company was to try and
reenter the camera market and be competitive in it. They introduced a
new 35 mm, lightweight camera, which they announced to be "the
lightest camera in the world containing a flash." Within a year they found
it necessary to diversify their products to remain solvent. They began
renting cameras at sight-seeing spots, started looking for subcontracting
business producing lenses, and tried to develop cameras for other uses,
such as in home security systems.

To date Unikon has manufactured single-lens reflex cameras, car
cigarette lighters, printed circuit boards, pocket cameras, underwater
cameras, binoculars, opera glasses, minicameras, and video camera conversion lenses. They have contracted with Pentax, Canon, and Hoya for
binoculars, Polaroid and Hitachi for video lenses, and Keystone for
minicameras. They now have eighty employees, six of whom continue
as full-time workers from before reorganization. The other seventy-four
are all part-time workers. The new Unikon union does not permit
part-time workers to be members, so the number of union members at
present is six. To cut labor costs they have opened two small "offshore"
factories, one in Taiwan making camera bodies and the other in southern
China doing assembly work.

My most recent correspondence with the people from Unikon came
from the former union president, Sasaki-san. He wants to talk with me
during my next trip to Japan because, "since the breakup of Eastern
Europe and the dissolution of the Communist parties," he has been
reflecting on his union's struggles and on the internal dynamics of the
organization. He says he feels freer now to talk with me about the
political dilemmas he experienced.

UNIVERSAL WORKERS' COOPERATIVE COMPANY

On November 18, 1986, Universal signed an agreement
with Custom Shoes which ended their dispute and won for themselves

the means to open Universal Shoes as their own worker-owned cooperative company. In the agreement, Custom Shoes gave the Universal union lease rights to one-fourth of the land upon which the factory stood, allowing them to reopen in the same spot, though with reduced space. They also gave the union all Universal's machines and ninety million yen (about $750,000) toward construction expenses. All buildings on the property were torn down, and on their 726 square meters, the Universal union erected new, two-story buildings to house their factory operations. Custom also agreed to pay back wages, social security, and severance pay to each worker and to pay the union eighty-seven million yen as a dispute settlement fee. This settlement was reached through arbitrated negotiation, and following its conclusion all court cases were withdrawn.

In March 1987 Universal reopened as Universal Workers' Cooperative Company and continues today to manufacture and sell shoes under this name. The workers at Universal were given the option of joining the new cooperative and continuing to work there, in which case they would buy shares of the company. Just under half did so, and the others quit either to retire or to seek other jobs.

The end of this struggle was not eventful, as Unikon's had been. Toward the end of it, however, there developed stronger disagreements about the wisdom of holding out for full reconstruction, a very ambitious goal. At the conclusion of the dispute came the reconstitution of the company as a workers' cooperative, and at this point individuals took different paths. All the older men retired. When the struggle began there had been men in their early sixties, but by the time they settled these men ranged in age from sixty-nine to seventy-nine. Universal's oldest worker at the time died at the age of seventy-nine, five years before settlement. One of their youngest, Nakada-san, the man who had led my contingent to the demonstration, died at the age of forty-eight just after settlement. Two of seven part-time women quit, one to take a different job as a kitchen helper in a downtown Ginza restaurant and the other to find a job closer to her home, which had moved during the struggle. The Universal struggle had, over its course, been constituted both by defiant political acts and by a very ordinary progression of lives through time.

Like Unikon, they have had to contend with the economic pressures which have threatened their company all along, but unlike Unikon, they continue to use unconventional distribution and sales networks, linking themselves to cooperatives throughout Japan. Universal faces severe competition from larger shoe manufacturers and from foreign products, which are increasingly common in Japan since the opening of that market at the time of their bankruptcy. To meet that challenge they have tried creative new ideas for products. They have made backpacks for children and have expanded to produce women's shoes as well as men's. Their most successful innovation and the one they are most proud of is their made-to-order shoe business. They began slowly, but have gradually expanded their reputation for quality and service. Customers come, have a mold made of their foot, and after that they can order whatever style they like and Universal will custom-make it. "In this day and age," says Kishi-san, "it is important to think about what customers want and to try and meet individual needs and tastes. The increasing demand for individual style or fit may be something a small company can take advantage of even better than a large one."

Organizationally, they have a committee to make management decisions. It is headed by Kishi-san, former union president, but his title is "representative," not "president." Decisions are made by the committee and in consultation with workers at regular meetings. The primary struggle, not unlike prior to reorganization, is to get people to speak up and take an active role in their own management. The habits of leaving management decisions to management continue to impede implementation of procedures for broadened worker control. The equality of the union relationships does not permit the usual hierarchy of a company. The Universal leaders, in designing their cooperative, decided that they would try to build a company on "partnership, independence, and confidence." They are self-consciously trying to "educate" themselves and to create a "tiny socialism" where workers can be independent of capitalists and where people can have confidence in their own abilities. It is a slow process, and Representative Kishi reports that he still has to work hard to get workers to call him "Kishi-san" or "Representative Kishi" instead of "President."

At present there are twenty-eight people working at Universal, fourteen from before reorganization. All are union members and own a small share of the company. They continue to be supported by a wide network of unions, cooperatives, and "friends" of the company. There are over five hundred members in their Solidarity Group (Soridarichi Kai), who continue to make small donations, gather for special events, and offer support to what many idealistically and hopefully still think of as a "tiny socialism."

"Tiny Socialism"

There was a precipitous drop in worker-control actions in the mid-eighties. Companies became more cautious in their efforts to carry out rationalization, plant closure, or bankruptcies in part because of these struggles. On the other hand, while their success was certainly noticed, their numbers and sizes were probably limiting factors.[2] The overall drop in labor disputes reflects the tightening of the economy, the fear of job loss, and the more conservative political environment of the time. The dissolution of Sōhyō, the most radical labor federation and the primary supporter of these struggles, is another obvious factor. In 1989 Sōhyō joined other federations in forming Rengō, the largest labor federation in Japanese history, ushering in an era Andrew Gordon refers to as "friendly opposition" (1993b: 451). The Universal and Unikon unions joined this federation, complaining of its inevitable shift toward the political right but seeing no feasible alternative. They acknowledge that disputes will be harder to fight, particularly for smaller unions. It was already hard for smaller unions to get the support they needed to carry on viable dispute actions, and in their estimation it will continue to become more difficult over time. Rengō has an important stake in working with government and industry on behalf of labor, thus tacitly accepting labor as a "partner" in the capitalist system. Rengō is learning to work effectively as sole national negotiator for labor, and its power as representative of nearly 70 percent of all unions gives it the ability to work in national networks of government, bureaucracy, and industry in ways that "both stabilize the economic system and enhance Rengō's influence in it" (Tsujinaka 1993: 213). In this organization many see the hope of a more powerful labor advocate on the national stage, one able to move beyond the enterprise-specific union actions and concerns and negotiate for labor as a whole. Others fear that there will no longer be any source of national support for struggles which challenge the basic structures of capitalism.[3] The more particular fear of those in small unions like Unikon and Universal is that this even larger federation will be an even larger sea in which concerns specific to their firms get diluted by the concerns of the industry giants.

2. For an assessment of the importance of these disputes on the labor movement, see Inoue 1981b.

3. Taira 1988 gives an extensive analysis of Rengō's development and the prospects for labor.

The significance of the Unikon and Universal struggles is still being discussed in Japan by academic researchers, observers, and those in the labor movement. Some think they were significant challenges to capitalism, specifically, that they represented a challenge to capitalist control of labor. The workers and union organizers themselves captured both the strength and the weakness of these struggles in their favorite term for them, "tiny socialism." Totsuka points out that the control of labor by workers during these disputes challenged important principles of capitalism with an innovative protest strategy (1980). Unikon and Universal workers did not merely demand the right to control their own livelihoods, they created factories which did in fact operate under their own control, in open defiance of orders to disband and liquidate assets. Their victories and subsequent patterns of settlement, however, paint a more mixed picture.

The Universal outcome continued the "tiny socialism" model and even expanded it by becoming a wholly legal workers' cooperative. These are still uncommon in Japan. There are about three hundred, with a total of just twenty thousand workers. Producers' cooperatives are building on a retailers' cooperative movement which also challenges usual capitalist forms of ownership. Universal leaders, while optimistic, idealistic, and proud, continue to look with a realistic pleasure on their accomplishment. They are, after all, tiny. Their product is sold very locally, and they struggle continually for survival. The meaning of this effort is most certainly an open oppositional act meant to challenge some basic structuring principles of capitalism. It is, however, also a very small-scale operation, one which the Japanese state and its capitalist economy can easily survive. The workers at Universal continue, as before settlement, to be slightly more cynical than their leaders, smiling at their small size, and reiterating the impossibility of creating socialism in a factory which operates in a capitalist economy.

At Unikon, while the struggle itself challenged assumptions about who has rights to control labor, the new company does not. Having returned to the form of an "ordinary company," leaders there are engaged in the same struggles for survival that Universal's are, but they do not share the idealism or sense of oppositional purpose to their enterprise. They talk instead of becoming "realistic" and doing what was necessary to survive in the "harsh" economic climate of contemporary capitalism.

Inoue, citing the work of Tadashi Hanami, claims that these worker-control struggles are the outcome of the Japanese labor unions' refusal to relinquish to managers and owners all rights of management. These struggles, says Inoue, represent a challenge to the control of labor by capitalists. Hanami has previously pointed out the radical nature of Japanese labor union tactics like work slowdowns, refusing to do certain tasks but coming to work anyway, and generally taking control of services to protest against management (Hanami 1979 and 1984). Such tactics, rather than strikes where workers refuse to work altogether, are themselves a refusal to abandon the workplace and a refusal to abandon certain entitlements to take part in running it. Inoue sees the worker-control movements as the most radical extension of this strain in Japanese labor relations (Inoue 1991).

Whether these struggles were for full worker participation in a capitalist enterprise or for worker control of labor in opposition to capitalism was a contested issue within both unions. The indignation and anger which motivated rank-and-file workers at the outset of their struggles stemmed less from the fact of economic collapse than from their exclusion from negotiations and consultations about it. Unikon leaders spoke openly about their indebtedness to the insensitivity of their owners in mobilizing rank and file. They felt that had the union been consulted and included in working out provisions for workers following bankruptcy, they probably would have been unable to convince people to fight. This issue, the right to be included in the administration of their companies, was one which returned in the end to confront Unikon workers with ironic frustration. When leaders took steps to settle on plans for a postsettlement company without consulting rank-and-file workers, the result was the indignation and anger which sparked the internal crisis discussed in chapter 4.

This points to one of the great dilemmas of the Unikon union and one area of difference between Unikon and Universal, namely, the ongoing negotiation of the meaning of worker control. The Unikon leaders used worker control to achieve the goal of company reconstruction, without striving for a new company controlled by workers. Unikon leaders told me that although there were debates about it within their own leadership ranks, most of them knew all along that their goal was to create a new "ordinary company," and they pride themselves on having managed alignments with both socialist and communist political parties during their struggle. For them, the form of opposition for labor had to be one which opposed and threatened to disrupt the control of labor by company owners and financial institutions. That was a tactic, however, not a final goal. It was, rather, their judgment that it is not feasible for labor to challenge capitalism and succeed or even survive, except for a short-term strife. In other words, worker control of production is possible only because a vast network of unions supports it on a daily basis, and only in extreme and unusual circumstances like their bankruptcy struggle. It is a powerful enough threat to owners and financial institutions to force negotiation. The negotiation, however, was about compensation, equal participation, and the right to employment within the existing economic order. Totsuka has suggested that the Unikon struggles were in fact a much more powerful threat than the union intended. That is to say, the workers and leaders began their struggles as protest against exclusion from negotiation over potential bankruptcy, against loss of jobs without proper compensation, and for financial settlement allowing them to restructure their enterprises. The form of their struggles, however, posed bolder and more critical threats to capitalist enterprise than anyone had imagined. In addition, it became clear rather early on that at Unikon the rank and file developed more radical demands and expectations than did their leaders.

Through most of the dispute, rank-and-file workers assumed that their participation in management decisions would continue and that the form of their company during the dispute would carry over into the newly opened Unikon should they succeed. To assure themselves that this would be true, the part-time women in the union actually raised the issue shortly after the struggle began and received assurances that this would be the case. After the struggle ended I interviewed the former union president and asked him about the motivation of leaders and about their reassurances to workers about the goal of the struggle. His response was thoughtful, somewhat troubled, and clear. "They would never have fought had we told them that we couldn't continue running the company the same way after settlement as during the dispute." Following this, he talked about how impossible it would have been to maintain solidarity without the goal of full participation in decision making for workers and about how hard it is to survive in a capitalist world without an "ordinary" structure to the company. As may be clear from my account in chapter 4, this judgment on the part of the Unikon leaders may have been flawed. Rank-and-file workers expressed a willingness to cope with the necessities of becoming an "ordinary company." That might well have been accepted as "inevitable." What was not accepted as inevitable, and what they were unwilling to accept, was the loss of their jobs following such a long struggle to secure them.

At Universal, workers and leaders alike knew that their union's goal was to achieve a "tiny socialism" both during their dispute and in the company they hoped to open after settlement. Theirs was conceptualized as an oppositional act, as an idealistic one, and as an effort to escape from the structures of power which threatened their jobs. There was a sense both of political opposition and of a yearning for a small enterprise on the model of the *machi kōba* which dot the *shitamachi* area, the old-fashioned small companies of their "old Tokyo" neighborhoods. The yearning for the independence from industry, bureaucracy, and state echoes many of the themes of the labor movement in the early twentieth century, when capital, bureaucracy, and government had to work so hard to manage rebellious and independent workers (Garon 1987; Gordon 1988 and 1991; Moore 1983). Universal was affiliated solely with the Socialist Party and was ideologically committed to realizing a new form of work organization, even if on a small scale. There were some rank-and-file workers in the union, however, who felt weary of the length of the fight and pessimistic about its outcome. In that context they would argue that a financial settlement with their parent company might be wise, that holding out for reconstruction could make them lose everything.

This is probably the single most common debate within worker-control struggles in the seventies and eighties (Totsuka 1984) and one which characterized the worker-control struggles of the immediate post-war period as well (Moore 1983). It is a fundamental question about control of labor and about the nature of opposition. Within Unikon and Universal, there was no question raised about the preference for worker control of production. The questions were about feasibility, and the answers to those questions governed goals and strategies. Moore points out that in 1945 and 1946, the outcome of many such struggles was the organization of management councils that institutionalized worker input into administration of the firm. In Japanese firms today, nine of ten companies with labor unions also have joint consultation bodies, and in six of ten companies labor negotiations and joint consultations are mixed (Tsujinaka 1993). It is part of the current debate over the power of Rengō to ask whether or not more consolidated power within the established capitalist order is really more power for labor, or whether labor is more powerful when it can protest against that system itself (Mochizuki 1993; Taira 1993; Tsujinaka 1993). Rank-and-file workers at Unikon and Universal lived these contradictions, worrying about their viability as companies on the one hand and enjoying their increased sense of ownership, control, and independence under their own management on the other.

The Formation of Consciousness

Unikon and Universal workers created decisive collective actions with some decidedly uncollected thoughts. Class consciousness was neither present nor absent. Commitment to their struggles was felt "naturally" at some points and became weak and plagued with doubts at others. Thoughts and feelings about equality, solidarity, and protest shifted through time. Straightforward questions aimed at understanding consciousness led to argument. With very few exceptions, responses to questions like "Do you think of yourself as belonging to the working class?" were "Sometimes" or "No, not really, but it depends on what you mean by class." The discussions which followed such questions were much more revealing, not of a simple, yes-or-no answer to the question of consciousness, but of the terrain of the conceptual world where social consciousness was being shaped, challenged, and reshaped through time. My questions, for instance, about reasons for such a long-term commitment to a radical struggle were met with lengthy discussions, many of which I have reported here. One common response, given with irony and humor, was "First let me tell you what we always tell people who come asking that question." Following a comment like this were remarks about working for the improvement of life for Japanese workers, fighting for respect and dignity for workers, and taking a stand so that capitalists wouldn't be able to eliminate jobs like this in the future. Then people would start discussing what they claimed to be the "real" answer to the question, an answer which almost always had two parts. The first was about doubt. Nearly everyone admitted thinking of quitting many times over the course of these three- and ten-year struggles, so the decision was made not once but several times. The second part of the answer was longer and sketched what was felt to be most responsible for their perseverance. They had been together with their coworkers for many years, had been through very hard times together, had struggled together, had all faced orders to leave their jobs together, and just couldn't quit when others were still fighting. Some said that they couldn't let down those who were so determined to fight, that they themselves weren't so convinced they could win but were inspired by the strength of purpose of particular individuals.

The relationship of "No, not really" as a response to questions of class identity to "We've been together for so long that I couldn't quit" as a motivation to fight a radical labor dispute lasting several years is intriguing. This apparent discrepancy suggests the embeddedness of consciousness in practice, raises the question of the formation of discursive consciousness from the experience of practical consciousness, and points to the importance methodologically of the qualitative analysis of social process. The formation of consciousness, at the very least, involves three things: argument, usually between articulated viewpoints; implicit social knowledge, sometimes assumed absolutely and at other times explained or doubted through example or metaphor; and action, itself a performance and experience of social relatedness. In each case, there is a degree of involvement or of experience that is critical not only to some clearly differentiated world of "feeling" but to knowledge and consciousness as well. Making sense of social relations and of action involves sensation as well as reason.

The workers at both Unikon and Universal referred repeatedly to shared experiences within their own unions, simple daily experiences like working together for years, staying up all night together to meet deadlines, or suffering the fear and anxiety of job losses. Demonstrations and other protest actions made workers "see" that they were not alone, that other workers were also fighting, suffering similar problems, and supporting one another. The experiences of acting in concert with these other workers had powerful impact on consciousness of class identity. Social relationships themselves have a sensory dimension, a dimension of consciousness and knowledge such that in social action knowledge is rehearsed, argued, understood, or possibly doubted and challenged. As Michael Taussig suggests, "The sense data of raw experience [includes] not merely sensory impressions of light and sound and so forth, but also sensory impressions of social relations in all their moody ambiguity of trust and doubt and in all the multiplicity of their becoming and decaying" (1987: 463). The daily acts of working the same time schedule, working together to produce objects, sharing the vulnerability to owners' decisions to rationalize production and eliminate jobs, and later sharing the streets in protest and exchanging members with other unions for meetings, work, or celebrations created a practical consciousness of class.

That consciousness was itself, however, vulnerable to changing events and circumstances, one of the most obvious and significant of which was the involvement of Unikon and Universal workers in protest. Their consciousness of class during the time covered in this book cannot be separated from their involvement in labor struggles and worker control of production. During times of protest, however, building union solidarity out of individual commitment is a central task for leadership, and Unikon and Universal leaders believed it to be the most critical element deciding the fate of their disputes. One of the federation officials working with Universal saw the development of class consciousness as the evolution of a kind of "wisdom," and believed that through workers' "wisdom" solidarity grows and that, conversely, through collective activities workers' "wisdom" grows. After more than six years of their ten-year struggle, he wrote that in his experience it is not the success of the Universal strife per se that is most meaningful, nor is it the way it might be viewed by others in the future. "The greatest joy," he writes, "comes from knowing that workers can see, however vaguely, what they previously could not."[4] He expresses, in the language of his own experience, the emergence of solidarity in protest and of the visibility of relationships of class and class consciousness that Universal workers gained through their meetings, demonstrations, and other solidary activities. The dialectic of consciousness evolving in practice, of class consciousness evolving through solidary activities, echoes the perspective of E. P. Thompson (1963) on the formation of class, of Raymond Williams (1977) on the emergence of consciousness through structures of feeling, and of anthropologists and sociologists on the formation of consciousness in the complex and mundane activities of daily life (Comaroff and Comaroff 1991; Fantasia 1988; Giddens 1979; Myerhoff 1992; M. Rosaldo 1980; R. Rosaldo 1989; Taussig 1987; Turner 1967, 1969).

Unikon and Universal workers answered the question of why they decided to stay by saying that they had struggled together. Leaders in both these struggles claim that they didn't really give people a choice about beginning the worker-control struggles; they just announced that the union was going to fight and asked everyone to stay and join them. Their faith was in the ability of solidary activities to create the solidarity needed for more solidary activities. At the same time, as is evident in the discussion of Unikon's history, there were intensive efforts at education through meetings, discussions, and newsletters, and it was the interaction of discursive activities and practical experience which formed consciousness.

Class struggle and the power and importance of worker protest, workers' interests, and their right to be employed in particular compa-

---

4. From a Universal union publication.

nies were keenly debated, as was the form of an egalitarian and democratic workplace. The conceptual life of the Unikon and Universal workers reveals the conflictual and formative engagement of argument with common sense. Workers at Unikon and Universal were at times more discursively persuaded by democratic notions of participation than by paternalistic or, in their words, "feudalistic" notions of perseverance and silence. For many workers, that battle was one waged openly, explicitly, and discursively. Reading that text over their shoulders, however, took me only so far in understanding eventual silences or decisions to "make trouble" or to "speak up" in internal disputes. The struggle was sometimes a nondiscursive one about the power of forms of knowledge as well. The confusing and unsettling response of Unikon workers to the crisis discussed in chapter 4 suggests that collective memories, habits of moral significance, and daily life routines of relating to one another can be more powerful, if not necessarily more convincing, and can carry people into actions or away from them even while they continue to wonder why. Silence is often an eloquent form of communication and has particular meanings in Japan (Miyoshi 1974). Jokes play on the obvious. Tones of voice, gestures, and certain looks exchanged speak to that which needs no words while all the time people are talking, thinking, and wondering what to do. Points of contention between assumptions and argument arise as the discursive touches the world of the obvious and assumed.

Class relationships were more visible to workers when collective actions involved wider networks or when owners of their companies used legal and economic powers to rationalize production, bankrupt their companies, and eliminate their jobs. This is not to suggest that class relationships were utterly invisible within the routines of daily life, but to point to the greater ease of recognizing these relationships when they actively restructured experiences. It is also to suggest that the visibility gained in demonstrations or through experiences of bankruptcy carried over into the more habitual experiences of daily work routines and were there made more convincing and certain if reinforced by routines of daily life. This interplay of special, unusual experience and familiar daily routine shaped arguments, discussions, and considerations throughout these protests.

Former Unikon and Universal workers now employed in a wide variety of companies, most without unions, much less collective action, continue to see themselves as workers, to use the language of their disputes, and to speak critically of class politics both in their new workplaces and in Japanese society. They still wonder about the ultimate meaning of these disputes, and they all speak of a personal sense of accomplishment, many referring to their participation as *jinsei keiken*, or life experience. Their lives now, however, don't motivate the kind of reflection that demands for collective action did or the kind of crisis consciousness that bankruptcy evoked, and they need not make sense of ongoing involvement in labor actions. The distance from struggle and protest has not eliminated the meaning of that experience, but it has removed the intensity of daily confrontation with questions of action and of meaning and has left them instead with a critical and often cynical vision of relationships of class and power. What is seen to be "inevitable" for workers, unions, and small industry now is more extensive than in the late seventies and eighties, when these struggles occurred. Union leaders and rank and file alike see the drop in numbers of labor disputes as a sign of decreased resources to support disputes.

Ethnography, Argument, and Everyday Life

Situated as it is in extended labor disputes, this ethnography has looked at transformations on several levels, and both practice and consciousness were complex and shifting. I have considered the living and imagining of daily life within social relationships of unequal power and cultural relationships of contested meaning. For several years Unikon and Universal workers lived daily lives constituted by mundane routine, vigorous protest, ideological debate, emotional struggles, the certainty of common sense, and the confusion of change. Rather than search for a single, coherent, "Japanese" way of thought, I have tried to examine the pathways to conviction, common sense, and social transformation within the wholeness of lived experience, with all its contradictions and dilemmas. At Unikon workers who participated in openly harassing the homes of owners felt compelled to use the most indirect forms of communicating their opposition when their union leaders took unpopular actions. People who cared deeply about labor and about transforming capitalism into even a small socialist experiment worried about efficiency and productivity in such an alternative organization. Consciousness of class was grounded in a feeling of "being one," a feeling exemplified by working through the night to meet production deadlines, suffering job loss together, and sharing years of daily work routines. The intellectual life which filled conversations and motivated opinions and decisions thrived in the complex and contradictory experiences of institutional life. Bankruptcy presented workers with a legal order to disband, while bankruptcy administrators allowed that until all related issues were resolved and settlement reached, workers could operate their own companies. Their unions faced rank-and-file workers with a centralized leadership that was able to manage production and fight successful disputes over their very livelihood while at the same time maintaining hierarchies of authority and power within the organizations that mediated against the very egalitarian and democratic workplace practices they aimed to achieve.

The tensions over defining control and participation and over forms of egalitarian, democratic, and productive organizations structured the debates, experimental practices, and protests constituting these lengthy struggles. Many of these have been chronicled in the chapters of this book. They provide pictures of idealism, opposition, and emergence. Ideals were shared more widely than were ideas about their implementation or evaluations of their feasibility. Notions of democracy and equality were grounded firmly in notions of daily life processes of institutional and social life. People were talking about and trying to create a community of equals built on *aijō* (love), on *giri* (mutual obligation), and on *ninjō* (human feeling) without breaking down the hierarchy which seemed necessary for organizational efficiency in capitalist enterprises. They questioned whether or not a company that feels like a "comfortable place to live" could survive. Rank-and-file workers tried to decide whether they could trust their union leaders to work toward realization of their own interests or whether they themselves needed to protect them.

Attempts have been made to find an interpretation which can set these concerns to rest, settle the debates, and resolve the contradictions. Unfortunately, they have sealed off from view the efforts of ordinary people to understand and to create social relations within daily life. Contradiction has long been a theme in writing on Japan, the most common being those between harmony and conflict, horizontal and hierarchical relationships, democratic institutions and authoritarian practices. In social science literature, the management of context has been used as an explanation for the persistence and lack of resolution of such contradictions. Equality and hierarchy have been seen to coexist within workplaces, and context has been relied upon to explain the harmony which reigns in spite of it. In office groups or work teams, hierarchy governs company operations, while equality characterizes the social circle of after-work partying. Chaotic abandon characterizes informal gatherings and deferential, reserved behavior the workplace. Successful leadership in organizations becomes a matter of skillful management of context and appropriate meaning. The contribution of such analyses is to isolate some of the more critical elements in social thought and practice and to point to their resilience. The picture of social relations, however, is static and the people—all but the managers, owners, and others on top of their respective hierarchies—are invisible, voiceless, and without conceptualization, reason, or decisive action.

At Unikon and Universal, people were spared neither confusion nor the responsibility to act. They were confronted with everything most of the time, and they usually knew it. That is, contradictions and dissonance were not problems of management of context for a handful of leaders or managers; they shaped the cultural reality of social life for everyone. People were not faced with equality at after-work parties and hierarchy at work, nor were they unabashedly enthusiastic at demonstrations and mild and reserved in daily routine. They were not wrapped up in harmony on their trips and conflict in their meetings, or feeling "oneness" at the demonstration and then losing it in crisis. Workers were coping with all of these most of the time. Situations of equality evoked the problems of hierarchy, feelings of community recalled feelings of individual self-interest, and harmony was inevitably linked to images of conflict. Contradictions and dilemmas did not arise between contexts so much as out of social life, and social life was formed not of a static structure but of fluid relations of power and action.

The intellectual issues and practical problems of conceptualizing and acting in protest and in daily life were not about great clashes or careful contextualizations. They were about small, daily clashes and about efforts to make connections between contexts which embody unresolved contradictions, or to "find a sensible frame for the interpretation of daily practice" (M. Rosaldo 1980: 223). The strain between hierarchy and equality appears frequently throughout this book in explicit argument, in comfortable assumptions, and in uneasy confusion. Efforts to create and maintain democratic processes of decision making were similarly idealistic and troubled. Ties of solidarity for collective action and ties of loyalty and affection for coworkers overlapped in sometimes contradictory and at other times complementary ways. The Unikon and Universal efforts to sustain lengthy labor protest and to create their own firms sustained complex debates for the workers involved, debates central to the social relations, organization, and control of industrial work in Japan. Their concerted efforts as ordinary people involved in extraordinary actions were cultural and social struggles for power and dignity deeply grounded in concerns for making feasible changes toward a more livable, "human" society.

References

Abegglen, James C.
  1958   *The Japanese Factory: Aspects of Its Social Organization.* Glencoe,
          Ill.: Free Press.
Apter, David, and Nagayo Sawa.
  1984   *Against the State: Politics and Social Protest in Japan.* Cam-
          bridge: Harvard University Press.
Bourdieu, Pierre.
  1977   *Outline of a Theory of Practice.* New York: Cambridge Univer-
          sity Press.
Chalmers, Norma J.
  1989   *Industrial Relations in Japan: The Peripheral Workforce.* Lon-
          don: Routledge.
Clark, Rodney.
  1979   *The Japanese Company.* New Haven: Yale University Press.
Clifford, James.
  1986   "Partial Truths." In *Writing Culture: Poetics and Politics of Eth-
          nography,* edited by James Clifford and George Marcus. Berkeley
          and Los Angeles: University of California Press.
Cole, Robert.
  1971   *Japanese Blue Collar: The Changing Tradition.* Berkeley and Los
          Angeles: University of California Press.
  1979   *Work, Mobility, and Participation: A Comparative Study of
          American and Japanese Industry.* Berkeley and Los Angeles:
          University of California Press.
Comaroff, Jean, and John L. Comaroff.
  1989   "The Colonization of Consciousness in South Africa." *Economy
          and Society* 18, no. 3:267–95.
  1991   *Of Revelation and Revolution: Christianity, Colonialism, and
          Consciousness in South Africa.* Chicago: University of Chicago
          Press.

DeVos, George, and Hiroshi Wagatsuma, eds.
  1966   *Japan's Invisible Race: Caste in Culture and Personality.*
          Berkeley and Los Angeles: University of California
          Press.
Dore, Ronald.
  1973   *British Factory—Japanese Factory: The Origins of National
          Diversity in Industrial Relations.* Berkeley and Los Angeles:
          University of California Press.
  1986   *Flexible Rigidities: Industrial Policy and Structural Adjustment
          in the Japanese Economy, 1970–80.* Stanford: Stanford University
          Press.
  1987   *Taking Japan Seriously: A Confucian Perspective on Leading
          Economic Issues.* Stanford: Stanford University Press.
Fantasia, Rick.
  1988   *Cultures of Solidarity: Consciousness, Action, and Contemporary
          American Workers.* Berkeley and Los Angeles: University of
          California Press.
Fujita Keizo and Takeuchi Masami.
  1977   *Chūshō-kigyō-ron* (Small and medium-sized industries). Tokyo:
          Yuhikaku Sōshō.
Garon, Sheldon.
  1987   *The State and Labor in Modern Japan.* Berkeley and Los Ange-
          les: University of California Press.
Geertz, Clifford.
  1973   *The Interpretation of Cultures.* New York: Basic Books.
  1983   *Local Knowledge.* New York: Basic Books.
Giddens, Anthony.
  1973   *The Class Structure of the Advanced Societies.* New York: Harper
          and Row.
  1979   *Central Problems in Social Theory: Action, Structure, and Con-
          tradiction in Social Analysis.* Berkeley and Los Angeles: Univer-
          sity of California Press.
  1987   *Social Theory and Modern Sociology.* Stanford: Stanford Univer-
          sity Press.
Gordon, Andrew.
  1987   "The Right to Work in Japan: Labor and the State in the De-
          pression." *Social Research* 54, no. 2:248–72.
  1988   *The Evolution of Labor Relations in Japan: Heavy Industry,
          1853–1955.* Cambridge: Harvard University Press.
  1991   *Labor and Imperial Democracy in Prewar Japan.* Berkeley and
          Los Angeles: University of California Press.
  1993a   "Contests for the Workplace." In *Postwar Japan as History,* ed-
          ited by Andrew Gordon. Berkeley and Los Angeles: University
          of California Press.
  1993b   "Conclusion." In *Postwar Japan as History,* edited by Andrew
          Gordon. Berkeley and Los Angeles: University of California
          Press.

Groth, David.
  1986   "Biting the Bullet: The Politics of Grassroots Protest in Con-
           temporary Japan." Ph.D. diss., Stanford University.
Hamabata, Matthews Masayuki.
  1990   *Crested Kimono: Power and Love in the Japanese Business Family.*
           Ithaca: Cornell University Press.
Hanami, Tadashi.
  1979   *Labor Relations in Japan Today.* Tokyo: Kodansha International.
  1984   "Conflict and Its Resolution in Industrial Relations and Labor
           Law." In *Conflict in Japan,* edited by Ellis S. Krauss, Thomas P.
           Rohlen, and Patricia G. Steinhoff. Honolulu: University of Ha-
           waii Press.
Haraway, Donna.
  1988   "Situated Knowledges: The Science Question in Feminism and
           the Privilege of Partial Perspectives." *Feminist Studies* 14, no.
           3:575–99.
Inoue Masao.
  1981a   "Rōdōsha jishu kanri no nihonteki isō" (Features of Self-
           Management in Japan). *Gekkan rōdō mondai* (Tokyo: Nihon
           Hyōronsha) 12:78–85.
  1981b   "Nanajyūnendai tōsan sōgi no seika to kongo no kadai"
           (Achievements and future of bankruptcy disputes in the 1970s).
           Gekkan rōdō mondai 3:24–34.
  1987   "Keiei-hatan to rōdō kumiai undō—rōdōsha jishu kanri no shisa
           suru mono" (Managerial failure and labor union movement—
           implications of self-management). In *Nihon no rōshi kankei no
           tokushitsu* (Characteristics of Japanese labor-management rela-
           tions), edited by Nishioka Yukiyasu, 31:35–55. Tokyo: Ochano-
           mizu Shobō.
  1989   "Rōdō kumiai undō no tensei: sōhyō no kaisan ni sokushite"
           (Transformation of the labor union movement: upon the disso-
           lution of Sōhyō). *Shakai seisaku sōsho* (Tokyo: Keibunsha) 13.

  1991   *Nihon no rōdōsha jishu kanri* (Self-management in Japan). To-
           kyo: Tokyo University Press.
Ishida, Hiroshi.
  1993   *Social Mobility in Contemporary Japan: Educational Credentials,
           Class and the Labour Market in a Cross-National Perspective.*
           Stanford: Stanford University Press.
Ishida, Takeshi.
  1984   "Conflict and Its Accommodation: *Omote-Ura* and *Uchi-Soto*
           Relations." In *Conflict in Japan,* edited by Ellis S. Krauss,
           Thomas P. Rohlen, and Patricia G. Steinhoff. Honolulu: Uni-
           versity of Hawaii Press.
Kawanishi Hirosuke.
  1981   *Kigyō-betsu kumiai no jittai* (Enterprise unions). Tokyo: Nippon
           Hyōron-sha.

Kinzley, W. Dean.
   1991   *Industrial Harmony in Modern Japan: The Invention of a Tradi-*
           tion. London: Routledge.
Koike, Kazuo.
   1983   "Workers in Small Firms and Women in Industry." In *Contem-*
           porary Industrial Relations in Japan, edited by Taishiro Shirai.
           Madison: University of Wisconsin Press.
Kondo, Dorinne K.
   1990   *Crafting Selves: Power, Gender, and Discourses of Identity*
           in a Japanese Workplace. Chicago: University of Chicago
           Press.
Lipset, Seymour Martin, Martin Trow, and James Coleman.
   1956   *Union Democracy.* New York: Anchor Books.
Miyoshi, Masao.
   1974   *Accomplices of Silence: The Modern Japanese Novel.* Berkeley
           and Los Angeles: University of California Press.
Mochizuki, Mike.
   1993   "Public Sector Labor and the Privatization Challenge: The
           Railway and Telecommunications Unions." In *Political*
           Dynamics in Contemporary Japan, edited by Gary D. Allinson
           and Yasunori Sone. Ithaca: Cornell University Press.
Moore, Joe.
   1983   *Japanese Workers and the Struggle for Power, 1945–1947.* Madi-
           son: University of Wisconsin Press.
Myerhoff, Barbara.
   1992   *Remembered Lives: The Work of Ritual, Storytelling, and Grow-*
           ing Older. Ann Arbor: University of Michigan Press.
Najita, Tetsuo.
   1974   *Japan: The Intellectual Foundations of Modern Japanese Politics.*
           Chicago: University of Chicago Press.
Nakane, Chie.
   1970   *Japanese Society.* Berkeley and Los Angeles: University of Cali-
           fornia Press.
Odaka, Kunio.
   1966   "The Middle Classes in Japan." In *Class, Status, and Power:*
           Social Stratification in Comparative Perspective, edited by
           Reinhard Bendix and Seymour Martin Lipset. New York: Free
           Press.
Ouchi, William.
   1982   *Theory Z.* New York: Avon.
Pascal, Richard, and Anthony Athos.
   1981   *The Art of Japanese Management.* New York: Warner Books.
Rohlen, Thomas P.
   1974   *For Harmony and Strength: Japanese White-Collar Organization*
           in Anthropological Perspective. Berkeley and Los Angeles: Uni-
           versity of California Press.

Rosaldo, Michelle Z.
1980   *Knowledge and Passion: Ilongot Notions of Self and Social Life.* Cambridge: Cambridge University Press.
Rosaldo, Renato.
1989   *Culture and Truth: The Remaking of Social Analysis.* Boston: Beacon Press.
Saxonhouse, Gary.
1979   "Industrial Restructuring in Japan." *Journal of Japanese Studies* 5, no. 2:289–320.
Shirai, Taishiro.
1983a   *Contemporary Industrial Relations in Japan.* Madison: University of Wisconsin Press.
1983b   "A Theory of Enterprise Unionism." In *Contemporary Industrial Relations in Japan,* edited by Taishiro Shirai. Madison: University of Wisconsin Press.
Smith, Thomas C.
1988   *Native Sources of Japanese Industrialization.* Berkeley and Los Angeles: University of California Press.
Steven, Rob.
1983   *Classes in Contemporary Japan.* Cambridge: Cambridge University Press.
Taira, Koji.
1988   "Labor Confederation in Japan." *Current History* 87, no. 528: 161–78.
1993   "Dialectics of Economic Growth, National Power, and Distributive Struggles." In *Prewar Japan as History,* edited by Andrew Gordon. Berkeley and Los Angeles: University of California Press.
Taussig, Michael.
1987   *Shamanism, Colonialism, and the Wild Man: A Study in Terror and Healing.* Chicago: The University of Chicago Press.
Thompson, E. P.
1963   *The Making of the English Working Class.* Harmondsworth, England: Penguin Books.
1967   "Time, Work Discipline, and Industrial Capitalism." *Past and Present* 38:56–97.
Totsuka Hideo.
1978   "Chūshō kigyō tōsan hantai sōgi jirei chōsa" (Anti-bankruptcy disputes in small and medium-sized companies). *Shakai kagaku kenkyū* 30, no. 1:206–21.
1980   "Chūshō kigyō no rōdōsōgi" (Labor disputes of small and medium-sized companies). *Chūō rōdō jihō* 4:2–13.
1984   "Kokusaiteki ni mo susunda nihon no tōsan tōsō" (Japan's advanced anti-bankruptcy disputes). In *Asshira no ase kagayaitemasu: kishu keisan katakai no kenjitsu to kenkai* (Our sweat glistens: evolution self-management and struggle in a labor

dispute), edited by Hataraku Nakama no Kōjōsai Jikkō Iinkai. Tokyo: Rōdō Kyōiku Sentā

Tsujinaka, Yutaka.

1993   "Rengō and Its Osmotic Networks." In *Political Dynamics in Contemporary Japan,* edited by Gary D. Allinson and Yasunori Sone. Ithaca: Cornell University Press.

Turner, Victor.

1967   *The Forest of Symbols: Aspects of Ndembu Ritual.* Ithaca: Cornell University Press.

1969   *The Ritual Process.* Chicago: Aldine.

Turner, Victor, and Edward M. Bruner, eds.

1986   *The Anthropology of Experience.* Urbana: University of Illinois Press.

Upham, Frank.

1987   *Law and Social Change in Postwar Japan.* Cambridge: Harvard University Press.

1993   "Unplaced Persons and Movements for Place." In *Postwar Japan as History,* edited by Andrew Gordon. Berkeley and Los Angeles: University of California Press.

Williams, Raymond.

1977   *Marxism and Literature.* Oxford: Oxford University Press.

Index

Accommodation: as adaptive strategy, 10, 140–41, 199, 201, 216–17, 218, 238; as reaction to conflict and change, 96, 97, 112, 113, 115, 122–28, 131, 139, 140; role of social activities in, 124–28. *See also* Conflict

Affective ties among workers: and appreciation of individuality, 85–86, 109–110, 121–22; and commitment, 59–60, 91, 157; strengthened during social activities, 38–39, 70–74, 87–89; as workplace characteristic, 100, 111, 192, 223–24, 234–35. *See also* Community; Solidarity; Unity

Age of workers: and attitudes toward antibankruptcy dispute, 6; and employment and workplace status, 188, 191, 211; and implications for union strength, 104–6, 155, 209, 210–11; and innovative management, 105–6; and participation in collective action, 105, 201, 202–4

All-Japan Leatherworkers Federation: Universal as member of, 16; and Universal's support of, at Sōkōdō demonstration, 188

All-Japan Metalworkers Federation: presence of representatives at union social activities, 75; support of Unikon's dispute, 4, 5, 6, 8, 41; Unikon as member of, 16, 36

Anger. *See* Collective action; Workers' rights

Bankruptcy: increase in incidence of, 4–5, 16n.11; as insufficient motivation for collective action, 56; and Japanese labor laws, 17; workers' attitudes toward, 6

Banks: relative vulnerability of, in Sōkōdō demonstrations, 191, 192, 198, 209, 210; as responsible for security of workers' livelihood, 45, 46, 197, 215; as targets of labor protest, 42, 45, 46, 186, 188, 190, 196–97

Bourdieu, Pierre, 19

Class consciousness: and accommodation, 117–18; in contemporary Japan, 10; as function of experience and education, 137, 138, 169; and identification with the middle class, 10–11; impact of collective action on, 51, 184, 249, 214–15, 250, 251; as lacking in Japanese workers, 25–26, 176, 237; and need for consensus, 11; as practical consciousness, 18–19, 249; as shaped by everyday life, 18, 249; strategic importance of, 158; and workers' affective ties, 60; among workers in small-medium sized firms, 11. *See also* Collective action; Consciousness; *Rōdōsha*

Responsibility: of banks and employers, toward workers, 45, 46, 56, 75, 136, 196, 197, 214, 215, 234, 235; multiple meanings of, 214–16, 235. *See also* Workers' rights

Rōdōsha (workers), 6, 163, 167; effect of demonstrations on identity as, 51–54, 205–8, 217; vs. *hataraku hitobito*, 235. *See also* Class consciousness

Rohlen, Thomas, 10, 12

Sake, 71, 76, 88, 161; deference and ritual aspects of, 77, 90, 91, 125, 162, 178; as stimulus for releasing emotions, 86, 87

Sekinin. See Responsibility

Small-medium sized firms: and bankruptcy, 4, 16n.11, 130; defined, 14; and democratic processes, 108; discrimination in, 23; and dissolution of Sōhyō, 243; lack of benefits in, 174; loyalty of workers in, 11; and membership in Tōkyō Sōgidan, 41–42

Smith, Thomas, 11

Socialist Party, 1, 57; as supportive of unions, 3, 44, 149, 157, 237, 247

Sōhyō Federation, 2, 6, 16, 62; dissolved, 16n.11, 243; as external source of union support, 40, 41, 156

Sōkōdō: defined and described, 41–48, 138. *See also* Collective action; Demonstrations; Tōkyō Sōgidan

Solidarity, 18, 60, 175; vs. community, 133; as enhanced by democratic processes, 109; and importance of shared time and space, 39–40, 111; as reinforced by collective action, 51–54, 205–6, 209; as reinforced during social activities, 66–69, 81–82, 84–89; and symbolic importance of demonstration attire and action, 52; as union goal, 33, 37, 67, 104, 132

Taira, Koji, 9, 12

Taussig, Michael, 19, 88, 249

Thompson, E. P., 238, 250

"Tiny socialism": role of meetings in, 149; as union goal, 146–47, 149, 180, 233, 234, 242, 244, 247. *See also* Workers' control of production

Tokyo: financial district as labor protest site, 41, 44, 45; neighborhoods, characteristics of, 21, 247; status distinctions by geographical area of, 213–14

Tōkyō Sōgidan (Tokyo Labor Dispute Association): as organizer of Sōkōdō demonstrations, 41–42; professional demeanor of officials in, 195; as promoter of solidarity, 51. *See also* Sōkōdō

Totsuka Hideo, 4, 6, 17, 138, 244, 246

Turner, Victor, 18, 48, 64

Unikon Camera: characteristics of work force, 14, 15; enterprise union, 15–16; history of, 13; labor disputes in, 16–17, 34–37; reformed as "ordinary company," 239; union as model for others, 3, 5, 41, 75, 101–2, 128, 129–30, 147, 209; union goals, 36–37; union newsletter, 35, 95; union picture albums, 42, 50, 66; uniqueness of union's dispute strategies, 42, 57–58, 104–5; women and part-timers as union members, 16, 36, 63, 107, 119; women and part-timers excluded from union, 134–37, 240, 246; workers' attitudes toward work, vs. Universal's, 226–30; and workers' post-settlement sense of betrayal, 113–15, 119, 122, 133, 140

Unions: age and gender of membership as index of strength of, 210–11; distance between top and bottom of, 133, 164, 175–77; enterprise, 15, 16, 174, 175; postwar growth of, 34

Unity: contrasted with solidarity, 101, 133; demonstrated in *sanbon jime*, 8, 77, 127; and demonstrations, 198, 204–6, 207, 209, 210; factors contributing to fragmentation of, 6, 96, 97, 101, 111, 122, 132–33; as fostered through affective ties, 38–39; importance of, to workers, 100, 101, 103, 122, 132; importance of workers' shared time and space in promoting, 111, 221–22; as inhibiting democratic participation, 178, 179; promoted through ideology of equality, 106–8; as reinforced during social

Unity (*continued*)
  activities, 7, 8, 66–69, 87–89. *See also* Community; Equality
Universal Shoes: characteristics of work force, 15, 22; description of physical plant, 145–46; description of workplace routines, 222–26, 228, 229; enterprise union, 15–16; history of, 13–14; labor disputes in, 16–17; reconstituted as workers' cooperative, 241–42; and settlement agreement with Custom Shoes, 240–41; women and part-timers as union members, 16

Warikirenai (things don't add up), 97, 124, 139–41; as analytical starting point, 19–20. *See also* Accommodation; Conflict
Williams, Raymond, 250
Women: employment and workplace status of, 70, 106–7, 188, 211; and participation in collective action, 6, 7, 106, 188, 191, 201–204; as part-timers, 15, 119, 135, 136; and workplace discrimination, 106–7, 118–19, 135–37
Workers. See *Rōdōsha*
Workers' control of production: differences in perceptions of nature and

extent of, 57, 129, 138, 230–34; difficulty of, in capitalist economy, 57n.6, 117–18, 129, 130, 146–47, 239–40; historical precedent for, 4
Workers' participation: in context of strong centralized leadership, 40, 119–20, 137, 138; enhanced by education and practice, 150, 159, 169; enhanced by feelings of equality, 108–9; limited by formal union procedures, 171, 177–79, 180; limited by linguistic forms of deference, 176–177; limited by role and status differences between leaders and workers, 164, 175–77, 230–31; limited by workers' feelings of powerlessness, 118, 169, 170–73; limited by workers' sense of economic vulnerability, 173–75; in meetings, 109, 150, 152–59 passim, 163, 169, 233. *See also* Democracy; Hierarchy
Workers' rights: to control their own labor, 233, 244–48; in Japanese labor law, 17, 53; to respect, as fully human, 49, 56–57, 58, 61, 63–64, 216; to secure livelihood, 56, 57, 215, 234, 235

Compositor:	Braun-Brumfield, Inc.
Text:	10/13 Galliard
Display:	Galliard
Printer:	Braun-Brumfield, Inc.
Binder:	Braun-Brumfield, Inc.